She/Him/Us

She/Him/Us

*A Psychiatrist's Search for Her Daughter
in the Transgender Sea*

Lisa Bellot, MD

PITCHSTONE PUBLISHING
DURHAM, NORTH CAROLINA

Pitchstone Publishing
Durham, North Carolina
www.pitchstonebooks.com

Copyright © 2025 Lisa Bellot, MD LLC

All rights reserved.
Printed in the United States of America

Library of Congress Cataloging-in-Publication Data

Names: Bellot, Lisa, author.
Title: She/him/us : a psychiatrist's search for her daughter in the transgender sea / Lisa Bellot, MD.
Description: Durham, North Carolina : Pitchstone Publishing, 2025. | Includes bibliographical references. | Summary: "Psychiatrist Lisa Bellot, MD, documents her journey as the mother of a trans-identified teen whom she did not believe was transgender. Her narrative takes a deep dive into the moral, psychological, and medical complexities of our society's current approach to the treatment of trans-identified children and challenges us to reconsider what we think we know about the gender-affirming model and the polarizing landscape inhabited by the most vulnerable among us"— Provided by publisher.
Identifiers: LCCN 2024046517 (print) | LCCN 2024046518 (ebook) | ISBN 9781634312646 (paperback) | ISBN 9781634312653 (ebook)
Subjects: LCSH: Parents of transgender children. | Gender dysphoria in children—Social aspects. | Gender identity in children—Social aspects. | Transgender children—Psychology. | Parent-child relationship.
Classification: LCC HQ759.9147 .B45 2025 (print) | LCC HQ759.9147 (ebook) | DDC 649/.1564--dc23/eng/20241004
LC record available at https://lccn.loc.gov/2024046517
LC ebook record available at https://lccn.loc.gov/2024046518

For Jordan

and the others

*"Truth doesn't mind being questioned.
A lie does not like being challenged."*
—fortune cookie wisdom, circa 2016

Contents

	Preface	xi
1.	The Disclosure	3
2.	This Will Pass	8
3.	Some Kind of Treatment	18
4.	This Place We Call Home	34
5.	Marriage	50
6.	Nobody Knows How to Help Her	57
7.	Show and Tell	75
8.	Collateral Damage	85
9.	Calling for Reinforcements	102
10.	The Cliff and the Ocean	115
11.	Recruitment	130
12.	The Intervention	141
13.	The Aftermath	150
14.	Reflections	165
15.	The Future	180
	Epilogue	197
	Glossary of Terms	199
	About the Author	

Preface

This is a story about losing my child and finding her again. It details my experience as the mother of a trans-identified teen who I did not believe was transgender. As a psychiatrist who has treated transgender individuals in my practice, I approached the situation with an open mind and a desire to explore what was happening with my daughter. I have learned a great deal along the way. What started out as a simple declaration—"I have gender dysphoria; I feel more like a boy than a girl"—set us down a path that culminated in a battle for the life and well-being of my child. Like many parents before me, I strove to support and protect her from permanent harm, to find resources and allies where very few existed, and to do so without destroying her in the process.

Although it involves the transgender movement, this is not a book about transgender individuals. I support the LGBTQ+ community, and I recognize that the suffering endured by those with gender dysphoria can be enormous. Fortunately, treatments are available to decrease their suffering, and many people have been helped.

My training as a psychiatrist has both helped and hindered me in understanding my child's dilemma, but the story is told primarily from my perspective as a mother. I have incorporated some of my professional knowledge and experience because I think it makes the narrative richer and the explanations more understandable, but the focus remains on the difficulties we faced as a family.

The people and events described in these pages are real, although the names and details of certain places and individuals have been modified to protect the identities of those involved. I have authored this book under the pseudonym Lisa Bellot to safeguard the anonymity of others, several of them children. Dialogues depicted in quotations are based on my best recollection of conversations, since I do not make audio recordings of my daily interactions. I have incorporated humor when it seems appropriate, not to make light of the topic or circumstances, but to add occasional levity to an experience during which I often felt hopeless and very much alone.

I want to remind readers that this is *my* story, not the story of all parents with trans-identified teens. During this three-year ordeal, I came to discover—*slowly*, as if emerging from a darkened room—that I was not alone. The details will resonate with many parents who have either stood or are currently standing where I was. It is my hope that this book will bring comfort and empowerment to those who are still struggling and that it will add to the conversation that we should be having as a society about whether our current approach to trans-identified teens is in the best interest of the long-term health and wellness of our children.

She/Him/Us

Chapter One: The Disclosure

From Magical to Messy

We rolled into town in a U-Haul, my husband Zack working the steering wheel of the twenty-six-foot monstrosity while I followed behind in the SUV. As we merged onto Main Street, a sign greeted us: "Welcome to Dante's Watch." I read the words out loud to eighteen-month-old Jordan, who was checking out the scenery in retrospect from her rear-facing car seat. I couldn't see the ocean, but I could smell it through the open window, the fog rolling through town like an empty stagecoach, the seagulls riding the breeze or gathered in small, watchful congregations in restaurant parking lots.

I surveyed the landscape in my peripheral vision as we lumbered past the surf shop, the pizza joint, and the town cinema advertising *Raiders of the Lost Ark* as one of its summer retro movie features. A teenage boy in a wetsuit rode past us on his bike, a nine-foot longboard nestled in the makeshift cradle attached to its frame.

"Gotta get you a surfboard," I told Jordan.

She rattled her toy shark in her tiny fist. "*Smurfboat!*" she echoed, and I snorted at that as the laughter rolled through me. "*Smurfboat! Smurfboat!*" she chanted, giggling from her car seat behind me.

I drew a deep breath and took in the scent of it, this place we would now call home. It smelled like popcorn and saltwater taffy, seaweed and Pacific Ocean mist. I had spotted the eucalyptus trees from the highway, spread out like sentinels along a coastline that would soon become speckled with evening bonfires as the sun dipped below the horizon.

After years of medical training in Philadelphia, I was excited to be returning to Coastal California and a town that was closer to my roots.

I did not grow up here, but we used to visit when I was younger. I remember the tide pools, the aching cold of my feet submerged in the water, the way hermit crabs used to skitter right over them if I stood still for long enough. When Zack and I had talked about settling down at the end of our training, Dante's Watch had been on the short list. The people, as I remembered from my teenage years, were kind, welcoming, and inclusive. I wanted our daughter to grow up in this kind of environment, a small town that was big enough for magic and wonder.

Over the next few months, it was strange how quickly we became part of the place. We moved into our house, enrolled Jordan in preschool, and Zack and I both started local jobs that we loved. As first-time parents, we marveled at every milestone Jordan achieved. She had a flavor for drama from the beginning, starring as Maleficent in a kindergarten depiction of Sleeping Beauty. ("*Oh, ho! If it isn't the lovely Princess Aurora…*") She embraced art, creating such spectacular works as *Pig in a Bikini*, which I had professionally framed and presented to Zack for his birthday. One of Jordan's childhood watercolors of a momma frog and her baby still hangs on the wall of my living room, a painting people sometimes mistake for the work of Eric Carle.

Watching her grow, we enjoyed listening to her chatter about the things she was interested in (mermaids, Princess Merida, puppies) or uninterested in (soccer, *Chitty Chitty Bang Bang*, spiders). Jordan watched seemingly endless episodes of *My Little Pony* and *Dora the Explorer*. She made pretend tea and muffins from sand on the playground and served them to us during our make-believe tea parties. She loved telling her friends that both of her parents were doctors. "My dad helps people when they're bleeding. My mom helps people when they're mad or sad."

Our daughter was the opposite of a tomboy. She gravitated toward anything fancy and loved bling: the more sequins, the more shine, the fancier, the better. She wore tiaras and headbands adorned with plastic jewels or large tropical flowers that matched her outfits. Her favorite shoes were her pink Uggs and ruby red slippers, both gifts from my brother. She had a velvet red Christmas dress that she literally wore to pieces, and the puffy satin blue dress that replaced it became her all-time favorite. To Zack's suggestion that she save the blue dress for special days, her memorable response was, "Daddy, every day is a special day." She had us with that one. We let her wear the dress every day it was clean.

As she matured, Jordan nurtured our aging dogs with maternalistic ease. We went apple picking in the fall and baked cakes and apple pies together. She helped me make soup from treasures we gathered at our local farmer's market: a wide array of vegetables fresh from the craggy, foggy coastal farmlands. She wanted to wear the aprons I'd inherited from my grandmother: beautiful garments with pink and yellow gingham patterns, bordered in lace and tied in the back with large white bows. We took a mommy-and-me ballet class. Her favorite part was wearing the pink tutu.

On cool, coastal, foggy evenings, we would drop by the beach on our way home from school and watch the sun set and the waves crash. I had a Volkswagen convertible that she adored, and it was perfect for our evening sightseeing. At night we would settle in for a movie of her choosing, and it was usually *Mary Poppins*, *The Little Mermaid*, *Cinderella*, or the like. I was lucky enough to find a complete Disney collection at a local thrift store. Together, Jordan and I explored the movies, characters, and lessons involved in those enchanted tales.

And then ... Jordan grew up. Her interest in Princess Aurora morphed into a fascination with Taylor Swift, and her infatuation with Snow White became a love of Camila Cabello. Colorful pictures of mermaids were replaced with photos of narwhals, swordfish, and other non-make-believe creatures. Making fun of the boys in her class turned into crushes on teenage heartthrobs, going so far as to say, "Justin Beiber looks like a prince," and, "Draco Malfoy is hot." Dr. Seuss was replaced by John Greene and J. K. Rowling, and later, by the works of Stephen King.

Things were changing. And then, sadly, things changed some more. We lost both of our beloved dogs, one of them tragically and the other unexpectedly. The acute inpatient psychiatric unit where I had invested so much of my time and passion closed. I followed a logical career path, but one that did not feed my soul. Our marriage, which had been limping along for the last few years, finally crumbled. The split was amicable, and Zack and I shared Jordan easily and remained friendly. We tried to minimize how much this transition affected our child, but the sadness of our parting lingers in all of us still. During the process of separating our lives and homes, Jordan found herself in a new school district and starting junior high at a school where she had no established peer connections.

Jordan was eleven, almost twelve, and teen angst had settled upon her. Her playlists included songs like "I'm Not Okay (I Promise)" by My Chemical Romance, "Misery Business" by Paramore, and "I Will Follow You into the Dark" by Death Cab for Cutie. It was in this vulnerable phase of life that Jordan started junior high school in a new district with one acquaintance but zero friends.

Things had already gotten messy. They were about to get worse.

What She Said

It was an unseasonably cold spring day in Dante's Watch. Jordan was twelve and had recently engaged in a bit of self-injury: cutting behavior that was new to her. Zack and I were naturally concerned and had decided we needed to talk to her about it. In hindsight (always so painfully clear), this was garden variety tween girl acting out. It probably didn't need an official sit down with both of her parents. We thought that we were doing the right thing, of course, based on the information available to us at the time. I wish we could go back to that day and handle it differently.

We sat in hard, uncomfortable chairs in the outdoor seating area between a closed Mexican restaurant and a bustling coffee shop. I had ordered a latte, and I hunkered over it against the intermittent bursts of wind. Zack had grabbed a juice, but Jordan had declined any refreshment, which was unusual for our trips to Coffee House. *She's not getting anything?* I wondered to myself, accustomed to her typical orders of an iced mocha or a decadent pumpkin scone. I remember thinking even then that something must be wrong with my daughter, a stomach bug or the first symptoms of the flu perhaps. Whatever it was, she looked pale and unwell sitting across from me. I half-expected her to vomit.

"So, what's this all about?" Zack asked her. "What's going on with you?"

She danced around it for a while as we sat there, waiting for her to say something meaningful.

Eventually, she came out with it: "I have gender dysphoria; I feel more like a boy than a girl. I've always known something was wrong with me. Now I've discovered what it is. I'm going to start living my life as a male—my authentic self—and I want you to use he/him pronouns when you refer to me."

I stared at her. The things she was saying were so ridiculous that I almost laughed. As a psychiatrist, I've been trained not to do that, but still, it almost happened. She could have said, "From now on, I'm going to communicate only through puppets, and I'll be wearing a hat with rotting fish on my head," and I would not have been more surprised than I was in that moment. Zack shifted in his seat, as if he was experiencing a bit of intestinal malaise, and again I almost lost it. The laughter wanted to bubble out of me, but I pushed it down and told myself to be still. I wonder what might have happened if I hadn't. How would she have responded if I had laughed out loud and said, "Okay, cut the shit and tell us what's really going on with you." How might that have changed everything that followed?

She was prepared, I'll give her that. She described the discomfort she experienced in her own body, how she wanted to escape her female form but couldn't. She had polished and articulate responses to all our questions, and she assured us that now that she had "come out" there would be no more self-injury. Jordan educated us about the risk of suicide for individuals with gender dysphoria who were not affirmed and supported by their immediate family. Although she was not overtly threatening, the threat of ongoing self-injury hung in the air between us. She advised us that several months earlier she had come out to a small group of friends at her new school (of which I estimate about 75 percent identified as LGBTQ), and they were all accepting of her new identity. There had been a time, she told us, when she had explored the possibility that she might be gay, but she had "grown out of it." Things were clear to her now.

I sat there and held my tongue, nodding when it was appropriate. *All of this from a twelve-year-old*, I marveled. How could she know anything about her gender identification and sexuality for certain? She was right about one thing, though: it was important for us to be supportive. The worst thing we could do was to push back against what she was telling us. *This will be nothing*, I thought, *an inconsequential blip in her self-exploration*. We would sit with this for a while and see how it unfolded. There was no harm in that, I reasoned, but I was wrong. I just didn't know it at the time.

Chapter Two: This Will Pass

Coming Out

What's a parent to do when their child comes out as transgender? In the year that followed Jordan's proclamation, I did my best to make sense of it and to figure out my role in the process. I was supportive, of course, but it took time to process my thoughts and emotions. I did so privately or during conversations with Zack. My political views are moderate but left of center when it comes to social issues, and I started out by drawing upon what I knew and believed. I was aware of the centuries of social injustice endured by transgender and other LGBTQ individuals. As a physician, I'd received training and education on the complicated dynamics of gender dysphoria and the importance of the gender affirming model when it came to transgender individuals. Ideologically, I supported and celebrated human diversity, and I lived in a part of the country renowned for its acceptance and support of the LGBTQ community. I'd attended Pride parades in my town of Dante's Watch, waving rainbow flags as people from all walks of the LGBTQ community celebrated their heritage and identities.

    I would prefer to say that my response was born of all those things, but the truth is much simpler and more primitive. I supported my child because I loved her. (I use the pronoun "her" at this point because we were new to this, and I had not yet transitioned my brain into using the male pronouns that would come later.) I supported my child because it was my responsibility as her parent. I had *always* been on her side, and I always would be. I didn't understand everything she was telling me—

and *yes*, there were doubts in my mind—but I supported her because it was the *right* thing to do. I would figure this out. We would explore this together. The decision to do so was as natural and unwavering as my own heartbeat. I could feel it in my chest, this steady determination. It whispered to my daughter: I love you, I love you, I love you …

Do I have to explain the kind of love that I am talking about? If you're a parent, I assume that you understand. For those who are not, suffice it to say that a child's safety, happiness, and well-being are not just part of a parent's day-to-day considerations; they are everything. Nothing is more important. At its most basic level, a parent's love and protective reflexes for their child come from the brainstem (metaphorically speaking, and perhaps literally as well). We internalize that from the moment our child enters the world until our very last breath on this Earth. That's the deal, and it isn't subject to change.

There's an old joke that a good friend will help you move, but a great friend will help you move a body. Replace the word "friend" with "parent," and the joke loses some of its humor. Why? Because it's no longer a joke. Burying a body, or the willingness to do so, is something parents might consider. That's disturbing, I know, and I can assure you there are no bodies buried in *my* backyard. (None that I would tell you about, anyway.) But when it comes to protecting the health and safety of one's child, most parents would willingly kill or die for their child without hesitation. It's how we're built. From an evolutionary perspective, it protects the sustainability of the species. So … if the day ever comes when my daughter tells me she's in trouble and needs help burying a body, what's a loving mother to say? "We'll talk about this later, young lady. But for now, wrap that thing in plastic and go get the shovel."

Ahh, but the situation wasn't quite so desperate. My daughter ("Call me he/him," she'd instructed me) had just come out to us as transgender. *Transgender*, I thought, and I was already replaying the years in my mind: the fancy dresses and tutus and sequins and everything bling; Jordan's pink Uggs and red ruby slippers; her preference to have her hair arranged in pigtails or French braids; the sea of mermaids and princesses and American Girl dolls that she had played with throughout the years; the make-believe tea parties; her rapt attention through the many adventures of *Dora the Explorer*. It was difficult to place this new information in the context of the person I'd known and raised for the past twelve years. *She's being funny*, I thought, *or sarcastic*. But I could see the pinched and serious look on her face, and I knew that she wasn't.

"I haven't decided what name to use yet," she told us. "But it's not going to be Jordan. Jordan is my dead name. I'm done with that. That part of my life is over."

We sat there for a while, listening to words that sounded like a well-rehearsed speech rather than a conversation. I was skeptical and curious—not yet truly alarmed by the things she was saying, although that would come later—and we asked many questions to which she had well-prepared answers. She told us that she had known from a young age that she was a boy, although the details of *how* she had known and specific examples of moments of gender dysphoria were lacking. She advised us that she had already been through a questioning period and had emerged on the other side. Questioning was now behind her, she said, and she was glad to have gotten through that. She was "100 percent sure," and told us that all doubt had already been eliminated by the time of this disclosure. Using online resources, Jordan had extensively educated herself about gender dysphoria, and she presented the information using terms and lingo indicative of the vast amount of time and research she had put into it. I wondered aloud if maybe she was going through a time of confusion and uncertainty. She was, after all, entering her years as a teenage girl, a span of development notorious for struggles with self-image and identity, but Jordan had no interest in discussing that. She assured us that she was not confused about her gender, and she neither needed nor wanted help in thinking through this or sorting out such a complicated matter in a logical or methodical way. She wanted to tell us that she was certain, and there was no going back. It was a consistent, unwavering message. This was not a discussion. "This," as she said, "is me letting you know."

In the weeks that followed, as I struggled to come to terms with this, I wondered why Jordan had never brought any of this up to me or her father before. If she had *truly known* (or at least suspected) from a young age that she was a boy, why hadn't she spoken of it until now? Why had she never asked the questions that would've clued us in to the possibility that something was different?

The first decade of life is replete with examples of children saying exactly what's on their mind, often to the horror and mortification of the hapless parent standing next to them. Waiting in line at the post office, a young child might blurt out anything—"What's wrong with that guy's leg? Why does that lady smell funny? Mommy, I just farted"—and the best you can do is turn to the people standing around you and shrug. "I'm sorry," you tell them. "She's five."

It's not their fault. Kids aren't born with the ability to self-edit. It takes years to develop, and some people never really seem to get it down. There's something genuine about the way young children communicate that gets tarnished and distorted as they become older and more self-aware. Children say what they want. The words pop out of their mouths like jackrabbits on a trampoline, and if my child had been struggling with gender dysphoria at the age of six or eight, I would've expected *something* before this. A simple statement perhaps—"I don't like girl things; I wanna be a boy"—but there had been none of that with Jordan. She was genetically, physically, emotionally, and socially a girl for all the years that I had known her. And now, as if out of the blue, she was asserting that she wasn't.

Here's something else: Jordan *knew* that I was a psychiatrist. She was aware of the nature of my work and the fact that I saw patients with gender dysphoria in my own clinical practice. Who better to talk to? But she hadn't come to me; she'd gone to the internet. Only after months of online consumption had she brought this before us as something fully formed, unmalleable, and not to be questioned. What did it mean, I wondered, and where would it lead? What role would we play in a thing that had, supposedly, already been decided? I chose to wait and to give it some space. Things will become clearer, I thought. We will see how this develops.

Waiting

As spring gave way to summer, Zack and I waited to see what would happen next, silently wondering how long this would last. We were progressive people. We recognized the existence and struggles of transgender individuals, but I also knew my daughter, and on some fundamental level I felt that her transgender proclamation was not an accurate reflection of what she was going through. This was *something else*—a life phase, perhaps—and phases are unavoidable in adolescence. Still, we decided to refer to our daughter (our "son," if you will) using masculine pronouns, as requested. I went along with it to be supportive and because I had learned in my medical training that this was the best approach. We implemented the gender affirming model full force. I did not think that resisting it or arguing about the validity of Jordan's self-diagnosed gender dysphoria were good things to do, and I wondered if resistance would lead to oppositional behavior that would be disruptive to her life in general and disruptive to her relationship with us as her parents. I told nobody outside of the family, not because I was ashamed or concerned about how they would react, but because I was not yet convinced it was authentic.

Making a departure from the "traditional" path was common in Dante's Watch. It is a big draw for those who live here. One can be whoever they want to be, and people generally find love and support in doing so. Jordan was trying out a different, trendy identity. I would support her, love her, and see her through it. That was my responsibility as her mother.

We were five months into this process of passive waiting, and already things had gone on for longer than I had expected. Jordan was becoming more entrenched in her new identity instead of less. A few weeks earlier, for example, I had signed her up for a summer cooking class at the local community college. When I arrived to pick her up that first day, the instructor told me what an excellent student Ash was, and what a joy it was to have a young person like Ash in her class, so attentive and interested in cooking. "Ash?" I asked her. "I think you have me mistaken with a different parent." No, the teacher assured me, we were both talking about Jordan, the name listed on the student roster. It's just that ... well ... Jordan had asked to be called Ash, so that's what they were calling him.

"You're going by Ash now?" I inquired when we got home.

"Just trying it out," she told me.

I nodded and took a bite of the quiche she had prepared in class that afternoon. "You want me to call you Ash for a while?"

"No," she said. "That's just for the class."

Just for the class, I told myself, but I didn't forget it. Later that summer she became "Crow" during a weeklong co-ed basketball camp during which she discovered the energy-enhancing powers of Flamin'

Hot Cheetos and Gatorade.

Other summer activities came and went, and she adopted a different name for each of them. She tried out "Twix" and "River," among others. When I think about it now, none of these were names that authentic gender dysphoric individuals would typically choose. In my professional experience, I have observed that patients with true gender dysphoria tend to select a name for themselves that is traditional for their authentic gender. A female-to-male individual (born female but identifying as male) typically chooses a masculine name that is prototypical and unambiguously consistent with his gender identity. Conversely, the names Jordan had tried out that summer—Ash, Crow, Twix, and River—were gender ambiguous, just as the name Jordan itself is gender ambiguous and could be the name of a boy or a girl. *What's the point*, one might ask, *of switching from one gender-ambiguous name to another, especially if the goal is to unequivocally align oneself with a gender that's different from the one assigned at birth?*

Jordan was not alone in her preference for a name that ran contrary to her stated intent. Trans-identified and nonbinary teens and young adults often change their name when they declare a new identity, but that name is not always consistent with their proclaimed gender identity. If an individual is a biological girl named Joanne, for example, and she changes her gender identity to nonbinary, what would be the purpose of changing their name to John, a traditional male name? For a nonbinary individual, it seems logical that a gender-ambiguous name would be preferred. Or, if the stereotypical gender connotation of the name does not matter to a nonbinary person, why not just keep the given name Joanne, a name already known to friends and family? Choosing an opposite-sex name to go with the change to nonbinary status is not consistent with one's claimed authentic self. And yet, I've seen this a lot. Jordan's biologically female friend Kaitlin announced that she was nonbinary and changed *their* name to "West." A year later, they began to identify as male and changed *his* name to "Lucy," an illogical choice for someone identifying as male. I can think of many other examples. The point is, the choices we make are often more revealing than the things we proclaim. Confusion, exploration, and the search for self are important aspects of human development. Along the way, sometimes we must plant a flag in the ground to see which way the wind is blowing.

The summer rolled on, and over the course of the year my daughter became a boy, not because she had boy tendencies or demonstrated a long history of stereotypical male preferences in activities or interests, but because she had decided to call herself that and we were too afraid of the potential consequences to contradict her. The danger of doing anything different was reinforced by numerous experts over the years. It never occurred to me that I could be inflicting damage by *affirming* this new identity. No professional ever advised caution in doing so. Zack and I used he/him pronouns when referring to our child in the third person, and Jordan settled on the name "Ash." The next school year started, Ash announced his new identity to the world, and his friends, family, and teachers fell into compliance.

Looking for Help (the Expert)

As concerned parents who wanted the best thing for their child, Zack and I decided to have Ash evaluated by a gender specialist. In Dante's Watch, there is no shortage of therapists citing expertise in working with transgender teens. If you stand in the center of town and throw a stone in any direction, chances are you will hit one.

I researched our options and took Ash to someone whom I respected and knew to be a true gender expert with specialized training and a long history of practicing in that field. The plan was for him to do an assessment and offer us his opinion on whether he thought our child's gender dysphoria was genuine. If so, he would give us his recommendations and Ash would be referred to a different gender specialist for further ongoing therapy.

The day of the appointment came, and I was filled with a tremendous sense of relief to be talking to someone who was an expert in the field. I'd known this specialist for years. Hearing his voice when I called to speak with him and schedule the appointment had provided me with the only shred of hope I'd experienced since this whole thing began. I anticipated that Ash would perceive him to be an authoritative figure as well, and I felt certain that the therapist would see past my child's thinly constructed façade and would compassionately advise her that she was misreading the messages from her mind and body and labeling them in an inaccurate way.

Already, I was beginning to revert to female pronouns within the relative safety of my own mind. I hoped that the specialist would shed some light on the root cause of the problems that were afflicting Jordan and offer us suggestions as to how we might get her the help that she truly needed. After months of emotional turmoil, here was a chance for healing and for us to at least start the process of getting our child back on track.

The entire appointment was sixty minutes, and the specialist explained that it would be separated into four parts. First, he would meet with all three of us together, then with Jordan alone, then with me and Zack alone, and finally with all three of us again. The time spent alone with Jordan doing an individual assessment for the presence or absence of gender dysphoria would be about fifteen minutes.

During the first part of the appointment, I sat silently and listened while Jordan told her story. She went through her narrative, omitting key components of her history and emphasizing others. She discussed information that she had found on the internet. I listened in horror while Jordan told a story we had all laughed about during her childhood. She was about three years old at the time and had spent the day with similar-aged children at a local playground. One of the boys—as boys are sometimes prone to do—decided to urinate in the pond, removing his penis from his pants to urinate standing up. Jordan had witnessed the act, and she inquired later as to what "that thing" was. I explained it to her in very basic terms. "Will I grow a penis?" she wanted to know. "No," I told her. "Boys have penises and girls have vaginas." She wrinkled her nose at me. "It's weird," she said. "Pee came right out of there." We laughed together at the oddness of how boys and girls are different. In Jordan's retelling of the story in the specialist's office that day, however, she explained that she had seen the penis and had wanted one *so badly*, as if she'd known, even then, that she was missing a key part of her body. It was in that moment, she explained, that she had *known* that she was a boy, and she reported to the therapist that she had thought about it countless times since then, obsessing about her relentless desire to grow a penis of her own. It was one of the only childhood memories she would later claim to have, a pivotal moment in the realization of her true self.

During the second part of the appointment, Jordan met with the specialist alone while Zack and I sat in the waiting room, making half-hearted conversation but mostly thinking of things we wanted to mention before the session was over. Fifteen minutes later, the specialist invited us back into his office while Jordan took our place in the waiting room. During our discussion, Zack and I shared our concerns in detail regarding the disparities between Jordan's self-diagnosis as transgender and the person we'd known for the past twelve years. We recounted our observations as her parents (as best we could during our fifteen allotted minutes) over the course of Jordan's life, revisiting fancy dresses, sequins, and everything bling; pigtails and French braids; mermaids and princesses and make-believe tea parties. We enumerated one telling example after another, a string of memories held up as witnesses on behalf of the authentic nature of our daughter, but more than anything it was my overwhelming certainty that I tried to convey. *This thing that she's latched on to—it's not real*, I wanted to tell him, but didn't. *You can see that, can't you? She's a girl. She's our daughter. We know her better than anyone else on this planet. We can bring her back into the room now and you can explain it to her. We can do it together. It won't be easy, but we can make her see.*

He sat there for a moment, studying us. My hands were folded and motionless in my lap.

"From everything Ash has told me, this seems to be real," he said. "Your child is a transgender boy, or at least I think he is. I'm ninety-nine percent sure."

The air slid from my lungs, a slight and quiet thing, and with it the thin ribbon of hope that I'd been clinging to since the day I first called him. I shook my head, or maybe I nodded. He took that as a sign to continue.

"He's answered my questions in the way I'd expect from a person with gender dysphoria. Ash says you've been supportive, and that's good. We call this the 'gender affirming model.' If you want what's best for your child, it's the only way to be."

I glanced at Zack, but his attention was on the therapist. Zack was leaning forward, as if he was afraid of missing some crucial detail, a small bit of advice that could make the difference between this moment and everything that came after.

"If you haven't done so already," the specialist continued, "you should make every effort to use he/him pronouns when referring to your child in the third person. It's what Ash has requested."

He/him, I thought. *Ash*. We were no longer talking about my daughter.

"Ash would like to start testosterone, which would help him transition and feel better about his body. If you're not ready for that, there are also estrogen blockers, which would allow us to put puberty and the development of female sexual characteristics such as breast development on hold for a while. You don't have to decide now, but it's something you should think about. Generally speaking, the sooner kids start these treatments the better."[1]

"Why is it better?" Zack asked. "Estrogen blockers. Testosterone. It seems extreme. What if she—what if Ash changes his mind?"

The specialist seemed to consider this. "If he changes his mind, he can stop taking the hormones. Estrogen blockers are relatively safe. They've been used successfully for decades for children with precocious puberty, a different medical condition. But you should be aware that most kids don't change their minds. Once they come out as transgender, they know who they are."

He sat back, laced his fingers together. "This will be a difficult time for Ash. Transgender teens have a much higher risk of suicide. Studies tell us that more than eighty percent of transgender teens have considered it, and about forty-one percent attempt suicide during their teenage years. The gender affirming model and supportive parents: these are the things that make a difference." He paused for a moment, allowing us to think about that. "Ash has decided on a gender, and we want to do everything we can to support him," he said. "Anything less can be extremely damaging. We want Ash to survive this."

He looked at each of us in turn. "Would you rather have a healthy son or a dead daughter?"

---

1. Several studies have found that most teens who opt for hormone blockers continue on to cross-sex hormones (e.g., testosterone). One such study is Catharina van der Loos et al., "Continuation of Gender-Affirming Hormones in Transgender People Starting Puberty Suppression in Adolescence: A Cohort Study in the Netherlands," *Lancet* 6, no. 12 (2022): 869–875.

Chapter Three: Some Kind of Treatment

Looking for Help (Jordan)

"Would you rather have a healthy son or a dead daughter?"

The question hung in the air like a helium-filled balloon, its blood-red membrane stretched taut to envelop those terrible words. It hovered silently between the three of us—me, Zack, and the specialist sitting across from us—threatening to explode at any moment. I sat there and watched it, this thing that had appeared out of nowhere and could destroy us if we let it. Its rubber sides expanded and contracted, ever so slightly, as if it was breathing.

The fingertips of my right hand rested against my abdomen, remembering the way my uterus had expanded as she had grown inside of me, a fragile life with so much potential and so much that could go suddenly and catastrophically wrong. I glanced at Zack, but he was lost in his own dreadful imaginings, and so I turned my attention back to the balloon, this pregnant thing that would come to dominate every decision that was yet to come. A slim whisp of string dangled from its underbelly like an umbilical cord and hung six inches above the floor. I was afraid to reach for it, afraid to *even move* in its direction, as if the slightest disturbance might set the balloon in motion. *It'll drift upward*, I thought, *its delicate skin coming to rest against the sharp metal slats of the air duct ...*

"This," the specialist said, and I jerked back a bit, startled to find him still sitting there.

He peered at me through the red lens of the rubber sphere between us. "This ... is what we are up against. We have to do everything we can to help Ash survive this. The choices you make from this moment onward can make that difference."

Zack nodded. I could see the bob of his head out of the corner of my eye.

"If it's okay with you," the specialist continued, "I'd like to have Ash join us now."

Be careful about the balloon, I thought. *Try not to disturb it*. But a moment later she was back in the room and the imaginary balloon had faded from existence. It was just Jordan now, this child who was created inside of me and had grown and grown until I could no longer contain her. She had entered the world and we had started our dance: together and apart, apart and together. With each passing year the distance between us had grown broader. *She no longer clings to me*, I thought, *and even when we are together, I can feel the world pulling at her*. What had it done to her when I wasn't watching? Why had I thought it would be safe to leave her alone with it?

When I consider my shortcomings as a mother, my thoughts scatter in all directions. I believe with all my heart that I am a *good* mother, but I am not a perfect mother. I am a *good enough* mother.[1] I can think of times when I've made the wrong decision, out of ignorance or fatigue, inattention or exasperation. There have been times when I've held her too closely, and times when I haven't held her close enough. I share responsibility for the dissolution of my marriage to Jordan's father, for contributing to a situation in which my child lives in two houses with two separate families.

I do not think of myself as a part-time parent to my daughter, but our parenting is fractured by the reality of divorce and all that comes with it. Jordan is shuttled back and forth between our two households,

---

1. The "good enough mother" is a useful term coined by the famous object relations psychoanalyst D. W. Winnicott. Good enough mothering is being empathic, warm, and sensitive toward the child. It is being emotionally and physically available and meeting the child's needs responsibly. Good enough mothers provide a nurturing environment where the child can be safe, contained, and held, both physically and emotionally. As the child matures and becomes more able to tolerate frustration, the good enough mother is less likely to feel the need to intervene when the child encounters difficulty. In contrast, a "perfect mother" may be unable to tolerate her child's feelings of discomfort, frustration, or anger. She consistently steps in to make things better, which reduces a child's ability to become self-reliant.

singing enthusiastically to the lyrics of her favorite music, gazing out the window, or engaging us in thoughtful conversations along the way. She is a strong and resilient child, either because we raised her to be that way or because we created a scenario in which her emotional survival depended on it. Like so many children of divorced parents, she is a child in perpetual alternating transition. *It's our fault*, I sometimes tell myself, because maybe the divorce was the start of it, the initial wedge that contributed to the growing distance between us. Then again, maybe it would've happened anyway. As parents, we crucify ourselves for the things we could've done better. But the truth of it is that the world would've gotten to our child the way it gets to all of them: one way or another.

"*This will be a difficult time for Ash*," the specialist had told us. "*Transgender teens have a much higher risk of suicide. Studies tell us that more than eighty percent of transgender teens have considered it, and about forty-one percent attempt suicide during their teenage years.*"

In the weeks that followed, I kept returning to those cold and terrifying statistics and the images that accompanied them. They visited me at night mostly, while I lay in bed staring into the darkness. In my mind, I could feel the wooden panel of her bedroom door against my fingertips as I pushed it open. I could see her lower legs and feet clad in blue jeans and sneakers, the rest of her lifeless body sprawled across the carpet but not yet visible around the corner.

I sifted through the scientific literature, trying to get my head around it. The 41 percent statistic came from a 2011 survey conducted by the National Gay and Lesbian Task Force and the National Center for Transgender Equality.[2] In some ways, the statistic had taken on a life of its own, becoming a rallying cry and political talking point rather than the result of a flawed survey performed more than a decade ago.[3] The 41 percent finding was derived from a single question about suicide posed to transgender teens: "Have you ever attempted suicide?" The response options were "yes" or "no." It is a question I ask my own patients,

---

2. J. M. Grant et al., "Injustice at Every Turn: A Report of the National Transgender Discrimination Survey," National Gay and Lesbian Task Force, National Center for Transgender Equality (2011).
3. J. Tanis, "The Power of 41%: A Glimpse into the Life of a Statistic," *American Journal of Orthopsychiatry* 86, no. 4 (2016): 373–377; R. D'Angelo et al., "One Size Does Not Fit All: In Support of Psychotherapy for Gender Dysphoria," *Archives of Sexual Behavior* 50 (2021): 7–16

although I ask follow-up questions to understand their history more completely. Having interviewed thousands of patients, I have found that the simple answer is not always the most accurate one. Many patients have suicidal *thoughts,* some have made suicide *plans,* and some have committed acts of self-injury without an intent to die (often referred to as suicidal *gestures* or parasuicidal behavior). Strictly speaking, none of these are suicide attempts, although respondents answering a yes/no question about prior suicide attempts might answer "yes" without fully understanding the differences. There were no questions in the 2011 survey about whether the attempted suicide occurred before, during, or after transition, which seems to be an important consideration.

It is also crucial to understand that patients with gender dysphoria often have other psychiatric conditions with their own independent risks of suicide. This can result in a higher rate of suicide attempts than might be seen in patients with gender dysphoria alone. In such cases, it is impossible to know whether the suicide attempt was related to gender dysphoria, some other psychiatric condition, or the combined effect of all the patient's conditions.

Results from other studies present a murkier picture. There is data finding *no reduction* in suicide rates following gender affirming treatment,[4] while other studies have found that the risk of suicide actually *increases* following gender affirming treatment.[5]

None of this was mentioned during our allotted 15-minute discussion with the gender specialist. There was only the 41 percent, placed in front of us as an irrefutable fact. It did its job in scaring us into submission. It would be years before we truly saw it for what it was.

One silver lining from our session with the gender specialist was that I was able to hear Jordan tell her story to a professional using expressions and terminology she had clearly gleaned from outside sources. She'd discussed her gender identity with the confidence and vocabulary of someone who had spent countless hours on the internet: reading

---

4. M. Biggs, "Puberty Blockers and Suicidality in Adolescents Suffering from Gender Dysphoria," *Archives of Sexual Behavior* 49 (2020): 2227–2229.
5. C. Dhejne et al., "Long-Term Follow-up of Transsexual Persons Undergoing Sex Re-Assignment Surgery: Cohort Study in Sweden," *PloS One* 6, no. 2 (2011): e16885; J. Straub et al., "Risk of Suicide and Self-Harm Following Gender-Affirmation Surgery," *Cureus* 16, no. 4 (2024): e57472.

blogs, watching YouTube clips, slipping in and out of chat rooms. She had learned all about a subject from the perspective of others, like a tourist collecting information about a country he or she has yet to visit. Was it fair to think of her that way? Had she not experienced some of it herself: the unhappiness with her body, the warm embrace of social acceptance, the lonesome and desperate feeling of being set adrift in the vast ocean of adolescence in search of a safe harbor?

Left to her own curiosity and personal development, Jordan might have explored the concept of transgender identity and decided it was not for her. What I failed to recognize until it was too late was the range and scope of her online exposure and the unrelenting influence of the internet. It seems obvious now, but it wasn't then.

She dived into it full force, a sea of transgender internet personalities and gurus, levying advice (the term grooming comes to mind) to anyone who would listen. Especially vulnerable were teenage girls who were attempting to navigate the troubled and confusing waters of adolescence in search of an identity. It was only later when I watched the YouTube videos myself that I realized the extent of the brainwashing that had taken place and continues to take place in households across the country. "Are you feeling awkward and emotionally troubled? Do you struggle to make friends? Are you uncomfortable in your own skin and looking for answers?" "Well," the YouTube personalities suggest, "maybe the reason for your emotional anguish is that you're actually trans. There's a whole community of people just like you, ones who have come to this realization and have finally found happiness in accepting themselves for who they are. Your trans community is the only family you can trust," they insist, "and we love and accept you for who you really are."

I allowed myself to imagine some of the search-engine queries that might be entered by an emotionally struggling teenage girl at midnight, an hour less amenable to logic. I pictured Jordan in her darkened room, hunched in front of the screen of her desktop, her fingers quickly flitting across the keyboard, the projections of her face illuminated by the synthetic glow of the screen. I sat there myself in the darkness, reenacting the moment. "I am twelve; am I transgender?" I typed. The results that populated the monitor were not recommendations to seek an evaluation by a professional, advice about exploring the question with one's parents or a trusted adult, or even a list of questions to consider when trying to grapple with such a profound and complicated subject. Instead, my online searches took me to YouTube personalities or websites advertising gear necessary for social and medical transition.

As far as I could tell, none of the YouTube personalities whose videos I watched had any kind of medical training, but they were quick to give medical advice. Even more notable, none of them seemed to have any psychiatric training, but they were quick to assist with diagnosis. In the videos I viewed, *every single one of them* encouraged self-diagnosis. One went so far as to tell anyone viewing, children included, that a person doesn't have to know for sure if they are trans to take hormones. "Take T and see how you feel," was the reckless advice, and I could all but hear the cheers from the online community backing them up.

The number of medically and psychiatrically false statements made by these individuals was voluminous, but the information was presented as if it was an absolute truth. The fact that mood fluctuates during adolescence (and, let's face it, throughout the muddled and unpredictable course of life in general) was absent from the discussion. Mood fluctuations were a sign of a deeper pathology—a problem with gender identity—and not one of the trans gurus mentioned the obvious, which is that puberty sucks and some degree of emotional suffering is normal. These individuals, who may or may not be trans themselves, freely discussed genitalia, breasts, and secondary sexual characteristics pertaining both to themselves and their viewers. Some had means by which a viewer could contact them privately to ask questions and seek tutelage. Watching these videos left me feeling surprised and disturbed that adults are allowed to discuss sex organs with children by way of the internet without consequences.[6]

These internet videos, websites, and chat rooms had a lot to offer. An adolescent girl proclaiming a trans identity could quickly, almost immediately, become part of a massive online community offering support, advice, and "unconditional acceptance" (as long as the individual

---

6. I imagine the time will come when we decide as a society to go after such adults by way of lawsuits or criminal charges. Until then, we live in a society in which you are more likely to be labeled a sex offender for public urination at a rock concert than you are for having online discussions with children about genitalia under the guise of instructing them about their trans identity.

continued to identify as trans, that is).[7]

The ads that accompanied my "I am twelve; am I transgender?" search were also noteworthy. One can find breast binders, packers (an artificial protuberance that's designed to be worn under the pants for that much-coveted penis-beneath-the-pants look), and STP devices (that's "stand-to-pee," if you didn't know), many available in discrete packaging to avoid parental discovery when the item arrives in the mail. When I typed "signs you're FTM" (that's "female-to-male," in case I'm losing you) into the search engine, I found an interesting article near the top of my search list entitled, "21 Signs That I Was Transgender and Just Didn't Realize It," published on July 31, 2020. The FTM trans writer mentioned things that really tipped him off, such as hating girls' clothing; secretly detesting photos of himself; being distraught when puberty struck; feeling angry the day he got his period; being obsessed with male classmates; being bothered by cisgender romance portrayed in the media; and being annoyed with expectations of female beauty standards. I imagine most teenage girls would agree with at least a few of these dislikes and preferences, but checking some or even most of these boxes seems like a far throw from being transgender. The obvious problem with the "21 Signs That I Was Transgender and Just Didn't Realize It" deduction is that it is not uncommon for an adolescent cisgender girl to experience all the items on the list. I'm not aware of an adolescent girl who loves her body, enjoys how she looks in girls' clothing, likes the way she appears in pictures, and looks forward to her period every month. If you find one, let me know. It might be our first contact with an extraterrestrial life form.

Following our session with the gender specialist, I thought a lot about what had transpired. Jordan had been evaluated individually for about fifteen minutes. It's amazing how brief fifteen minutes can seem. In my work as an adult psychiatrist, I do sometimes have 15-minute appointments, but they are very specific in nature and are known as "15-minute med checks." In such cases, I already know these patients well and we've already completed an extensive history and at least two 50-minute intake evaluations. I have spoken with the patient's family and prior mental

---

[7]. Be careful. Online announcements that you're not trans can get you excommunicated pretty quickly. Like most of our tribal identifications, if you want to be part of the team, you've got to wear the jersey.

health specialists, have reviewed the patient's past medical history, surgeries, allergies, social situation, history of drug and alcohol use, previous psychiatric hospitalizations, and any other pertinent information. All of this lays the groundwork for my clinical diagnosis and to establish an agreed-upon course of treatment that I have discussed with the patient. A "15-minute med check" is not a formal psychiatric evaluation. It's simply designed to check in with patients who are well known to me, clinically stable, and in need of a medication refill or slight adjustment in their medication. I would not rely on a fifteen-minute encounter to make a diagnosis as complicated as bipolar disorder, schizophrenia, major depressive disorder, generalized anxiety disorder, or gender dysphoria, and I would not feel comfortable recommending life-altering hormone treatment or surgical interventions based on that single encounter. And yet … that was what happened during Jordan's brief appointment with the gender specialist.

Had there been any assessment of other possible causes for Jordan's self-reported symptoms and psychological angst? It seems to me that there had not been enough time to discuss depression, anxiety, any history of trauma, peer pressure, social dynamics at her junior high, or the pain and complexity of going through the divorce of her parents. There were no collateral phone calls made to other family members, teachers, prior day care providers, or to a former therapist she had briefly seen. No educational records were sought, and no medical records were gathered from her pediatrician.

Patients in psychoanalysis spend decades of their lives working with a therapist to uncover the answers to such questions as, *"Who am I? How do I interact with the world? What are the underlying motivations for my behaviors? What insights can I gain about myself that will set me down the best path for a fulfilling and meaningful life?"* These things take time. Complex life-changing psychological discoveries shouldn't be preloaded and spit out with the rapidity of a PEZ dispenser.[8]

On a personal level, I think the world of this gender specialist. Still,

---

8. A patient enters a psychotherapist's office for the first time and tells him, "I'm a busy guy, doc. What do you say we skip the twenty years of therapy and you just tell me what I need to know in fifteen minutes."

"Fine," the therapist tells him. "Your father's an asshole and you have a complicated relationship with your mother. That'll be two hundred and fifty dollars."

a fifteen-minute assessment isn't enough time for a diagnosis of gender dysphoria, especially for a child. When medical and surgical transition is being recommended, a clinician must be sure. The consequences of being wrong are too significant. I wondered if it was common, this frenzied dash to a diagnosis and treatment. For the time being, I assumed that it was.

The Gender Specialists

In the wake of our appointment, I was propelled by a new sense of urgency to get Jordan into some kind of treatment. We had a gender-identity situation on our hands, and I needed to find a gender-identity-focused solution. In my mind, part of me was still back there in the office, staring at the bloated red mass of the balloon that hung in the air and dared me to mess with it. Someone had written the words, "This is what we are up against," in black magic marker along its thin latex hide. I was afraid of it, afraid enough to do whatever it took to keep it from exploding. *The balloon gets what the balloon wants*, I remember thinking during the weeks that followed. If someone had advised me that the balloon wanted blueberry waffles, I would've been the one in the kitchen frantically stirring the batter.

We had been given a short list of possible therapists who specialized in gender issues. As Zack and I considered the candidates, I couldn't help but notice that at least half of them had gender ambiguous names. The therapist who was most highly recommended had a full practice, and we asked ourselves questions like, "Should we wait for the top recommended therapist to have an available spot in his practice, or should we take Jordan to someone else not on this list?" We weighed the pros and cons of switching Jordan to the preferred therapist at a future date if an opening became available. "Maybe she doesn't need a therapist at all," I suggested, but Zack balked at that, and I didn't blame him. He was picturing his own red balloon, I imagine, or something just as ominous.

In the end, we had a single appointment with the top recommended therapist (a female-to-male transgender individual), who met with us as a professional favor. Although his schedule was too full to take Ash on as a patient, this therapist agreed with the gender specialist that Ash was transgender, and he had enough good things to say about another therapist with an opening in their schedule (I say "their schedule" because that therapist was gender nonbinary and used "they/them" pronouns) to give us the confidence to move forward with an appointment. We were ready to embrace the idea of having a healthy son. It was the only reasonable approach, given the binary nature of the decision before us.

As I aggressively worked on securing a therapist for my soon-to-be healthy son, Ash continued to plod along down the path he had selected. He went to school every day and did his homework, but he was not particularly interested in any academic subject. His science teacher was kind and connected well with our child, and he always had snacks in his classroom for kids who got to school early. Still, Ash's interest in science was lackluster at best. He liked his history teacher because she spoke about Broadway plays during class time, but Ash told us that history was his least favorite subject. He was in the school play and performed his part with gusto, but other than that, he did not express real excitement about anything. He had made some friends at his new school, most of them professing some form of LGBTQ affiliation. They were great kids and presumably fun to hang out with, but Ash became increasingly withdrawn and spent large amounts of time in his bedroom. He told me about his occasional panic attacks, which usually occurred late at night. He described feelings of overwhelming anxiety that culminated in pacing, crying, and hyperventilation. During the day, I observed melancholia: the sullen expression, a vacant look in his eyes, his head tilted downward toward the floor. He didn't seem to want to do anything with me, even things we had enjoyed together in the past. Ash's weight fluctuated considerably. Unbeknownst to me, he continued to self-injure, slicing thin cuts along the length of his upper thighs and forearm.

Ash had come out to us. We were using male pronouns and the name he had requested. We were facilitating a therapist specializing in gender dysphoria. And yet … there was no cathartic change in his mood, no sign of relief in his lost and strained expression. He seemed *more* miserable instead of less. *A child in transition*, I thought, but he didn't seem to be in transition at all. He was sinking, fading away from me and the world around him. I couldn't reach him, couldn't take him by the hand and pull him out of it. He slipped from my grasp almost willfully, like someone who did not want to be rescued or could not see the point of making it to the other side.

"This will be a difficult time for Ash," I could hear the specialist telling us. "Transgender teens have a much higher risk of suicide. Studies tell us that more than eighty percent of transgender teens have considered it, and about forty-one percent attempt suicide during their teenage years."

It's coming, I thought, but I didn't know what to do about it—*even me*, with my years of training and extensive experience as a psychiatrist. *What was it all good for*, I wondered, *if I couldn't make a difference in the life of the person I cared about the most?* I prayed that things would change when Ash started seeing the gender affirming therapist. I attempted to limit internet time, fighting with him about it but feeling that it was for the best. *Things will get better*, I promised myself. *This will not be the end of him.*

In the weeks before Ash's first appointment with the therapist, I thought a lot about the person I hoped would make things better for our child. The term "gender specialist" is defined differently depending on the reference. I had created a concept in my mind of what a gender specialist was, based on the title, my professional experience, and what I wanted it to mean. My naïve construct was this:

Gender specialist (noun):
A professional trained in psychotherapy who uses clinical assessment skills, diagnostic criteria, collateral information obtained from a patient's family and previous mental health providers, as well as critical thought in the evaluation and treatment of patients expressing concerns or discomfort regarding personal gender identity. A gender specialist is trained to rule-in or rule-out the diagnosis of gender dysphoria over time, based on careful consideration and assessment of the patient and diagnostic criteria from the DSM-5,[9] and through the detailed process of ruling out other potential diagnoses that might mimic or contribute to gender dysphoria. If the diagnosis is uncertain, a gender specialist may refer a patient to a psychiatrist specializing in the field of gender dysphoria and related disorders.

---

9. American Psychiatric Association, *The Diagnostic and Statistical Manual of Mental Disorders*, currently in its 5th edition (2013). This is the authoritative diagnostic standard used by mental health specialists throughout the world.

A gender specialist benefits patients through counseling and support, and works with patients on strengthening self-confidence, resilience, stress management, and the development of mature coping skills. The specialist has a thorough knowledge and understanding of strategies and treatments utilized to facilitate social, medical, and surgical gender transition/reassignment, including the ability to counsel a patient (and, in the case of minors, their parents or legal guardians) regarding the long-term risks, benefits, and alternatives to these treatments.

In an ideal world, all of this would be true. But the disparity between my concept of an ideal gender specialist and those we encountered turned out to be considerable. For our first session with the therapist Ash would be seeing on a weekly basis, we decided it would just be the three of us (me, Zack, and the therapist) without Ash. We wanted to get to know the therapist, to speak freely, and to express our concerns. We remained skeptical about the diagnosis, and we did not want *this* therapist (who would be initiating long-term therapy with our child) to take the diagnosis at face value. If they agreed with the other two specialists, so be it. It was best to make our reservations known, however. Maybe a fresh set of eyes was all that was needed.

The psychotherapy office was in a trendy area of Dante's Watch. The sidewalk outside was speckled with locals carrying cups of designer coffee while wandering in and out of used bookstores, antique shops, and restaurants serving produce harvested from our beloved neighboring farms. Artists chatted with a few passersby who had stopped to peruse their colorful collections of paintings or jewelry. A man dressed in blue jeans and a flannel shirt was perched on a concrete bench, his fingers picking out the melody of a song I didn't recognize from the strings of his well-loved guitar. With his long beard, baseball hat, and sunglasses, he could've been twenty or fifty-five, it was hard to tell.

Yes, I decided, *Ash will be comfortable coming to this office*, and I had a good feeling too. With the warm sunlight on our shoulders, the previous assessments felt more like a dream that was dissipating in the light of day. *This might be different*, I told myself, and I clung to that possibility as Zack and I rode the elevator to the building's second floor, proceeded down the hallway, and located the office.

For some reason I can't recall, we opened the door and glanced around the waiting room but then returned to the hallway and decided to wait there instead. Perhaps the waiting room was too small for two people who were once intimate partners but had both moved on to other relationships. Perhaps it was already occupied. Either way, it didn't matter. I did not want a cup of water or warm tea from the dual dispensers sitting side by side on the table next to the window. I had no need to distract myself with *Newsweek* or the latest celebrity scandal. Although I may have needed them, I did not want to avail myself of the various brochures in the office advertising resources such as the LGBTQ Network's Community Center or the local high school Rainbow Alliance. I was still in denial, perhaps. Or maybe I was about to make my case to the only person who could help us, and I was considering the best way to do it without coming across like a bigot or a crazy person.

The therapist came to fetch us from the hallway and was kind, professional, and well-intentioned. We told them our story ("they/them" being the therapist's chosen pronouns, something they announced to us at the beginning), and I again expressed my concern about the lack of previous objective evidence during Ash's life to support a diagnosis of gender dysphoria.

"Well, I treat it as if it's real," was the therapist's response.

"Every time?" I asked, "Always? Regardless of the evidence?"

"Yes," they said. "It's called the 'gender affirming model.' It's the best thing for the patient."

I sat there and thought about this. The therapist hadn't performed an evaluation—hadn't *even met* the patient—and yet the diagnosis was confirmed because the patient had proclaimed it to be so. Our child was trans. End of story.

Really? I thought. *That's all there is to it? We no longer do assessments or think critically about a case because the patient has done the work for us?*

I'd like to pause for a moment to explore the wisdom of this approach in other medical scenarios:

- A forty-year-old man loses control of his car and crashes into a tree at seventy miles per hour. A CT scan performed at the hospital shows that his spleen is ruptured and bleeding severely. The trauma surgeon explains to the man that he requires an emergency life-saving procedure. The man tells the surgeon that he read on the internet that the best treatment for a ruptured spleen is vodka and orange juice. The surgeon agrees, mixes him a cocktail, and sends him home.

- A female patient is referred to a psychiatrist for evaluation of possible anorexia nervosa. The patient, who is 5'9" and weighs eighty pounds, presents to the psychiatry office and tells the doctor she's there for help with her morbid obesity. The psychiatrist quickly concurs (affirms?) and prescribes weight loss medication, an exercise regimen, and a calorie-restricted diet.

- A mother brings her six-year-old to the ER after he falls off a swing. X-rays show a broken arm that needs to be straightened and placed in a splint. The child wants a cookie instead, since he'd seen that work for broken bones in a cartoon. The doctor shrugs and gives him a chocolate chip cookie. "If this doesn't fix it," he tells the mother, "bring him back and we'll see if an oatmeal raisin cookie does the trick."

- A neurosurgeon orders an MRI for a patient with recurrent headaches. The MRI is normal, but the patient is convinced that she has a brain tumor anyway. The surgeon, following the *brain tumor affirming model*, schedules her for surgery.

Since when did we decide that the best thing for the patient is to agree with them, *always*, regardless of the evidence? Our anorexic patient may think she is obese, but that does not make her obese. She is at risk for sudden death due to the many complications of starvation and severe malnutrition. As for the patient's psychiatrist, he or she should be reminded that blindly agreeing with a patient's proclamation despite all evidence to the contrary isn't what it means to be an expert. If everyone just agrees with the patient, what's the point of having an expert at all?

What we *should have* done was thanked the therapist for their time, paid them, and gone on to find someone else. After all, they were lacking what I thought was at least one key component of being a gender specialist: to assess my child based on critical thought and diagnostic criteria. We should have left, but we decided to stay. *Why?* I ask myself, and the answer is because we were running out of places to turn. This was our third session with a gender specialist. All of them were saying the same thing: follow the gender affirming model; if a patient says they're transgender, treat them as such.

Maybe I was the one making a mistake, and so we sat there and agreed with them. *Gender affirming model. Let's do this. Best thing for the patient, right?* We were choosing a healthy son over a dead daughter.

In the quiet space of that office, Zack wept—not because he was transphobic or because he was losing a daughter, but because he was afraid of losing our child altogether. "*Transgender teens have a much higher risk of suicide,*" the specialists kept telling us. We were taking it seriously, getting ahead of it, starting some kind of treatment, although I didn't know where that would take us or how quickly we might get there.

I took Ash to his therapy every week. He liked the therapist and the trendy neighborhood. We used he/him/Ash and thought we were doing the right thing at the time. I told my extended family to do the same and conveyed the risk (is "threat" a better word?) of suicide if we didn't get this right. The specialists advised me to instruct my toddler daughter to refer to her big sister as "he/him/Ash/brother." It broke my heart. What kind of confusion was I placing upon sweet Zoe in telling her to refer to her sister in this way? I was reassured by the experts. "It's so easy for little kids," they said. "They're very adaptable." It was like dress-up or a day at the playground.

About once a month, the therapist wanted to meet with just me and Zack, or sometimes with all of us together. They supported Ash in breast binding, and Ash started to bind. During one of our sessions, the suggestion was made that Ash should be excused from running in PE, since binding made it difficult for him to breathe during increased exertion. I drew the line there, suggesting that I get Ash a sport bra that he could wear instead of his binder during PE class. That didn't go over well. I also drew the line at the therapist's suggestion that we buy Ash a "packer." One appointment in which we were all present was solely dedicated to the therapist providing moral support so that Ash would feel comfortable asking us for a different kind of binder. The concept of the therapist needing to be present for moral support for such a request seemed completely unnecessary. Ash had independently asked me for his first binder, and I had obtained one for him without much question or fuss. He had thanked me when it came in the mail. Perhaps something had changed, but I couldn't help but notice that the meeting had an "us vs them" feel to it, as if two teams had been formed when I wasn't looking. Ash hadn't chosen me to be on his team.

I wish I could go back to the day of Ash's initial disclosure and do everything differently. The decision to take my child to this therapist despite what I learned about their therapeutic approach still bothers me. I was entrusted to choose a competent therapist for my daughter, and I failed her. These days, I try not to entertain the notion that I did not act in my child's best interest. It visits me at night, though, when I lie awake and think about the approach that I should've taken but didn't.

I am a board-certified psychiatrist and have a license to practice medicine, but I do not know what specific therapeutic goals were set for my daughter during that time. I should have asked for clarification. I do not know what they were trying to accomplish. It's a reasonable question to ask a therapist. I am ashamed that I was not more assertive, that I did not protect her or at least work harder to understand the path that was being set for her. On my bad days, the narrative is that I was too stupid, too tired, too busy, or too intimidated by fear of the unthinkable to even ask.

Chapter Four: This Place We Call Home

Community

I've already mentioned a few things about this place we call *home*. Every journey begins somewhere, and where it began for the three of us was in Dante's Watch. It is, in my admittedly biased but genuine opinion, an extraordinary place. Nestled between the Pacific Ocean and the deep, pine-studded arms of the Inferno Mountain range, Dante's Watch is a land of rugged, breathtaking beauty. Surfing, hiking, mountain biking, and all forms of artistic expression are integral parts of the town's culture. I once saw my dentist in her starched white coat for a checkup at 8 a.m., and then later saw her paddling out to catch a wave in her wetsuit and booties as the late afternoon October sun descended toward the horizon. During my interview for my first job there, I was told by my future boss that the schedule would be flexible. "Some of us surf before work," he told me, his face serious and earnest, "and some of us surf after."

On a typical morning, the coastline is blanketed by a thick layer of fog that burns off by midday. Pelicans fly low over the open water, and marine animals congregate amidst the wooden piers of the town's rickety wharf. It is a *wild* place, spectacular to its core, and for those who prefer more cultured recreation and amenities, there is a broad selection of restaurants, theaters, outdoor concert venues, a prestigious university, as well as multiple national sports teams, world-class ballet, two symphony orchestras, and opera all within a short drive from our quiet suburbs.

We are a multicultural community and a place where differences are warmly embraced. The day we went to tour Jordan's elementary school, there was a group of children in the outdoor amphitheater learning a traditional Chinese dragon dance, their bodies swaying back and forth to the steady cadence of the big drum, the sporadic clash of cymbals, and the deep-bellied resonance of a gong. In addition to recognizing more traditional American holidays, public schools expose children to festivities from other cultures. Day of the Dead was popular with the elementary students. During a conference I attended one evening in the school's multipurpose room, I spotted a picture of Bacchus, our Great Dane who had died two years before. The stage had been set up as an *ofrenda* for Day of the Dead, and Jordan had prominently placed a large picture of Bacchus upon the altar. It took me by surprise, seeing Bacchus there, amidst a collection of pictures of other students' animals and relatives, all of whom had been loved and lost. I cried a bit in the car before heading home that evening, as if I'd been given an unexpected gift of gentle kindness that clung to me like the fog and left me feeling cared for and full of gratitude.

As you might imagine from where it sits along coastal California, Dante's Watch is a progressive, liberal-minded town full of well-meaning people with political views that tend to be a few standard deviations left of center. In the last presidential election, more than three-quarters of the residents voted Democrat. The Federal Election Commission reports that financial contributions toward Democratic and liberal campaigns outpace contributions to Republican and conservative campaigns by roughly five-to-one. On one hand, residents are living in a forward-thinking, inclusive, and progressive town. On the other hand, the tendency to embrace all things liberal has its own set of drawbacks and consequences. There is a common hesitance to impose moral judgment on any behavior, and a tolerance for crime that casts perpetrators as the true victims in need of protection. Drug use, property theft, and petty crime are all above the national and state averages. Mass homeless encampments are tolerated, if not enabled. The disease of addiction is not called out for what it is. Dante's Watch is a broken place by many societal standards, and it is frustrating to me personally that so many people seem to prefer it that way. These are complicated issues, and I do not profess to have all the answers to the problems that plague our community. But just mentioning the issues is often met with open hostility and an air of distrust, as if any attempt to make things better (or to at least name the problems) is a direct assault on the community's much-loved liberal agenda.

School

In the early years of her public education, Jordan attended a small and charming primary school close to our home. The front of her elementary school was adorned with a large, bright mural of an underwater sea world containing dolphins, an octopus, multiple schools of fish, and even a sole hermit crab flailing on the cusp of the shore and sea. The mural was refreshed every year by parent volunteers. There were, in fact, so many parents interested in this volunteer job that there was a sign-up sheet for the activity, and any unfortunate souls who did not sign up on the first day were turned away and assigned to more mundane tasks. The school is in a residential neighborhood perched atop a hill. There are nearby hiking trails where I walked our dogs on cool afternoons, and a "secret glen" well known for its air of mystery and mischievous (real or imagined) fairy inhabitants.

For Jordan, kindergarten began at the age of five with the extraordinary Ms. Stenson, who won me over quickly and completely at the parents' back-to-school night when she lost her train of thought in front of the crowded classroom and impulsively said, "This is my worst day of the year. I hate talking to grown-ups." (If she later thought the better of making that statement, she never let on.) Ms. Stenson was the quintessential kindergarten teacher, and she began every school day with a story in the cozy reading corner that was outfitted with brightly colored pillows, small patchwork blankets, and a few stuffies. One morning the children would start the day hearing about the journey of Max into the magnificent world of the Wild Things, and the next day they would recite the methodical, soothing words of *Brown Bear, Brown Bear, What Do You See?* I always wondered where those stories took the mind of a five-year-old. It had been many years since I was that age, but I lived vicariously through my daughter, and when I dropped her off at school I often longed to stick around a bit in this place of eternal safety and comfort. *Maybe for just one story*, I would think. But I would tell myself *no* and return to my car and the adult world of responsibilities and disappointments, monotony and failures, brief moments of sunshine, and everything in between.

The elementary school had activities such as the well-attended Fall Festival, where children could ride a pony, have their face painted, try their hand at a myriad of arts and crafts, jump around in the bounce house, hang out with animals at the petting zoo, or dunk their principal in a tank of water with a well-placed softball throw. Jordan was particularly drawn to the petting zoo, returning to it each year to sit on a bale of hay and gently express affection to the chickens, bunnies, and goats that populated the small corral. She had a natural way with the animals, allowing them to come to her when they were ready. She loved school, and she loved to dress for school. Although the satin blue dress was her favorite, she rotated through a collection of several others, each with matching hair accessories. She proudly sported her blue unicorn book bag that was equipped with an ergonomically friendly handle and wheels for rolling.

Reports from Ms. Stenson about Jordan's academic progress were mostly positive. During her kindergarten year, Jordan had effortlessly learned to read—*as if by magic*—and she developed a fervor for books. "She's intelligent and studious," Ms. Stenson told us, "although she does like to talk, and Jordan does not always stop talking when the teaching begins." She'd been moved to other tables with different children, Ms. Stenson advised us, but Jordan talked to everyone. So yes, there was a problem with being quiet and paying attention during lessons. But given the realm of possible problems, this one seemed to be minor.

Jordan finished with kindergarten and moved on to the first grade. During her kindergarten year, I had parked in the nearby neighborhood (which posed less traffic than trying to navigate the school parking lot) and had walked Jordan to her classroom each day. About halfway through first grade, I began dropping her off in the parking lot roundabout, as did most parents, and Jordan walked to her classroom alone or with a friend. She would always turn around and wave to me though, just a few paces into her short journey. Until one day … when she didn't. I remember sitting there in the car that day, shocked and emotionally crushed as I watched her disappear into the building. *She didn't wave*, I thought. I had half a mind to go get her, to pull her out of the classroom and take her to a private place where I would tell her, "*Hey! You wave to your mommy when you walk to school. When you get to high school—or maybe college—you don't have to wave. But for now, you wave. This is first grade and you're only six years old, and I am not emotionally prepared for you not to—*"

BEEEEEEP.

I looked up. The car behind me was getting impatient. I thought about rolling down the window, sticking my head out, and looking back at the driver behind me (a parent themselves, no doubt). "*She didn't wave,*" I would say, pointing accusingly toward the building. Instead, I put the car in gear, nudged the gas pedal, and drove away, all too aware of what I had just witnessed: a tiny baby step on Jordan's long road to independence.

That first-grade year was filled with very interesting things because Jordan's first-grade teacher, Ms. Chandler, was interested in *all* things. She embraced that sense of wonder in her students, even though it would have been easier and more time efficient to stick to the bureaucratic restrictions of state guidelines. The class would be studying a unit on oceanography and doing a lesson about seaweed, and the question would be brought up by one of Jordan's peers, "What is the fastest fish in the ocean?" Perhaps far off the curriculum, unrelated to seaweed, but Ms. Chandler met the kids where they were and made it into a complete integrative learning experience that was vivid and memorable. (For the interested, the fastest fish in the ocean is the stunning sailfish.) On another occasion, although the kids were making their way through a science unit on insects, a first grader found an interesting rock near the play structure at recess, and Jordan came home an expert in spelunking, using the words "stalagmite" and "stalactite," and using them correctly. Her class planted and lovingly tended what they called "the salad garden" and grew vegetables in the spring. Each day was a new adventure. Each child was treasured, and healthy relationships were nourished.

First grade gave way to second, and one year rolled into the next as Jordan made her way through elementary school. In each year, there was a gain and a loss. I remember the talent show, in which Jordan performed "Let It Go" from the Frozen soundtrack; a spelling bee, in which she was one word away from going to the state competition (who knows how to spell cauldron anyway?); and annual parent-teacher meetings in which it was always pointed out how "social" Jordan was, which could be interpreted positively or negatively depending on the teacher. Slumber parties, roller rink gatherings, parent-guided outings to a local pottery studio, and shriek-infused birthday celebrations peppered the years. I look back on those times with nostalgia and fondness, and I am reminded of the adage, "The days are long, but the years are short." I remember in a vague and unimportant way that it was an exhausting journey, but I hold a deep love and affection for that time in our lives that is over now but was so incredibly precious. In what seemed like the blink of an eye, my daughter was finished with elementary school and would soon be entering junior high, a time I did not look forward to with quite so much unbridled enthusiasm. We were leaving the relative safety of the harbor now, and I could already make out the words on the channel marker as the shoreline receded into the distance. ROUGH WATER AHEAD, it said, and I knew enough to be ready for it, but not enough to anticipate the form that it would take, or how quickly it would be upon us.

When Jordan came out as trans, she was no longer at the primary school perched atop the hill adjacent to an enchanted, fairy-inhabited secret glen. Gone was the welcoming bright sea mural. Her junior high school was a grouping of gray buildings that resembled massive tombstones that appeared to be melting into the landscape beside the busy street. Although the school had a good reputation, it had an institutional feel to it with its heavy gray doors, large chain-link fence that surrounded the perimeter, and fields of once-green grass that had turned partially brown due to drought and neglect. It did not feel good to me, and I would venture to say that it did not feel good to my daughter. Whenever I dropped her off, I would hear honking and tires on gravel and see awkward children milling about, either alone or in small groups, each child with a token gray or black backpack. Many had hair that obscured their vision. Nobody's bookbag featured Hogwart's School of Witchcraft and Wizardry. In junior high, the sweetness was replaced by peer pressure, bullying, cruelty, a tendency toward the dramatic, cliques, an inability to self-regulate emotions, body odor, pimples, and other dreadful things. The excitement to get outside to play kickball was taken over by body shame that came with changing before PE. The satisfaction of eating lunch after a long morning of learning was eclipsed by the self-consciousness of consuming food in front of others. The thirst for books:

gone. In its place arrived social media, an evil I did not fully recognize until it was much too late.

Trouble struck quickly, one gut-wrenching melodramatic crisis after another. Choices that were once easy and unencumbered, such as what time to arrive at school or which hoodie to wear, were now fraught with anxiety and a host of social implications. In the midst of Jordan's self-proclaimed trans-identification, it was crucial, we were told, to superimpose the gender affirming model on this already complex and confusing situation. We were assured by the experts that this would make things clearer for our child. The school must be notified of "his" gender identity, preferred pronouns, special bathroom requirements, and other needs. I didn't understand how drawing attention and making special requests would ease his social pain or make life simpler or better for him (it seemed counterintuitive), but we were reminded that this was "an integral part of social transition" and thus "important for his psychological process." Our child's welfare and safety were at stake, the experts reminded us, and of course there was the ever-present red balloon, something I hated but dared not ignore.

In the early days of his social transition, I talked with Jordan—now Ash—about what he would like to happen at school to make him feel more comfortable as a trans male. I encouraged him to speak with his teachers about his preferred name and pronouns. "That's a given, Mom," he informed me with an air of condescension. Without consulting me or his father, he had made such requests months ago. I was surprised that nobody at the school had informed us. It was a stark difference from our honest and open communications with Ms. Stenson. Six years had passed since kindergarten, but Ash was still a child. Shouldn't the school have reached out to us, not to tattle on him but to bring his parents into the conversation? Instead, Ash was being guided by in-the-know YouTubers, self-proclaimed experts on the emotional world of trans teens.[1]

"These people know what they're talking about," he advised me, his voice tense with irritation and more than a dash of exclusionary haughtiness. "They've been through it."

I've tried to look at things from the school's perspective. They were

---

1. "How Accurate Is Mental Health Advice on TikTok?" *PlushCare*, November 18, 2022, plushcare.com/blog/tiktok-mental-health/.

creating a "safe place" for my child, avoiding the possibility of parental conflict by leaving Zack and me out of the discussion. "Our allegiance is to the student," the school's reasoning might go. "Children can discuss their gender identity with their parents when they're ready."

At first glance, this seems like a prudent and reasonable approach. Not all parents are immediately supportive of their child coming out as trans. There could be trouble, and neither the child nor the school wanted any part of that. The problem with this strategy is that the parents of these students do not live on Neptune. What happens when the next report card comes out and the child's name is listed as "Twix" instead of Melody? What will a parent's reaction be when they open the theater playbill to discover a picture of their daughter Amanda next to a bio that uses male pronouns and the name "Castle"? Bewilderment, shock, anger, and a sense of betrayal are not the best starting points for these conversations. Wouldn't it be better for both students and their parents for the school to engage the family in a controlled and supportive environment, to answer questions and offer resources, and to treat parents as a trusted partner with their child's best interest at heart? Parents do not appreciate being kept in the dark. They do not like other adults colluding with their children in secret.

Issues like bathroom and locker room choice and which gender sports team to play on seemed more complex, had bigger consequences, and thus needed more thought than a one-size-fits-all-parent-demonizing-eight-minute video on YouTube. Ash politely listened while I encouraged him to think about what it might feel like to change for PE while wearing a binder and having a female body in a room full of teenage boys. His answers had limited scope and insight and included such meaningless utterances as, "Uh-huh," "Whatever," and "It's fine, Mom." I asked him to take some time to consider the many ramifications of these choices, but he would always return to me after a perfunctory waiting period, wanting it all, having briefly and superficially tolerated my annoying, uninformed, trans-hating concerns. He wanted as much as the school was willing to give, as much as *we* were willing to give. All his answers were conversation enders. All his responses sounded like they were coming from somebody else's script.

Zack and I were not yet aware of how many options and advantages our public school district awarded a transgender child, or a child claiming to be transgender. Ash had come out as transgender at the end of his sixth-grade year. His hope was to start seventh grade as a fully socially transitioned boy. We met with the effervescent school counselor who pleasantly and compliantly facilitated some interventions. Ash was granted access and opted on a few occasions to use the boys' restroom. He was granted access to the boys' locker room as well, although he ended up changing in the school's nursing office for PE. Regardless of how he claimed to feel about it, I knew it would not be an emotionally positive experience for a seventh-grade teenager with female anatomy to change with boys in their locker room, and I was perplexed by the lack of concern on the school's part regarding liability in allowing that to happen, even if we *had* supported it.

Ash was not interested in sports, so which team to be on did not become an issue. His teachers and school administrators were instructed to use he/him/Ash, and he was given a lead male role in the school play. No physician's note was required to document that he had been diagnosed with gender dysphoria, so there was no medical documentation to justify that any of these interventions were necessary or even appropriate for his mental health and well-being.

By the time eighth grade arrived, the school had adjusted Ash's records so that his teachers would never see his birth name (aka his "dead name") in school documents. It was only Ash now, and his gender was listed as male. Unless they asked around or cared to investigate (they didn't), Ash's teachers would never know that he was once a girl named Jordan who liked mermaids and large hibiscus-adorned hair pieces, who chanted, "Swiper, no swiping!" as she watched *Dora the Explorer*, and who adored Pinkie Pie and Rainbow Dash. Only the paperwork that the school sent to the state would have his name listed as Jordan. The school counselor told us excitedly that Ash was her test case in how to accomplish concealing the birth name and gender from teachers. I attempted to share in her exuberance, but it was impossible. She had wiped my daughter from the face of the Earth. Ash was becoming a star.

One thing was clear to me from early on: if there was a psychological upside to coming out as trans, Ash didn't seem to be benefiting from it. His mood had deteriorated significantly since he'd come out to us and his peers. Rather than the anticipated social and emotional relief that experts touted, our "healthy son" was more moody, more angry, more sullen, and more withdrawn in the wake of his outing.

When asked about this, Ash didn't agree. "No, I'm much happier now. I'm living an *authentic life*," he told me, but again I was struck with the feeling that these were not *his* words reflecting his true reality. "*Who told you to say that?*" I wanted to ask him, because the evidence to the contrary was sitting right there in front of me: hiding behind a swathe of hair that covered his eyes, his private moments filled with recurrent, compulsive incidents of self-injury that I would discover later. "You're much happier now? Why are you still cutting?" I asked him. "Why are you not eating? Why do you lie in your bed with the lights out in the middle of the afternoon, hour after hour, sobbing into your pillow? Talk to me. Explain to me how you are better. Give me an example. At least consider the possibility that maybe you're not."

And what had been so *inauthentic* about his earlier years, I wondered: the laughter and friends and joy of frolicking in the surf on a warm summer day. When asked, he rolled his eyes at that. "I have almost no memories of my childhood," he told me. Boom. Another door slammed shut in my face.

Ash's world was becoming smaller and less accessible to me. His only real interests surrounded the LGBTQ community and its issues. Efforts to engage him in things that he'd previously enjoyed (photography, for example) resulted in a brief, superficial response before he turned the topic back to LGBTQ. It was as if he had fallen into a well, and I stood there peering over the edge, calling out to him, straining to see him in the darkness. "I like it down here," he would mutter, and instead of gripping the rope that I had thrown down to him, he let it slip from his grasp and allowed it to hang limply beside him. "You can go now," he would say. "This is the place for me. *This* is where I want to be. I'm living"—his voice smaller now and thick with resignation—"my authentic life."

Education

It is only in the aftermath of all of this that I have dared to ask the question, "Why was the school so eager to honor every request from my trans-identified child?" Since when do schools have no limits, no accountability, and no responsibility for what can happen to these children in the context of blind, unthinking, absolute affirmation of any identity proclamation a child decides to embrace? Why has the use of the word "no" become so difficult in a public academic setting? Even in teaching about consent for sex, children are not taught the use of the word "no" because the "yes means yes" curriculum has become so trendy. The concept of "no" is an important visceral response. The word "no" is a powerful word and sentiment. It is prudent that everyone, including children—*especially* children—know how and when to use it.

Enter the California Department of Education (CDE) and the regulations put forth by this entity.[2] The CDE declares on its website that it provides "medically accurate" information. According to the website, this means information that is "verified or supported by research conducted in compliance with scientific methods and published in peer-reviewed journals, where appropriate, and recognized as accurate and objective by professional organizations and agencies with expertise in the relevant field, such as the federal Centers for Disease Control and Prevention …"

The DSM-5 is well-accepted as the gold standard for diagnoses, including gender dysphoria, yet the CDE regulations seem to have overlooked this major publication in formulating things they deem to be good ideas. School districts are instructed that they must respect either a student's assertion of his/her gender identity or other evidence that the gender identity is "sincerely held." Other evidence includes letters from family members and healthcare professionals, photographs at family events and other gatherings, or letters from community members such as clergy. The CDE goes so far as to say that "a school *cannot* require a student to provide evidence of diagnosis." Let's reflect on that for a moment. The school is prepared to make significant interventions to address a medical condition (gender dysphoria), yet no confirmation of a diagnosis is required. Is this the policy for every medical condition a student might have, or just the policy for gender dysphoria?

When Jordan was younger, she had a medical issue that required her to take one prescription tablet daily during school hours for four days. Not only did this require documentation of a diagnosis from a physician, but several other things had to happen. In addition to the origi-

---

2. California Department of Education, www.cde.ca.gov.

nal doctor's appointment during which the diagnosis was made and the medication was prescribed, I had to make a second appointment to get a doctor's note, since it was not intuitive to me that a doctor's note would be required to take medication prescribed by her doctor. The prescription bottle, in other words, was insufficient on its own, even though it included Jordan's name, birthdate, dosing instructions, pharmacy information (with diagnostic coding information included), and the doctor's name. The school required a doctor's note stipulating that the prescription that the doctor had written was okay for the child to take. *In addition*, I had to sign a separate permission slip/waiver for Jordan to receive the medication on school grounds during school hours for the four days that she needed to take it. In this relatively low-stakes scenario, Jordan had to have two doctor's appointments, a doctor's note, a separate parental permission slip, and a fully intact prescription bottle. On another occasion, in an even lower-stakes scenario, I had to sign the same permission slip/waiver for her to use the Costco brand sunscreen that the school provided.

Yet in the far more serious matter of gender dysphoria, the school took the liberty of enacting dramatic interventions but was *not allowed* to verify the diagnosis. Not only had Ash not received a medical diagnosis, but he had also never had a doctor's appointment relative to this issue. (The therapists and gender specialist he had seen were not physicians.) The interventions that the school was making on behalf of our child—a name and gender change, permission to use the boys' bathroom, permission to strip down to his underwear (maybe even shower?) in the boys' locker room while cisgender boys did the same—was readily granted based solely on our child's desire to do so. If Ash had decided to start taking testosterone or estrogen blockers, that would have been accommodated as well, with no permission slip, no doctor's note, no official diagnosis, and no consent from either of his parents.

The CDE states that gender identity is private and may not be released, even to parents. They do not comment on how it would be addressed if the parent expresses a concern about the veracity of an undocumented medical claim of gender dysphoria. The website does briefly mention the possibility of a student claiming transgender status when that is not the case, but a meaningful solution is not provided as to how that might be handled. The CDE gives schools no leeway on these matters. Gone in California's public school system is the ability to act and think critically, independently, and on a case-by-case basis.

If students or parents are not comfortable with trans-identified kids using gender segregated locker rooms, the solution, according to the CDE, is to work with the families of the *cisgender* students to create a culture that "respects and values all students." If your fourteen-year-old daughter, for example, comes home distraught one day because there's a fifteen-year-old boy who's allowed to strip naked in the female locker room while the girls are changing because he proclaims to identify as female, your complaint to the school administrator would be met with an offer to work with you and your family on respecting and valuing all students, regardless of gender identity. *You and your family*, in other words, are the ones with the problem. Your fourteen-year-old daughter is being insensitive. She's going to have to learn to deal with it.

All of this is not to say that some of these interventions are necessary and potentially lifesaving for authentic trans children[3] and children with gender dysphoria when the diagnosis has been medically established. But to emphasize, schools do not require, and in California they are *not allowed to request*, medical evidence of a diagnosis to support these social allowances and interventions.

A relatively new concept introduced to public education in recent years is "The Genderbread Person," a teaching tool that is touted to be useful "for breaking the big concept of gender down into bite-sized digestible pieces." The metaphor "simplifies" a person's gender-based characteristics into five areas:

1. Gender identity ("woman-ness" or "man-ness")
2. Gender expression (femininity or masculinity)
3. Anatomical sex ("female-ness" or "male-ness")
4. Sexual attraction (either to "women and/or feminine and/or female people" or "men and/or masculine and/or male people")
5. Romantic attraction (either to "women and/or feminine and/or female people" or "men and/or masculine and/or male people")

---

3. See chapter seven for a discussion of the differences between authentic and inauthentic transgender individuals.

If these bite-sized pieces seem murky, you are not alone in your assessment. It is not clear at what age and grade the Genderbread Person is designed to be introduced, but considering the imagery, I imagine it starts with elementary-aged children. The DSM-5 estimates the prevalence of gender dysphoria to be between 0.002 and 0.014 percent of the population. In light of this estimate and the fact that some elementary-aged children are struggling just to learn math and basic social skills, teaching the concept of gender identity and dysphoria to a class of young children seems like, at best, a waste of time. At worst, it opens a door that may lead to confusion and devastation. Normalizing these concepts to young children teaches a child with or without gender dysphoria that he or she can pick their gender, despite lack of evidence to support the selection or all evidence to the contrary. In this way, lessons in prepubescent gender and sexuality have become a fictional choose-your-own-adventure story. Unlike a choose-your-own-adventure story, however, it is not easy to start fresh from the beginning and choose a different adventure when things go horribly wrong. There are no second chances once certain aspects of medical transition begin, and the risks and complexities of social transition can be equally damaging.

For those who might find the the Genderbread Person fraught with trouble, "The Gender Unicorn" is another option for the teaching of young children. Some trans activists and gender specialists consider it to be a more inclusive model than the the Genderbread Person, which has characteristically masculine features. The cheerfully colored purple Gender Unicorn is cute enough to be a stuffed play toy, and the advantage according to its proponents is that it recognizes genders outside of the "Western gender binary" and uses a sliding scale rather than a checkbox format. The double helix of a strand of DNA is placed where one would naturally imagine the unicorn's genitals to be. The term "other gender(s)" is introduced to indicate the many genders that people might identify as, or be attracted to, such as agender, bigender, genderfluid, genderqueer, transgender, nonbinary, gender nonconforming, and two-spirit (as if life is not already complicated enough for young children who are just trying to make their way through *James and the Giant Peach*.)

Statistically, it is unlikely that there is a single gender dysphoric child in any given elementary school class. I fail to see how these concepts are helpful or even appropriate to discuss in this kind of detail with young children, who are not at a phase in their lives in which they are concerned with whom they may wish to have sex with years into the future, let alone wonder if they may be "asexual" or "queer." I would conjecture that many adults would struggle to accurately define such terms as "genderqueer" or "two-spirit." Thankfully, that will not be a problem in the future because the kindergartners can tell them. Whether or not the concepts are actually learned by these young children, or if the Genderbread Person and the Gender Unicorn just generate more questions and confusion, remains to be seen.

I do not wish to lose sight of the fact that some of these basic concepts are extremely important. (Not everyone is the same, for example, and not everyone is attracted to the same type of person. Sometimes people who are born one gender decide to live their lives as the other gender, and that's okay.) It is equally important that these basic principles of human diversity and acceptance are taught to children at a young age in the interest of inclusivity, compassion, and understanding. However, the full range and complexity of the Genderbread Person and the Gender Unicorn is confusing to most adults, and no doubt confusing to our children. At the risk of being labeled an ignorant transphobic bigot, I would just like to suggest that kindergartners don't need a PhD in gender identity, dysphoria, and human sexuality. They need to be reminded about basic decency and acceptance of others. Each of us is different, and it's important to treat people with kindness and respect.

(There, I did it, and without the help of a Gender Unicorn.)

These are the challenges we face in this place we call home: being sensitive and inclusive of others without bludgeoning our children in the process; establishing public spaces and safe schools that protect and respect everyone, *including* the majority; and developing school policies that partner with parents instead of working against them. I believe that we can get there, but it feels to me that we have lost our way. We are no longer in the relative safety of the harbor. The waters have become rough and choppy all around us.

I pull at the oars of the rowboat as the storm clouds gather on the horizon. Jordan was with me when we started, but I can no longer see her, only the brooding form of Ash with his black hoodie, restless eyes, and dark hair that hangs in his face and obstructs his features. I do not know him, do not understand why he lies to me, why he carves into his body with a sharp piece of metal and tells me that he remembers nothing of the person he was before. What has become of my daughter? Is she out there, flailing in the swell or sinking quietly beneath the surface? And the question that I have already begun to ask myself: What will I do to get her back?

Chapter Five: Marriage

Together

The obvious person to help me in dealing productively with Jordan's trans identification and subsequent psychological derailment was her father, Zack, the only person on the planet who loves her as much as I do. He had been present during her early upbringing and had observed the persistent stream of feminine interests and activities that Jordan had naturally embraced. We shared in the delight of having a daughter who insisted on sleeping in her teal sleeping bag with pink polka dots, followed by a longer stint during which she'd crawl into her purple-and-green Princess Tiana and Prince Naveen tent each night and would not emerge until morning. Zack had been there on the afternoon when Jordan belted out "Dreams" by The Cranberries and danced around our living room in her pink glitter-speckled tutu in front of an audience of her two parents and a carefully arranged congregation of stuffed animals. (Her tie-dyed teddy bear named Smoothie was one of my personal favorites.)

Jordan had been born of love and into love, and the years during which Zack and I were madly in love seem not so long ago. We met on the street of a third-world country, in front of dilapidated shacks selling chicken, fresh fruits and vegetables, strange sodas, and coconut cakes. Nearby wooden tables and rickety chairs provided a place where one could rest in the heat (not *from* the heat) and enjoy an afternoon snack. It was about 1 p.m., and the air was thick with humidity. I was not in the most pleasant state of mind that day as I walked along: hungry, hot, crabby, and looking from one shack to the next as I tried to decide what to eat. There is a certain decision-making paralysis that descends upon me during such moments. The hungrier I am, the harder it is to decide, and I could feel myself winding down, moving slower, the turn of the gears grinding to a halt.

"Are you going to have a little lunch?"

I turned and saw him standing there, a container of coconut curry in his hand. He'd caught me off guard. I hadn't been looking for "a little lunch." Food, yes. A little lunch, and what came with that: no. And starting with that question, our friendship began. I have no recollection of what I ate. It didn't matter. After lunch, I asked for his number. He wrote it down and I folded the small piece of paper and put it in my pocket. Only later when I got back to my apartment and emptied my pockets did I realize that the number he wrote was 1-800-HOT-BUNS. Luckily, we lived in a small village, and I knew I'd run into him again.

The relationship developed over time. We were both in medical school, so we shared a common interest, similar challenges, and an understanding of the sacrifices that came with the territory. While my brain has a propensity for darkness (think: Wednesday Adams), Zack's has a propensity for levity (think: Jim Carrey). I learned to sing in the shower. He learned the pleasure of vegetarian cuisine. I had never known anyone who I thought was as perfect for me as he was. I loved spending time with him and the effortless joy of being together. The problems that arose (he lived on the East Coast; I lived in California) seemed small and inconsequential. We dated across the country for several years as we made our way through our medical training, but eventually we found a way to be together and were married on the beach at sunset with a total of nine people present. There was a gentle ocean breeze, and I remember hearing the banana trees and palms blowing delicately in the background, a serenade to our commitment. I wore a black dress (again, Wednesday Adams) and had deep rose-colored orchids in my hair. Each guest had a personalized champagne flute that we'd designed and hand-painted in the weeks leading up to the wedding. My mother blew a conch shell and played the ukulele in our honor. Other than a Rastafarian trying to peddle ganja to my future brother-in-law (it would not have been their first business transaction that week) amidst the "I do's," the ceremony was beautiful and was one of the happiest moments of my life.

Our marriage thrived. We bought a townhouse while we were both residents-in-training. We painted the walls in shifts and enjoyed selecting the vivid colors. Our dining room was violet eclipse; our bedroom was bahia grass; and our finished basement was venetian plaster. In the spring of 2006, we decided that maybe it would be a good idea for me to go off my birth control. (You know, just to see what happens.) I was pregnant by the end of the month, and Jordan was born nine months later. Her future bedroom had been wallpapered with puppies and kittens by the previous homeowner, and we left it that way, realizing that there had been a place set aside for her—in our house and in our hearts—even before she was created.

We rescued a gigantic Mastiff named Monty who looked after me during my pregnancy and looked after Jordan for the first few months of her life until Monty unexpectedly died from lymphoma. As our residency training ended, Zack and I planned and executed a cross-country move, at my request, so that we could live closer to the place I still thought of as home. If Zack ever had a negative thought about moving away from his family and his childhood friends to establish a different life on the West Coast, he never shared it. I felt loved and supported, and I think he felt the same from me. We arrived in California when Jordan was eighteen months old, and we've lived there ever since.

From time to time, if life is kind enough and the wind is blowing just right, we are blessed with brief moments of realization in which the world suddenly becomes clear. ("Are you going to have a little lunch?") I remember being visited by such a moment when Jordan was five. I recall what I was wearing and exactly where I was standing in our large, well-lit living room, the sun pouring through the window and bouncing off the hardwood floors. I was alone in the house, gathering toys off the floor (a perpetual task with a five-year-old), when I stopped for the space of about thirty seconds and just stood there, looking at nothing in particular. *Oh my gosh*, I thought. *I am happy.*

The years in which I experienced that happiness are among the best of my life. I held onto them as long as I could. But this is not a fairy tale, and we did not live happily ever after. Eventually, Zack and I began to focus on other things: work mostly, and the incredibly rewarding but relentless demands of parenthood. Weekends were the best but most demanding hours of our week, and we took shifts with Jordan to give each other a little personal time and a chance to recuperate. Zack would take her bike riding or to the playground in the morning, and I'd take her to the beach or for a playdate with a friend in the afternoon. Zack's work involved sporadic weekends, and on those days, it was just me and our daughter, having fun together, of course, but I was also exhausted and running on empty. Sometimes, we did things together as a family, but Zack's upbeat, jovial nature engaged Jordan in a way that I could not. What started out as an activity for the three of us would often transition to an activity for the two of them with me feeling like a spectator, or even worse, like an intruder. I couldn't match their level of energy, enthusiasm, and general silliness. It wasn't in my nature, I couldn't compete with them, and I didn't want to. After a while, I started avoiding those outings. "You two go," I'd tell Zack. "I'm not feeling well." Then I'd feel sad and regretful for the rest of the afternoon, wishing I'd made a different decision but knowing it wouldn't have gone well. I loved being a mother, and I was still in love with Zack, but I felt a sense of loss and loneliness within my own family, and I realized that I was drifting with the soft pull of a current that was putting distance between me and my husband.

I suggested to Zack—asked; no, begged him actually—that we go to couple's therapy. To my great disappointment and frustration, he resisted. To this day, I don't understand why. He is intelligent, insightful, and psychologically minded. We would've done well in therapy. It might've given us the tools we needed to save our marriage. Instead, he responded with things like, "We've always been able to talk to each other. Why do we need someone else involved in that conversation?"

"There are things I am telling you that you are not hearing," I told him. "If this continues, the way things have been going … it's not going to lead us to someplace good."

Here's a tip for anyone in a meaningful long-term relationship that they'd like to hold on to: if your partner expresses a strong desire to start couple's therapy, you should go. It doesn't matter what you think about the process. Maybe you'll come around, or maybe you won't. But you should at least try, or risk losing them along the way.

I drifted for years, and Zack and I both distracted ourselves with other things. We took some vacations together, just the two of us, and during those times I felt closer and more hopeful in our marriage, and I think he did too. *Maybe we can salvage this*, I thought, but we'd return home and fall back into our usual patterns, and the thought began to occur to me that maybe we couldn't.

One evening, I announced to Zack that I was moving out. It wasn't rash or impulsive. I'd been contemplating it for months. I'd rented a place close by, a little cottage near the water. "It's a month-to-month lease, not forever," I told him. "I just need a break, some time apart to see how I feel when we're not living in the same house together. It could end up being a good thing. It might actually be the change we need to bring us closer together."

Zack seemed shocked, completely taken by surprise. "It's the beginning of the end," he told me. "Don't you see that? This will not lead us to someplace good."

It was like hearing my own words repeated back to me, something I'd been telling him for years. *How could this be a surprise?* I wondered. *How could he not have seen this coming?*

"I just want to be happy," I said, "and I've been unhappy for a really long time."

"Don't move out," he implored me. He was paying attention now. After all this time, he had finally heard me. "We can go to therapy," he suggested, as if this was a novel idea.

"Maybe we can," I said, "but I'm still moving out. Maybe it'll only be for a short while. In the meantime, we can figure out a schedule for what days we'll each have Jordan."

"You're taking Jordan?" he asked, his features once again transformed by shock and disbelief.

"Only some of the time," I said. "I'm her mother, and you're her father. She needs both of us."

He shook his head. "Don't do this."

"I have to. It's not forever."

"It's the beginning of the end," he repeated, and although I did not want to believe this, part of me understood that he might be right.

Apart

The marriage did not survive. Zack was right about that, although I do not agree that my decision to move out was "the beginning of the end," as he put it. Things had begun to unravel much earlier than that, building with a momentum that brought us both to a place where we did not want to be. I acknowledge my part in that, the things I could've done differently to change the trajectory of where we were heading. In our many conversations since, Zack has done the same. Falling in love takes two people, and falling apart happens pretty much the same way.

As it turned out, we did end up going to therapy—*finally*—but by the time we got around to it the opportunity to avoid disaster had passed. Our sessions with the therapist were more of an autopsy than a resuscitation. We rummaged through the remains of our relationship, turning things over in our hands, exploring the mistakes we made and the reasons we had made them. It was useful, enlightening in a way that helped us understand ourselves and each other, and I believe that the insights gained have allowed us to navigate subsequent relationships with greater skill and awareness.

It's hard to look back on a broken marriage and recognize the positive things that came from it. I still consider our failure to save it as one of the greatest tragedies of my life. *Our* lives. We were together for fifteen years, and *so much* of that was good. I wish it had been longer. But we produced an amazing child, and that's reason enough to rejoice. We've also remained friends, and I'm thankful for that. Somehow, we managed to protect the core of what we were, the thing that really mattered when the rest of it was stripped away. Our willingness to come together in the end—the respect, friendship, and love for each other that we still share—has made us stronger allies and more capable of working together for the benefit of our daughter. Parenting doesn't end with divorce. The love for our daughter is a common thread that still binds us. It pushes on, doing the hard work when nothing comes easy, and any path forward leads to a battle.

I don't know how much of Jordan's derailment was related to the dissolution of our marriage. It didn't help—I'm sure about that. Managing her crisis from two separate households was difficult. Our parenting styles and perception of the situation were so different. I felt strongly that Jordan was in serious trouble and needed our assistance in becoming unwedged from the predicament she had created for herself. Zack was less convinced, and his *laissez-faire* parenting style favored a watch-and-wait approach that did not match my own sense of urgency and desperation.

From that standpoint, the dynamics of our recently dissolved marriage seemed to be repeating themselves, and I felt unheard and unsupported in my mounting concerns. "There are things I am telling you that you are *not hearing*," I said again to him, and it was frustrating, the way we kept looping back to this when any change or intervention was likely to fail without his support. I had to recruit him. I had to get him to see the urgency in it. It would prove to be one of the most difficult parts of turning things around, but it was also one of the most important.

For now, I was alone in my struggle to try to save her, or so I felt. *I can't do this without him*, I thought. But meaningful help was a long time in coming.

Chapter Six: Nobody Knows How to Help Her

Looking for Help (the Mother)

Several months had passed since Jordan's initial evaluation, and it was around this time that I slowly came to realize something. As a parent who questioned the accuracy of my child's self-made diagnosis and the wisdom of going along with it, I was alone with my objections. The gender affirming approach that we'd been following thus far was clearly making her worse, but none of the specialists we'd spoken to seemed to be concerned with that, or even willing to entertain the possibility that we were heading in the wrong direction. To be clear, it wasn't that they'd taken the time to listen to my concerns with an open mind, had reevaluated Jordan and carefully considered the information at their disposal, and simply disagreed with me regarding the conclusion. Rather, they disagreed with me based on *ideology alone*, or so it seemed. It was as if these specialists had decided a long time ago that the world was flat, and they perceived my insistence that it wasn't as a nuisance that needed to be dealt with.

"*Don't you worry your pretty little head about that*," was the message I seemed to be getting from my string of conversations with a long line of specialists. "*These are complicated matters best left to the professionals.*"

"But *I am* a professional," I tried to tell them. "I graduated from medical school and completed a four-year psychiatry residency as well as a fellowship. I've been a practicing psychiatrist for over a decade. I see patients in my own clinic who are transgender and have gender dysphoria. It's not that I don't believe in the diagnosis. It's just that I don't believe it's correct in this case."

"*We disagree with you,*" was their collective response.

"How can you be so sure?" I asked. "What if you're wrong? What if the diagnosis isn't accurate?"

"*The history of transgender individuals tells us that—*"

"I'm not talking about the history of transgender individuals," I reminded them. "I'm talking about a *very specific* individual, my daughter, who's gotten herself caught up in a social movement with the rest of her teenage friends, many of whom *also* profess to be trans. Despite what she says, I haven't witnessed *any* objective evidence that she's transgender … and believe me, I've been looking."

I recounted the discussions and struggled with the arguments in my head. Why were the specialists so quick to recommend permanent life-altering medical and surgical transition to a teenager during the emotional rollercoaster of adolescence? Jordan's hairstyles and musical tastes changed like the weather. How could they know what she would want ten years from now? If she turned out to be trans, fine. But wasn't it best to wait on the medical and surgical interventions until she was older and *absolutely certain?* Wasn't that the more responsible way to approach this?

"*Some families do decide to wait.*"

"But you're not recommending that."

"*No.*"

"Why?"

"*The thing to understand,*" they kept telling me, "*is that we've been treating transgender individuals for decades, and the experience we've acquired tells us that the gender affirming model is critical to the psychological well-being of the patient—*"

"Then why is she getting worse?!"

"*—and in reducing the very high suicide rate among transgender individuals.*"

Yes. They had mentioned the suicide rates every chance they got. "But tell me," I asked them, "will she be less suicidal if we destroy her ability to have children, cut off her breasts, remove her reproductive organs, deepen her voice, cause her to grow back hair, increase her risk of certain cancers and cardiovascular disease, and replace her vagina with ambiguous genitalia, only for her to realize—too late—that she was an impulsive teenage girl prone to the social influence of her peers, and that she's not transgender after all? Where will she be then, with ambiguous anatomy in the wake of a horrible life-altering decision that cannot be undone. What will be her risk of suicide at that point?"

Blank stares. A placating smile.

"*We realize this is difficult. Many parents have trouble coping with the news that their child is transgender.*"

"I'm not having trouble coping. I'm just not convinced that what we're doing is the right thing for her."

"*There are parental support groups that many parents find helpful.*"

And so it went, the gist of every conversation with a gender specialist thus far. We talked past each other, and I was treated as someone to manage, an obstacle to my child's self-actualizing progress and psychological well-being. The school followed their liberal California-based protocols, eliminating Zack and me from the conversation altogether. I do not know what Jordan talked to her therapist about, but I imagine there was very little exploration of alternative hypotheses regarding her recently proclaimed change in gender identity.

Around this time, I happened upon the brilliant poem, "Diving into the Wreck," by Adrienne Rich. The poem describes a scuba diver descending into the depths of the ocean to explore a shipwreck. Enveloped by darkness, armed only with a camera and a knife, the diver has come to see the wreck itself and not the myth, the thing of stories that few had actually seen.

I thought of the poem frequently during this time in my life when I felt very much alone. Gone were the days in which Jordan and I attempted to navigate these waters together. For the months and eventually years that followed, I was by myself, alone in a small wooden rowboat with no view of the shoreline and no way of knowing whether I was even headed in the right direction. I worked the oars, and the muscles of my lower back and arms ached from the effort of each stroke. The waves slapped at the hull and crested the lip of the gunwale. Water spilled into my tiny vessel and slopped around at my feet. The emotional storms came and went, threatening to capsize me, and during the calmer moments the sun beat down on my shoulders and the gulls circled and screeched from overhead. The nights were the worst of all, the loneliest by far, the heavens vast and indifferent above me. I kept telling myself that someone would come for me, that sooner or later they would find me out here, still rowing, still looking for my daughter, still searching for a way out of this.

To be fair, there was no shortage of people who offered their assistance. Treating trans teens has become fashionable, almost elitist, with a sprinkle of self-righteousness thrown in for good measure. Some of these people seemed to want to help me too, but they didn't know how.

Everyone I disclosed her story to either knew someone who had transitioned or knew someone who knew someone ...

"Oh, my kid has been through something too. It can be difficult. Do you want Ash to talk with my nonbinary child? They're a volunteer at the Rainbow Center."

(No thanks. I don't think having Jordan hang out with yet another enabling peer will make things better.)

"My child is using they/them pronouns. We started testosterone three months ago."

(Why on Earth would you start your child on testosterone if they can't even decide what gender they are?)

"A guy I work with is a fully transitioned man. He's had everything done and you'd never know. Do you wanna talk to him? He's really cool and totally an open book."

(I don't think that would be helpful.)

"A woman in my office has a trans kid. She goes to a support group for parents of trans teens—I'll get you the information."

(As if celebrating my progressiveness on a weekly basis with a group of pretentious, enabling parents would serve me well.)

"Isn't it wonderful how kids have so many options these days?"

(And yet they're all so tortured.)

These were the thoughts that went through my head with every well-intentioned conversation. I said none of it, only smiled and thanked them for their kind advice and generous offers. I agreed to accept their assistance in a vague, noncommittal, open-ended way at an undefined, never-arrived-at future date. They seemed pleased to have helped, but I felt more hopeless and more alone with every conversation. On my worst days, I felt bitter and ungrateful and not worthy of the kindness bestowed upon me. Eventually, I stopped reaching out for support. There was only so much disappointment I could stomach.

It was a dark time for me, but even during my most hopeless moments it was hard for me to let go of the conviction that all of this could've gone a different way. I imagined the enlightening questions that might have been asked by the specialists, the gentle confrontations that could have been made.

"Can you tell us how it feels to be a boy? What does it mean to you on the inside to be a boy? What exactly is it about a boy's body that seems right for you?"

"You've stated that you have gender dysphoria. What does that mean to you? How did you learn of the term? What kinds of sources have you looked to when educating yourself?"

"What does, 'I've always known,' really mean to you, Ash? What might you like most about being a boy?"

"I'd love to have a conference call with the physician who diagnosed the gender dysphoria. Would that be okay with you?"

(Ahh, but first you'd have to find a physician willing to do a real evaluation and make that diagnosis with a high degree of confidence.)

"I'm curious, Ash, to hear more about your childhood. Can you tell me about other things that came up for you that may have signaled a problem with your biological gender? I'm sure there must be so many; I'd love to hear all the instances you can think of."

(What would he say to that? Would there be *any* examples that he could think of?)

"What kinds of things do you look forward to most during your life as a man? What specific things have you thought of and fantasized about in transitioning to your authentic gender? What would the transition allow you to do?"

(I'd expect silence, or a pleading look toward me or Zack.)

"Testosterone is a big step. I wonder, have you considered other ways to improve your dysphoria without medical transition? There is now evidence, for example, that focused psychotherapy without medical transition may be effective.[1] Do you think it might be worth giving that a try?"

"What would happen if you woke up tomorrow in the same body

---

1. Although there is evidence in published literature suggesting psychotherapy as a viable treatment for gender dysphoria, the modality was not recommended or even mentioned by a single gender specialist who spoke with us. Psychotherapy was recommended for assistance in coping with the transition, but not as a treatment for the dysphoria itself. For a general overview on the topic, see R. D'Angelo et al., "One Size Does Not Fit All."

but no dysphoria? Would you be happy then? Would that bring relief?"

"Now, Ash, I'm curious to know more about how your world has changed since you came out as transgender. Usually, things get so much better! Tell me all about it. How has your life changed? Tell me everything!"

(What could my child say about his deteriorating mood and behavior since coming out? *"It's going great! I lock myself up in my room, sit in the dark, and have frequent panic attacks. I spend hours crying every day, and I've been slicing into my body repeatedly as a primary coping mechanism."*)

These were the kinds of questions an interested, responsible, and caring clinician might ask, but I heard none of them during Ash's evaluations by the gender specialists. "Let's discuss the various forms of testosterone so we can get you started," was the primary focus, and anything outside the realm of medical transition was swept aside to make way for important topics like the surgical options already available.

The Gender Clinic

What's a mother to do when her child is sick and no one seems to be able or willing to help her? I doubled down, refusing to believe that the opinions and meager evaluations Ash had received thus far were the best the medical community had to offer. I chose one of the most respected medical institutions in the state. For the sake of anonymity, I'll call it the California Institute of Medicine (CIM), which had one of the oldest established gender clinics in the country with world-renowned experts doing research and treating patients. CIM had a gender clinic specifically for children and adolescents, and it was also close to home, although that was secondary. (I would've traveled to Madagascar if I thought it would help.)

To be honest, I was hesitant about making the appointment. *What if this doesn't help?* I asked myself. *Where will we go from there?* I had no answers, only a lingering uneasiness as I picked up the phone and contacted the clinic. The receptionist I spoke with was kind and friendly and seemed to understand that this was not an easy phone call for me. We did not pretend that everything was okay, and she did not treat my call as if I was scheduling a routine well-child check-up. Unlike other pediatric specialty clinics whose appointments filled months in advance, the CIM Child and Adolescent Gender Center was able to see Jordan within a few weeks. (For comparison, my younger daughter waited six months to be seen by a pediatric cardiac surgeon for a matter far more acute than this.) It is also worth noting that, in the era of managed care, no referral from a primary care provider was required.

Since this was during the COVID-19 pandemic, the appointment was via Zoom, so Jordan, Zack, and I all gathered in my private practice office to participate in the consult. My office is on the second floor of a three-story office building close to the ocean. The complex has bright exterior hallways and well-tended gardens with multicolored geraniums and a variety of succulents. Nearby, there is a coffee shop with rich, buttery, melt-in-your-mouth chocolate croissants, a quaint Mexican restaurant with vegetarian options, and a local mom-and-pop drugstore. From the open windows of the corner consultation room, I can see tall pine trees, their limbs swaying in the breeze. A gray heron often visits the grassy area between my building and the neighboring restaurant. I encounter him so frequently that I have come to think of him as a security guard stationed at his post.

On the day of the CIM appointment, I had the windows closed to optimize acoustics for my desktop's microphone. The sound of the leaves was absent, and so too was the heron, off to wherever it is that herons go when they are not patrolling the grounds of medical office buildings. I wish he had been there—a friend who had my back—but his contract with Gray Heron Security isn't specific about his working hours, and he tends to come and go as he pleases.

We gathered in my small office, the three of us. Jordan sat closest to the computer because she was the focus of the consultation. It was important to remind her of that. This was happening *for* her and *to* her. She had asked for this, and I was hoping that she would tell her story, ask her questions, and lead the discussion in a way that was most helpful to her. Zack sat to her right, and I sat to his right, both of us smashed into a large, square, overstuffed chair in an effort to be equally present. Jordan began the appointment, providing a brief history and recounting the same well-organized collection of symptoms that she'd enumerated during previous appointments with other specialists. She finished quickly, looking to us to fill in the rest, but this was *her* version of the story, one she had practiced and memorized and recited in my small office like lines from a play. The things she chose to omit were everything that we knew to be true about her personality and long history of preferences. I wondered if she even heard the words anymore as they slipped from her mouth like water and cascaded to the floor all around us.

It wasn't long before Zack and I had to take over. We talked briefly about our thoughts and experience through all of this, and about our skepticism pertaining to Jordan's highly edited account of her symptoms. We expressed our concerns regarding the accuracy of the diagnosis of gender dysphoria (she'd still not received any such diagnosis by a physician) and our concern about proceeding with any kind of medical intervention without a proper evaluation and diagnostic work-up.

"There won't be any treatment without a diagnosis, right?" I asked them, and I went through the DSM-5 criteria for gender dysphoria and how my daughter's reported symptoms fit none of it.

The CIM specialists at the Zoom meeting that day were an endocrinologist and a psychologist, and they both seemed to be compassionate, caring individuals trying to do the right thing. There was no discussion, however, regarding the diagnosis, why Jordan thought she was a boy, or other factors in her life that might be contributing or at least relevant to the situation. The many questions I'd imagined *might* be asked were not. Instead, they focused for a moment on Zack and me. "What sort of questions do *you* have?" they wanted to know, but the questions I'd already asked remained unanswered.

A discussion of hormone therapy ensued. There was no talk of less invasive treatments for gender dysphoria. The discussion included how the hormones were usually administered, whether Jordan would be able to give herself an injection, the "desired" effects of the hormones (growth of facial hair, clitoral enlargement, increased libido, decreased hip circumference, abortion of menses), and some of the undesired effects of the hormones (acne). Keep in mind, Jordan was thirteen at the time. I did not think increased libido or an enlarged clitoris were things that would be a desired effect for any child of that age. There was no discussion about the more severe and potentially life-threatening side effects of hormone blockers and testosterone therapy (infertility, cancer, stroke, and heart attack, to name a few). The endocrinologist briefly enumerated which of these changes would be irreversible should Jordan decide to detransition at some stage. "I'm not detransitioning," Jordan assured them, and that seemed to be good enough for the specialists.

Zack and I brought up Jordan's history of recurrent self-injury, and we worried aloud about the potential for further self-harm. We asked about mood fluctuations as a side effect of testosterone (since neither clinician had mentioned it), and we expressed our concern that erratic mood fluctuations might elicit suicidality or worsening self-harm. The evaluation of that potential life-threatening complication was encompassed by one of the clinicians asking her directly, "Ash, do I need to be worried about you?" Our child immediately responded, "No," and that appeared to settle it.[2]

We were told not to be too worried about cutting or other forms of nonlethal self-injury. The overarching concern was the increasingly tiresome warning of the suicide risk that would be posed by non-affirming parental behavior. The specialists briefly touched on the letter that would have to come from Jordan's therapist, and they offered "coaching" to assist her therapist in authoring the words that would qualify our daughter for medical transition therapy.

The appointment ended with the specialists asking Zack and me if we had any more questions (excluding the ones already ignored or dismissed, I suppose) and asking Jordan if she had any more questions (she didn't, although she hadn't asked any meaningful questions during the appointment at all). The session was concluded with the plan that we would give them a call when Jordan was ready to start hormone treatment. No concern was expressed by either clinician about Jordan's age, immaturity, or lack of ability to consider the risks, benefits, and alternatives of hormone treatment. In medicine, we call this "informed consent," and it's required for almost all treatments and medications. With very few exceptions, children cannot provide informed consent for themselves. A parent or legal guardian must do it for them. Apparently, we were letting a lot of things slide during today's consultation, and informed consent seemed to be one of them.

---

2. I was stunned with the brevity and dismissiveness of the CIM clinician's assessment of this concern. I was asking about a potential life-threatening complication of the treatment they were recommending. To sweep it aside so recklessly without any meaningful discussion or acknowledgment was one of the more egregious things that I witnessed that day.

A few words regarding the requested letter from the therapist. The World Professional Association for Transgender Health (WPATH) has established standards of care that are widely recognized by clinicians who offer medical and surgical transition to transgender individuals. WPATH requires one letter of recommendation from a "qualified mental health professional" prior to beginning hormone treatment or pursuing upper body surgery (aka "top surgery," which includes bilateral mastectomies for female-to-male transgender individuals or breast augmentation for male-to-female transgender individuals).[3] The letter must contain identifying characteristics of the individual, the duration of the clinical relationship between the patient and mental health professional, the type of evaluation or therapy already provided, a supporting diagnosis and psychosocial assessment, and an explanation of specific criteria met by the individual seeking hormone treatment or upper body surgery.

Specific criteria that must be documented in the professional's letter include:

1. Persistent, well-documented gender dysphoria;
2. Capacity to make a fully informed decision to consent for treatment;
3. Age of majority;
4. If significant medical or mental health conditions are present, they must be reasonably well-controlled.

For individuals seeking lower body surgery (aka "bottom surgery," which tends to be more complicated, more invasive, and fraught with potential complications),[4] WPATH recommends additional documen-

---

3. "Upper body surgery" (top surgery) and "lower body surgery" (bottom surgery) are euphemisms for complex and invasive surgical procedures. Naming the procedures themselves in a medically accurate way is often avoided, ostensibly due to the "icky" nature of the surgeries and the need of patients, families, and clinicians to distance themselves from the severity of the procedures. I use the colloquialisms here to be in line with the current commonly used language. More precise details of the surgeries themselves are included in the glossary at the end of this book.

4. Lower body surgery includes alteration of genitalia, attachment of a prosthesis resembling a penis, creation or closure of the vagina, and other complex genital surgeries. After creation of a penis or vagina, there is also the option of leaving the original genitalia intact, so that the patient has both a penis and a vagina. Genital nullification surgery ("nullo" or "eunuch procedure") is the surgical removal of all genitalia, leaving the patient with a small hole through which to urinate but no genitals. There are numerous clinics in

tation and evaluation of the patient by *two* mental health professionals. In addition, WPATH recommends that the individual consistently live within the gender role congruent with that person's gender identity for a minimum of twelve months prior to approval for lower body surgery. Twelve months of hormone treatment prior to a recommendation for bottom surgery is also strongly recommended.[5]

In Jordan's case, the CIM gender specialists recommended proceeding with medical transition and offered coaching on how to author a letter of recommendation in favor of medical transition, despite the following:

1. Jordan did not have a well-documented history of gender dysphoria; she had a recent self-report of the diagnosis.
2. She was unable to engage in a meaningful conversation regarding the risks, benefits, and alternatives of treatment, and therefore could not provide informed consent.
3. She was not the age of majority.
4. She had not been thoroughly evaluated for mental health comorbidities, so whether or not they were well-controlled could not be determined. The recent self-injury suggests that comorbid conditions were not well-controlled.

Informed Consent and Further Disappointments

I'd like to take a moment to explore the principle of informed consent as it pertains to the medical and surgical treatment of children with self-diagnosed gender dysphoria. "Informed consent" is a term used in medicine to describe the permission given by a patient to a clinician to provide a medical treatment. According to the American Medical Association (AMA), clinicians should assess the patient's ability to understand relevant information, to understand the implications of treatment alternatives, and to make an independent, voluntary decision. Permission for treatment is given and accepted only after the patient has ample

---

the United States and throughout the world offering these surgeries.
5. Amy Riese, "Writing Letters for Transgender Patients Undergoing Medical Transition," *Current Psychiatry* 20, no. 8 (2021).

knowledge of the possible risks of the treatment, the anticipated benefit of the treatment, as well as alternatives to the proposed treatment, which may include forgoing treatment altogether.

A patient with advanced terminal cancer, for example, might opt for no treatment after learning about the side effects of a proposed chemotherapy. In that case, a patient may decide that the benefit of the treatment (extending their life for several months) does not outweigh the likely side effect of intractable nausea and vomiting for most of that time.

To use another example, a patient must provide informed consent allowing a surgeon to remove his or her infected appendix. Such a surgery can be lifesaving, since an infected appendix can rupture if left untreated, and the ensuing complications can be fatal. It is also true, however, that there is a small risk of complications or even death associated with the surgery and general anesthesia. In this case, the patient may decide that the benefit of the treatment (removing an infected appendix before it ruptures) outweighs the small risk of potential complications.

Informed consent is always a risk-versus-benefit analysis. The expected benefit of a treatment is typically obvious. The risks and alternatives to treatment usually involve a more complex conversation. This conversation becomes even more complicated when it pertains to the medical and surgical treatment of children reporting gender dysphoria. This is not as simple as consenting for a Tylenol to treat a headache or declining a Band-Aid for a skinned knee.

I later learned that we were far from alone in thinking that there was not a sufficient informed consent discussion regarding medical transition treatments with hormone blockers and/or cross-sex hormones. In a recent study of patients who had decided to detransition following hormone treatments and testosterone for reported gender dysphoria, 45 percent of participants felt they were not properly informed of the health implications of medical intervention, 33 percent felt "partially informed," and 18 percent felt "properly informed."[6]

Unfortunately, things have not gotten better. Several years after Jordan's appointment, CIM held a training seminar on aspects of treating

---

6. Elle Vandenbussche, "Detransition Related Needs and Support: A Cross-Sectional Online Survey," *Journal of Homosexuality* 69, no. 9 (2022).

transgender and nonbinary youth. The training advocated for providing patients with *less information rather than more information* when it came to side effects pertaining to fertility. The reasoning? Providing the information in its entirety would somehow interfere with normal psychological development. Although physicians were, by their own admission, withholding information critical for informed consent, minors and their parents were nonetheless allowed to consent to treatment without a full understanding of what they were getting into. This runs contrary to the AMA's code of medical ethics, which states, "Informed consent to medical treatment is fundamental in both ethics and law. Patients have the right to receive information and ask questions about recommended treatments so that they can make well-considered decisions about care. Successful communication in the patient-physician relationship fosters trust and supports shared decision making."[7]

The CIM appointment left me feeling frustrated and disappointed. I had not been inclined to allow my daughter to hurl herself into the open arms of medical transition, and I was even less so now. For Jordan, it had the opposite effect. Once again, the gender specialists had encouraged her to move forward whenever she was ready, somehow forgetting that a medical and psychological evaluation were necessary, or that it might be a good idea to let her know that the treatment could leave her sterile and unable to bear children. "When can I start T?" she would occasionally ask, and I finally told her to stop asking, at least for the remainder of the school year. I was stalling, trying to wait her out, hoping it would all blow over. Still, I could feel the persistent crush of time pressing down on us, and I knew that someday soon she would not *need* to ask my permission.

"I've done it," she would tell me, opening her shirt to reveal the long scars where surgeons had removed parts of her body. "I thought I would feel better—*different* somehow—but I don't. It just hurts me now. I wonder if maybe they can put them back on again."

This Will Not Pass

The boxer Cassius Clay denounced his given name in 1964, shortly af-

---

7. American Medical Association Code of Medical Ethics, Opinion 2.1.1.

ter becoming the heavyweight boxing champion of the world. After his victory on February 25, 1964, he spent the evening with several friends, including Malcolm X. He publicly joined the Nation of Islam and identified his given name as having ties to slavery. One month later, he famously stated, "I didn't choose it and I don't want it. I am Muhammed Ali, a free name—it means beloved of God, and I insist people use it when people speak to me."

For many years after announcing publicly that he was Muhammed Ali, the press and his boxing opponents continued to refer to him as Cassius Clay. Ali fought boxer Ernie Terrell in 1967, three years after Ali's name change, in what became known as the "What's My Name?" fight. In the interview leading up to the fight, Terrell repeatedly referred to him as Cassius Clay, despite Ali's objections. The bout went fifteen rounds, and in the seventh Ali landed a left hook that sent Terrell to the ropes. It was a turning point in the match, and during the next round Ali dominated. "What's my name?" he asked Terrell again and again, blending the question with his punches. The question became a mantra, raining down on Terrell as he tried to defend himself. In the end, it was too much for him, and Ali won by unanimous decision.

In the horrible, restless days that came and went, I imagined myself to be on the receiving end of that persistent, unrelenting ferocity. My daughter continued to march down a destructive path with devastating consequences, and I could not help her, or even reach her. "What's my name?" she would ask in my sleep. "Jordan," I would answer, and my head would rock back with the force of her blows. I awoke most nights around 1 a.m., staring into the darkness, wrestling with my fear and agony. Every bleak day was the same, a parade of arguments in my head, objections articulated and dismissed. The day's mundane activities distracted me, and there would be moments of respite when it slipped away from me, only to be shattered by a fresh sense of panic. *Don't let go*, I admonished myself, breathless and sweating in the solitude of my car. *You're losing your child. Time is getting away from you.*

For a long time, I continued to harbor the small hope that Jordan might emerge from this on her own. Perhaps she would come across just the right person who would unexpectedly ask her just the right question in just the right way. She would be gently confronted with an undeniable truth, and things would change. I wondered if an influential teacher might see an opening and be brave enough to make a perfect intervention. Jordan would see where she'd gone astray, and the path back would become clear. She might run into an old friend who affectionately called her by her real name, and in doing so, would remind Jordan of what it felt like to be loved for who she is. Or maybe she would come across a YouTube video by accident that was made by someone who had detransitioned, and it would speak to her in some way that nobody else could. Others had found their way back. She could too.

"It'll get easier as time goes by," was the frequent reassurance from the community of experts. Only things hadn't gotten easier. I could see her imploding, losing herself in all of this, slicing into her body with relentless fervor, pulling away from us and everyone else as she became more and more withdrawn. I internally cringed each time I referred to her using cross-gender pronouns. It did not become "second nature" and I never arrived at a place of acceptance or resignation. On a particularly difficult day, one expert looked me in the eye with a laser-sharp focus, and under the auspice of compassionate motivation, he said, "You really need to be dealing with this more gracefully."

Yes, I thought. *My daughter is destroying herself in front of me. The best thing I can do for her is to deal with this more gracefully.*

There were times when I felt angry and resentful toward Jordan for putting us through this, but it wasn't her fault. She was an adolescent, and that was a difficult and turbulent period in most people's lives. My frustration was with the therapists and specialists. The more I spoke with them, the more frustrated I became. Nobody seemed to recognize (or at least admit) that being a trans-identified youth was becoming a fad. Could they not see it? Were they afraid to articulate what was right in front of their noses? "We live in a more open-minded society," was the frequent explanation.[8] "There is greater acceptance, less stigma, and better means of self-expression. We've come so far, isn't it wonderful?"

I want to reiterate that my colleagues are intelligent people with

---

8. Some have pointed out that social media platforms have increased the numbers because it is a safer and more private or anonymous way to "come out." See, for example, Marc Ramirez, "Many Young Adults Now Identify as Transgender or Nonbinary as Social Media Helps More People Come Out," *USA Today*, June 13, 2022. Fewer are willing to entertain the possibility that social media may be contributing to a social contagion and making the lives of these children worse, not better. "Psychoeducation or Social Contagion: Social Media and Self-Diagnosis," *Psychiatric Times* 40, no. 5 (2023).

postgraduate educations and a wealth of clinical experience. Many were clinicians who had seen multiple cases of authentic gender dysphoria. Shouldn't they have been the *first* people, therefore, to describe this new class of trans-identification in teenage girls (previously a minority of transgender individuals) with no objective evidence of gender dysphoria? This newest cohort of trans-identified children did not like being questioned and did not tolerate being questioned. These children were making demands, not seeking help, and they presented much differently than those with classic gender dysphoria.[9] Their sheer numbers far surpassed even a high-end estimate from the DSM-5. Weren't my colleagues in the *best* position to recognize and describe this new phenomenon? Shouldn't they be on the front lines protecting children from the obvious harm of overzealous medical and surgical transition?

In some ways, I understood their hesitancy. We live and work in a politically charged landscape. Meaningful scientific exploration of the phenomena runs the risk of censorship or being labeled as hate speech, and those who attempt it are often shouted down, fired from their jobs or removed from their academic posts, harassed to the point of receiving death threats, and professionally ruined.[10] Somewhere along the way, the scientific and medical community have relinquished our duty to carefully examine the evidence, to test hypotheses, to analyze data with rigorous scientific scrutiny, and to embrace an open and inquisitive dialogue focused on improving the health and well-being of our patients. Instead, we have turned the reins over to the shifting mob of public opinion. In some ways, we have become the mob.

One of the earliest lessons taught to new medical students is the doctrine *primum non nocere:* "First, do no harm." As physicians, we have powerful tools at our disposal to heal the sick and dying. But while medications and other treatments have the potential to heal, they can also cause great harm when they are used in a reckless manner. It is a respon-

---

9. For a brilliant description of classic gender dysphoria compared to what we are seeing now en masse, see "One Compelling Idea: Endogenous vs. Exogenous Gender Dysphoria," *Inspired Teen Therapy Newsletter*, July 14, 2022.
10. Lisa Littman, "Parent Reports of Adolescents and Young Adults Perceived to Show Signs of a Rapid Onset of Gender Dysphoria," *PLoS One* 13, no. 8 (2018); "Reader Outcry Prompts Brown to Retract Press Release on Trans Teens," *Retraction Watch*, August 29, 2018; Meredith Wadman, "Rapid Onset of Transgender Identity Ignites Storm," *Science* 361, no. 6406 (2018): 358–359.

sibility not to be taken lightly, and protecting patients from unintentional harm at the hands of the medical community is a core responsibility of every medical provider. We do not prescribe chemotherapy or perform open-heart surgery, for example, on anyone who wants it. We must first take a history, perform a physical exam, run tests, make a diagnosis, and discuss the risks, benefits, and alternatives of treatment with our patients. Not every patient with chest pain requires a triple-bypass. *"Treat first and ask questions later"* is seldom the best approach. It's a lesson learned during the first year of medical school, during the first death or serious complication from an unnecessary treatment. The healer is faced with the haunting realization that he or she has done great harm to the patient. In many cases, that harm cannot be undone.

It was during these terrible days, in the wake of the CIM appointment and the year that followed, that I finally came to understand that my daughter's fixation on medical and surgical transition would not pass without a major intervention. I could either stand aside and allow her to continue down a path that was destroying her, or I could begin the difficult and dangerous task of pushing her in the direction of the person I believed her to be. If I was wrong, if I pushed her too hard or with too much force, there was a possibility that she might break apart in my hands. "First, do no harm," I told myself, but much of the damage had already occurred.

I remembered the words of the first gender expert we had taken her to. "This will be a difficult time for Ash," he'd said. "Transgender teens have a much higher risk of suicide. … The gender affirming model and supportive parents: these are the things that make a difference." He'd paused for a moment and allowed us to think about that. "Ash has decided on a gender, and we want to do everything we can to support that. Anything less can be extremely damaging. We want your child to survive this."

Survival, I thought. It was the most important thing. *If I push her too hard, if I get this wrong and she ends her life because of it …*

I sat in the quiet of my house and shook my head, trying to shut down the thought before it could sink its teeth into me. Too late. It gnawed at my belly as my mouth filled with saliva. I gagged, ran to the bathroom, and hovered over the toilet as I emptied my stomach.

(Would you rather have a healthy son or a dead daughter?)

I will not abandon her. I will not give her over to a lifetime of regret. (You will kill her. She will be dead because of you.)

No, I thought. *There has to be another way.*

I wiped my mouth and rested my head on my forearm. The tile was hard against my knees. I remained that way for a long time before I attempted to stand. "I'm afraid," I whispered, but I was alone in the house and there was no one there to answer.

Chapter Seven: Show and Tell

Janet and Jack

At multiple times in this story, I have referred to individuals who are authentically transgender or have been diagnosed with gender dysphoria (diagnosed by someone other than themselves, that is) and who desire transition to a different gender. I mention these people because they are so different from the trans-identifying teenager who was residing in my house. The differences are not subtle, but they may be easier to convey by way of example. I will do so by introducing you to Janet, a fictionalized individual who is a constellation of several of my authentically transgender patients. Each individual story is unique in terms of its detail, life context, and clinical presentation, although the core of the gender narrative is often the same. After that, I will tell you about Dex and Con, two fictionalized individuals with traits I have observed in my own daughter and the sea of transgender-proclaiming teens from Dante's Watch. There are plenty of transgender activist groups who would have you think that Janet, Dex, and Con are inherently the same. Having spent considerable time with all of them, I would argue that they are not.

Janet grew up in a large, progressive urban area on the West Coast. She had several older brothers and loving, albeit flawed, parents. She came from a long line of hard-working people who were not wealthy but who worked steadily to provide their children with all their basic needs and some of their wants. Janet's mother was a vocational nurse, and her father was an accountant for the county. The family had a good-natured dog named Stan and an adventurous, mouse-hunting cat named Patches. There was also a guinea pig named Steamer, who Janet did not like to discuss in any detail due to the tragic nature of his untimely demise.

Janet and her brothers lovingly tended to the family pets, and her brothers also protected and looked after Janet. She was not a child who easily made friends, but she had a handful of friends in elementary and junior high school, many of them female. Although she was not naturally gifted in academics, Janet worked hard in school and was mostly a B student with one token A each semester. She was liked by her teachers but was never a teacher's pet. Being the only girl in the family, she did not have to wear hand-me-downs like her brothers were sometimes forced to do. The clothes she chose were similar to what her female friends wore, but she occasionally borrowed some of her brother's shirts, with her favorite being the forest green flannel that belonged to her brother Brian. The shirt was very large on her, but Janet liked the way it felt, and as she aged, she liked that it disguised her body. Janet once described herself as "pleasantly unremarkable" during those elementary years. Her friend group shifted some as she moved from elementary school to junior high, with some friends going to different schools or moving away. Some of her friends became "mean girls" in junior high, and Janet was dumped by a few friends for reasons unbeknownst to her. During one session, she comically reported with a good-natured laugh, "Who knows, maybe *I* was the mean girl."

When she entered high school, Janet had an equal number of male and female friends. Her childhood was mostly happy, punctuated by common and expected challenges. She often felt a stirring sense of internal restlessness, like something didn't quite fit—like *she* didn't quite fit—although she didn't know exactly what was causing the restlessness or what it might mean. What she did know was that she did not like what her body was turning into. As breasts developed and pubic hair grew, she described feeling that it was all wrong, but not really knowing what might feel right. Her hips and thighs were expanding, and she didn't like that. Her girlfriends frequently complained of "feeling fat," and she thought it was possible that her dislike of her hips was attributable to the teen girl's banal fear of fat. In the wake of that recognition, she developed an interest in athletics. She experimented with various sports such as soccer, softball, and track. She noticed within herself a passing interest in being on the football team, although she dismissed the thought quickly, knowing it would not be suitable for a female, particularly at that time. Janet liked the idea of having a larger, stronger, and more muscular body, although it was hard to imagine a realistic path in which such a thing was possible.

In the end, Janet settled on long-distance running. It started with a fear of being fat and became much more than that. She ran every day and enjoyed the leaner body that developed. Running also became a way for Janet to manage mood and anxiety during her high school years. The white noise of the gentle wind passing over her ears and the rhythmic pounding of her feet gave her time to quietly think without internal or external struggles. She ran every day with her school track team, and she was fast, gathering victories for the school. During the off season, she continued to run several times per week, often in the morning before school, enjoying the crispness of dawn, the way the sun rose to meet her. Her green oversized flannel shirt remained a favorite. With her interest in sports and boyish clothes, she wondered during high school if she might be a lesbian, although she experienced romantic and sexual attraction toward both genders.

Janet went on to attend a well-respected public university and she majored in social science. Her parents helped her as much as they could, but Janet also worked part time to get through college, and she graduated without any student loan debt. During college, the restlessness persisted. In her upper-level courses, she learned about some of the possibilities that might be contributing factors. Issues with gender identification were among them. Although Janet had learned about gender dysphoria vaguely when she was younger, she now began to seek out more detailed information about this complex and uncommon phenomenon. It was during college that she first wondered if this might be what was causing the stirring restlessness she'd felt early on.

Reflecting on it later, she acknowledged experiencing that discomfort as far back as elementary school. She thought back to her early feelings of unease and restlessness, that green flannel that served different purposes, how she felt about the broadening of her hips, her passing interest in the football team, and what she had decided was her bisexual orientation when it came to her romantic and sexual preferences. Although she had learned a lot about the nature of gender dysphoria and had considered that it might explain her feelings over the years, she did not impose that diagnosis upon herself. "It seemed very dramatic," she once told me. In her own words, Janet just wasn't sure.

Janet first presented to my practice as a middle-aged woman seeking help for depression. She described depressed mood, intermittent disturbances of sleep and appetite, and some degree of weight fluctuation. Her energy level and interest in activities varied depending on the severity of her depression. She reluctantly acknowledged that there were seasons in her life during which she'd contemplated suicide. "Sometimes," she admitted, "I felt like the only solution was to swallow the business end of a shotgun." I prescribed medication for her which she compliantly took, and she experienced some improvement in her symptoms of depression. Fortunately, the suicidal thoughts abated with the treatment as well, but her depression did not completely resolve.

After several years in my care, Janet finally trusted me enough to tell me about a "longtime restlessness" that she had not mentioned before. She reported that during early adulthood, she'd had several relationships with men that she described as having "flailed," but these relationships were more of a disaster if truth be told. She enjoyed sex and was able to climax, but she always thought it didn't feel "quite how it was supposed to." She noted that she had investigated gender dysphoria as a possible explanation for her symptoms, but she wasn't sure. She told me she'd had "inklings" of these feelings as a prepubescent child but disregarded them for the most part. The feelings, she said, were more confusing than anything. As she went through puberty, certain changes in her body were unwelcome, such as the onset of menses, but she thought, "Who wants to be on the rag anyways?" She did not dislike her physical development more than other girls, or so she thought at the time. Other changes were more than welcome, such as increased freedom from her parents, expanding her friend group, and exploring her genuine interests. In addition to her passion for running, she loved to read and enjoyed true crime. She had several potential career interests including becoming a teacher or a private investigator, although she eventually pursued a path unrelated to either one. Janet never married and instead had serial monogamous relationships with women after her early failed relationships with men. "I noticed early on that I was attracted to straight women," she told me, "and they were attracted to me." Her relationships with women were not disastrous like the ones with men had been, but they always seemed more dramatic than she wanted and were fraught with problems. Intimate relationships were not a source of safety or stability for her. Again, that persistent feeling that something just wasn't quite right.

During some of our sessions, she reflected on what she had learned about gender dysphoria during her early exploratory phase in college, and she compared this information to how she felt now. The subject resonated with her, and we would discuss it intensely for several sessions. Then months would go by, and the content of our sessions would focus almost exclusively on her depression and anxiety. After a particularly long stent during which Janet had not brought up discomfort with her biological gender, she disclosed one afternoon that she'd been thinking about it more seriously lately. "I've reached a point," she told me, "that I am thinking about it more often than not."

In the sessions that followed, Janet and I investigated the possibility of gender dysphoria and the various treatment options in greater detail. Although what she'd read about the subject resonated with her, it was also scary. She'd been glad to learn that she was not alone in her feelings, but she was terrified by some of the treatments (hormones and surgery) and had therefore never discussed it with a medical professional until now. We were at least four years into our treatment relationship when she finally told me about this. She disclosed slowly over several sessions, frequently seeking reassurance that it was okay for her to continue, as though testing the waters to see if I might reject her or minimize her experience in some way. Janet told me some of the things she'd read about and how they related to her personal experience, but she was always interested in my feedback and opinion. The concern of "Am I crazy?" was frequently present.

After a long period of processing her life experience up until that point, Janet finally flirted with the idea of changing her name and pronouns, which I supported. Following her initial disclosure about feelings of gender dysphoria, I had reviewed the diagnostic criteria from the DSM and had them in my mind frequently when I saw her. With regularity, I asked myself if Janet fit the diagnostic criteria for gender dysphoria. In addition to seeing me for medical management of her depression and anxiety, Janet was also seeing a therapist (not a gender specialist) to whom I'd referred her. I'd spoken to her therapist several times about Janet's clinical issues, and we agreed on the diagnosis of gender dysphoria and we both thought the initial social transition was appropriate. Janet also brought a long-time friend in for a session, who provided collateral information and observations that supported the diagnosis and treatment plan.

And then Janet became Jack. After an initial adjustment period of about eight months during which her symptoms of anxiety transiently increased, something beautiful happened. Jack's depression resolved. Over the past five years, Jack and I have continued to work together. He forgives easily when I accidentally and infrequently lapse to the name Janet, particularly when looking at Jack's medical file where the legal name is present for prescription purposes. Jack sometimes questions himself and asks my opinion if something he experiences does not quite fit the typical transgender narrative. He is grateful that I prompted the transition. Even so, Jack occasionally wonders, "Maybe I'm not transgender." I've not heard Jack speak of suicidal thoughts in several years, and he is now on a low dose of a single psychiatric medication. Jack has never threatened me with suicide or self-injury. When suicidal thoughts occurred, he *reported* them to me, and we addressed them together and head on. It was the two of us tackling the problem as a team, not Jack holding the threat of suicide over me like a bomb ready to explode should I accidentally used the word "her." Although he has considered medical transition, Jack has decided that social transition is sufficient for him. He has surrounded himself with people who love him, and he has a good life. Jack thrives socially and professionally.

It is important to note that Jack identifies as male, but not as a trans male. Jack supports the equal rights of transgender individuals but does not consider himself to be a trans activist. In fact, Jack has on occasion expressed significant discontent with the behavior of trans activists described in the media. Due to his decision to live a quiet and happy life as a man, he has been chastised in the past by trans activists with whom he has crossed paths. He has attempted to engage with the Dante's Watch Rainbow Center but told me that they are doing a disservice for trans people given their inflexible nature and their need to make his personal decisions political ones. It has been rewarding for me to be a part of Jack's journey, and I am proud of my patient for creating such an authentic life for himself. I consider his case to be a success.

This is Jack's story. It is a common story for transgender individuals, although it is not *every* transgender individual's story. Nonetheless, Jack's story highlights much of the inconsistency between an authentic transgender person's experience and the experience of what is happening now with our children. Let's review a few of the highlights:

- Jack did not "know" from a young age that he was a boy. He did wonder about this possibility, among others, and asked himself questions.

- Jack did not self-injure before or after his coming out. I never felt threatened by Jack's thoughts of suicide. The suicidal thoughts were not threats. They were a symptom that Jack reported so that it could be evaluated and treated.

- Jack sought to pass as a male, not to draw attention to his transgender status.

- Jack's symptoms of depression and anxiety dramatically improved following his coming out. I was able to minimize psychiatric medication. He experienced a remission of his depression for the first time since his treatment began.

- Jack never accused anyone in a hostile way (or in a non-hostile way) of "misgendering" him or using his "dead name." He is grateful for supportive friends, family, and medical professionals. He knows people are doing the best they can. He generously forgives.

- Jack questioned his gender dysphoria, sought advice from professionals, and continues to do so. He sought evaluation for his symptoms. He did not make demands to receive a specific diagnosis or treatment.

- Jack felt no urgency to medically or surgically transition, but rather perceived and described medical and surgical transition for what it was: "dramatic."

- Jack sought to discuss this personal and medical matter with his therapist, physician, and close friends; not with the world.

- Jack goes through life with many interests and involvements. His transgender status is not a single-minded obsession and is not the penultimate identifier of who he is.

- Jack questions modern-day trans activism. His opinion is that trans activists threaten medical treatment availability for those who truly need it. He is embarrassed on their behalf.

- Jack selected a male name for himself.

Dex and Con

Concurrent with Jack's treatment and prior to my own child's coming out, long before the magnitude of this troublesome issue was even on my radar, I did have two young adult patients, "Dex" and "Con," who were referred to me by local therapists for depression and anxiety. Both were referred at about the same time, although they were referred by different therapists. These patients happened to be transgender, which I was told by the referring therapists was "incidental" to their depression and anxiety.[1] Receiving two transgender patients at the same time was unusual but not completely surprising. My private practice has a reputation of being "LGBTQ friendly," which is a source of pride for me.

Although I was seeing these patients separately, I was struck by the similarity of their presentations. Both "Dex" and "Con" were closed off, suspicious, and they seemed heavily invested in being depressed, dark, and flippant during our sessions. Both brought up suicide and self-injury within the first fifteen minutes of our first session. Both reminded me

---

1. The concept of someone's depression and anxiety NOT having a relationship with their transgender status is naïve and untrue. Even if someone is authentically transgender, mood and anxiety symptoms will fluctuate before, during, and after transition. Referrals being prefaced with the declaration that a patient's psychological symptoms are "incidental" to the individual's transgender identity is yet one more manifestation of the defensive posturing of the alleged diagnosis and the experts making that diagnosis.

frequently of the risk of non-affirming behavior. Neither seemed particularly interested in relieving their symptoms, but were instead committed to what they assumed would be the lifelong melancholic plight of a transgender individual.

After several appointments, I compassionately and gently questioned these patients about their transgender status, but they had no interest in discussing the matter in a meaningful way. My attempts at exploration (usually a joy of my job) were perceived as hostile, undermining, and unsupportive. I addressed their irritation as best I could, but I needed to understand where their anxiety and depression were coming from and why the symptoms had not dramatically improved when they came out as transgender. One of the patients had a history of trauma, and I suspected that might be contributing to many of his symptoms. I explained to him that I would not be doing my job if I merely made assumptions without doing an adequate evaluation. He did not seem happy about that. I was his psychiatrist. It was, in his opinion, not my place to ask questions.

After several failed attempts to elicit any meaningful information, I tried a different approach, asking them to describe their feelings to me without using gender stereotypes. Rather than rise to the challenge, they rolled their eyes and refused to participate, and they both accused me of being too focused on gender stereotypes. Despite my reassurance that I had only their best interest in mind and that I genuinely wanted to help them, both patients eventually fired me as their psychiatrist with full support from their parents, who also seemed strongly invested in their child's transgender identity. One mother sent me a letter advising me that my services would no longer be needed, and informing me, "I'd much rather go shopping for dresses at Ross with Dex than attend baseball games with Nathan. <u>Shame on you</u>!" (The underlining is hers.)

The differences in Jack's presentation compared to the hostile, entitled, self-righteous behavior we are currently seeing in trans-identifying teens is remarkable. One could argue that Jack was a middle-aged adult when he first presented to my practice, while Dex and Con were in their late teens or early twenties. What did I expect? Teens need time to develop, evolve, and to sort themselves out. It's a slow and halting process that happens over the course of a decade, and often longer. All the more reason, I would suggest, to give them time to work it out.

By adopting a gender affirming approach to any minor who refers to themselves as "trans," the medical and mental health communities are doing these young, vulnerable patients a grave disservice. There will come a time when these individuals are no longer in their teens, when they must live with the hasty and troubled decisions they made as children. Facilitating and encouraging medical and/or surgical transition for children who have not been properly evaluated and who are already going through a time of rapid change is malpractice. Threatening parents with the prospect that their child will most likely kill themselves if the parent does not fall in line with the transition is cruel and unconscionable. It robs parents of their most important responsibility: safeguarding the health and wellness of their children, not just in the moment but for all the years that follow.

Chapter Eight: Collateral Damage

Spreading Like Wildfire

If we think of adolescence as a state of transition—a sort of developmental gauntlet between childhood and adulthood—it is not surprising that teenagers are particularly vulnerable to all kinds of social influence. Among these is the phenomena of social contagion. The community of Salem, Massachusetts, encountered this in 1692, when the 9-year-old daughter and 11-year-old niece of a Puritan minister began experiencing bizarre and erratic behavior: fits that soon spread to the other young girls in the village. Local doctors decided that the girls were being tormented by witches, and the quest to root out and eradicate those witches culminated in the deaths of nineteen women. Three hundred twenty-five years later, social contagion returned to Danvers, Massachusetts—the site of Old Salem—in an unexplained outbreak of chronic hiccups in twenty-four teenagers, mostly girls. The outbreak baffled local health officials, who investigated possible environmental factors and a host of other potential causes but came up with no clear explanation. Local opinion as to the cause of the phenomenon varied, including conspiracy theories related to the release of a biological weapon developed by the U.S. government and the suggestion that the symptoms were related to the contagious spread of a rare pediatric autoimmune disorder. Over the span of three months, state health officials conducted three environmental assessments, which turned up nothing. The idea that the outbreak was psychological in nature—a social contagion spreading among the teenagers—was widely discussed among investigators, although it did not make its way into their final report.[1]

In 1972, British psychologist Gerald Russell encountered a woman who presented to the hospital for self-reported symptoms of anorexia. Her clinical picture, however, did not match the diagnostic criteria for anorexia. She was of average weight and reported episodic purging behavior following binge eating, something that was not typical at the time for patients with anorexia nervosa. The young woman was the first of about thirty patients who would present to the clinic over the course of the next seven years with similar symptoms of binging and purging. The psychologist had discovered a rare condition—one he termed *bulimia nervosa*—that had not yet been described in the scientific literature.

Initial response from the scientific community was skeptical. The condition was too rare, the sample size too small, his colleagues argued, to be studied seriously. All of that changed over the next decade as bulimia nervosa swept across Europe and North America, finding its way into college campuses and affecting mostly young women. In women's dormitories, sororities, and college sports teams, the prevalence of the condition approached 15 percent, a staggering number for a condition that seemed to have emerged out of nowhere. Children in American high schools were the next to be affected, and the disease spread across the globe like wildfire: 400,000 cases in Egypt; 600,000 in Canada; 800,000 in Russia; 6 million in India; 7 million in China.[2] What was the explanation for such numbers, Russell wondered. Had the condition always existed with such widespread prevalence, and if so, how had it gone undetected for so long? "You might suggest it required somebody to come along and put two and two together before people felt safe talking about bulimia," Russell reflected, "but I don't believe that. Until then, the disorder was extremely rare. But after 1980, it became widespread in a very short period of time."

Following its inclusion in the *Diagnostic and Statistical Manual* in 1980, bulimia nervosa became a topic of discussion among psychiatrists and academics, but it also made its way into popular women's magazines such as *Mademoiselle* and *Better Homes and Gardens*. With its prolifera-

---
1. Dan Vergano, "The Hiccuping Girls of Old Salem," *BuzzFeed*, August 7, 2016, www.buzzfeednews.com/article/danvergano/salem-hiccups-mystery.
2. Lee Daniel Kravetz, "The Strange, Contagious History of Bulimia," *Cut*, July 31, 2017, www.*thecut*.com/article/how-bulimia-became-a-medical-diagnosis.html.

tion through popular media, the practice of binging and purging became a popular strategy for weight management.

The theory of media's effect on the spread of social contagions has been extensively described. By the mid-1990s, bulimia nervosa was endemic across the industrialized world, but almost nonexistent in isolated developing nations free from Western influence. The island of Fiji was such a place, with no documented cases of bulimia nervosa in the island's history prior to 1995. That changed in the mid-1990s with the arrival of television to the remote nation. Residents of Fiji were introduced to the influence of American culture through popular shows like *Melrose Place* and *Beverly Hills, 90210*. A study by Harvard Medical School Associate Professor Anne E. Becker found that, three years later, 11 percent of surveyed Fiji adolescent girls admitted to self-induced vomiting to control weight, and 83 percent cited television as a major influence in being more preoccupied with their body shape and weight.[3] By 2007, 45 percent of young women on Fiji's main island reported at least occasional purging behavior.[4]

Other examples of social contagion abound. In the late twentieth century, there was a remarkable and seemingly inexplicable surge in the prevalence of dissociative identity disorder (DID), also known as multiple personality disorder, an extremely rare condition that rose to the surface of public attention and, for a period of several years, was mystified, romanticized, over-diagnosed, and dramatized in entertainment and popular culture. Individuals with histories of severe psychological trauma often sought out the diagnosis from their therapists, and clinicians colluded with their patients in granting them a diagnosis that provided a way for patients to separate themselves from parts of their past they would rather not revisit.

During the COVID-19 pandemic, clinicians at eight different Tourette Syndrome clinics across the globe noticed a dramatic rise in females aged 12 to 25 years with no previous history of tic-like behaviors

---

3. A.E. Becker et al., "Eating Behaviors and Attitudes Following Prolonged Television Exposure among Ethnic Fijian Adolescent Girls," *British Journal of Psychiatry* 180 (2002): 509–514.
4. J.J. Thomas et al., "A Latent Profile Analysis of the Typology of Bulimic Symptoms in an Indigenous Pacific Population: Evidence of Cross-Cultural Variation in Phenomenology," *Psychological Medicine* 41 (2011): 195–206.

who presented to clinics and emergency departments with rapid onset of complex motor and vocal tics following exposure to social media content of others displaying a similar pattern of functional tics.[5] Multiple differences were observed in these patients compared with patients with Tourette Syndrome. Patients with rapid onset functional tic-like behaviors (FTLBs) experienced an abrupt and explosive onset of symptoms in their teens and early twenties, were predominantly female, had no family history of movement disorders, displayed high rates of self-injurious behavior, had high rates of prior anxiety and depression, demonstrated an atypical response to standard pharmacological treatment, and experienced symptoms that flared when around others and improved or ceased when the individual was alone.[6] Most patients with rapid onset FTLBs confirmed watching videos of social influencers displaying similar tic-like behaviors prior to the onset of their symptoms. Some patients had posted personal videos on social media of their own abnormal movements.[7] Many patients presented with motor and vocal tics that were identical to those displayed by popular social influencers, including the use of repetitive vocal tics like "*beans,*" "*woohoo,*" and "*knock-knock.*"

It is important to point out from these examples that recognizing the potential for a condition to spread by means of social contagion is not the same as denying the legitimacy of the condition itself. Hiccups, bulimia nervosa, dissociative identity disorder, tic-like behaviors, and gender dysphoria are all recognized within the scientific and medical communities to be real conditions. To say that bulimia can sometimes spread by means of social contagion is not the same as arguing that bulimia does not exist, or that it does not sometimes develop *de novo*. Furthermore, the concept of social spread of a condition is not meant to suggest that individuals with the condition do not suffer, or that their suffering is not justified. Patients with bulimia suffer greatly, and the goal of treating

---

5. T. Pringsheim et al., "Rapid Onset Functional Tic-Like Behaviors in Young Females During the COVID-19 Pandemic," *Movement Disorders* 36, no. 12 (2021): 2707–2713; M. Hull and M. Parnes, "Tics and TikTok: Functional Tics Spread Through Social Media" *Movement Disorders Clinical Practice* 8, no. 8 (2021): 1248–1252.
6. G. Amorelli et al., "Rapid-Onset Functional Tic-Like Disorder Outbreak: A Challenging Differential Diagnosis in the COVID-19 Pandemic," *Journal of the Canadian Academy of Child and Adolescent Psychiatry* 31, no. 3 (2022): 144–151.
7. T. Paulus et al., "Pandemic Tic-like Behaviors Following Social Media Consumption," *Movement Disorders* 36, no. 12 (2021): 2932–2935.

patients with this condition should be to reduce or eliminate suffering and to explore the underlying causative factors in an attempt to gain insight into how the patient developed the symptoms in the first place. These are complicated conditions with a variety of causes, and we do not understand them fully. Even chronic hiccups can be profoundly uncomfortable for patients, and treating them effectively can be complicated and frustrating for both patients and their doctors. Figuring out the best path forward for any of these conditions requires careful consideration and decision-making about what is best for the individual.

In her article "Outbreak: On Transgender Teens and Psychic Epidemics," Jungian psychoanalyst Lisa Marchiano compares the current social contagion of trans-identified teens to the Pied Piper of Hamelin.[8] The Pied Piper is the only story from Grimm's fairytales that is based on an actual historical event. The town of Hamelin is located in lower Saxony in England. Factual historical accounts indicate that sometime during the thirteenth century, a large number of the town's children disappeared or died, although the details remain unclear. One theory is that the children were lured away by a pagan or heretic sect to forests near Coppenbrugge for ritual dancing where they all perished in a sudden landslide. A different theory points to the occasional practice at the time of selling children to recruiters in Eastern Europe, a theory that could explain why the loss of the children was never documented. In the fairytale, the Pied Piper—a pipe-playing man wearing multicolored clothing—was hired by a rat-infested town to lure away the rats with his magic pipe. When the town refused to pay for his service, the Pied Piper used the power of his music to lure the town's children away, and they later disappeared into a cave and perished. Both the historical account and the fairy tale, Marchiano points out, suggest an archetypal situation in which adults allowed children to be seduced away into peril.

The Pied Piper analogy is one that stuck with me during our struggles over Jordan's trans-identification. Perhaps it is the recognition that every action has its consequences, or the fact that the decisions we make as a community have the power to either save us or doom us. More than anything, though, it is the image of the children themselves being lured

---

8. L. Marchiano, "Outbreak: On Transgender Teens and Psychic Epidemics," *Psychological Perspectives* 60 (2017): 345–366.

away by the enchanting melodies of that magical pipe, following each other blindly, as in a trance, their faces slack and devoid of comprehension. And where were the adults, the leaders, the guardians, the politicians, the parents? Was there no one to step forward to prevent this from happening? How did these adults and protectors come to abandon that most basic responsibility?

Guarding the Wall

For several years during my early clinical practice as a psychiatrist, I became interested in the psychology of cults. I was treating a patient at the time who had been indoctrinated into a cult in her early twenties and had been immersed in the group for several years. It wasn't until the birth of her daughter that she perceived the necessity and found the strength to break away. They escaped in the middle of the night together, moved across the country, assumed new identities, and started new lives. Remnants of my patient's old life still clung to her though, and she sought help for persistent feelings of guilt and regret, as well as frequent disabling panic attacks that tended to descend upon her in the middle of the night.

There were no local experts in our town, and so I researched the topic extensively in my attempt to understand the psychodynamics of a cult mentality and to help my patient as best I could. During that exploration, I came across a fascinating article entitled "An Object Relations Approach to Cult Membership"[9] in which the authors assert that nobody "joins a cult." During a well-intentioned search for meaning, new recruits believe they are joining a healthy group that will not mistreat them. Once a recruit joins, there is pressure to conform to the norms and behavior of the group. Paranoid thoughts about the outside world are planted and encouraged. These pressures coalesce to activate a primitive level of functioning in the individual, who utilizes immature defense mechanisms to cope with their new reality.

We all use defense mechanisms daily in our lives, and the use of these

---

9. J. Salande and D. Perkins, "An Object Relations Approach to Cult Membership," *American Journal of Psychotherapy* 65, no. 4 (2011): 381–391.

defenses is almost entirely outside of our conscious awareness. Defense mechanisms exist on a spectrum from immature to mature. Altruism and humor are examples of mature defense mechanisms. Altruism alleviates negative feelings about one's situation or oneself by helping others. A person with a gambling addiction, for example, might volunteer for a gambling help hotline. Humor allows a person to express feelings about uncomfortable, difficult, or distressing situations without adding to their personal discomfort or negatively affecting others. A hospice patient near the end of life might respond to a friend's offer of a cigarette with, "No thanks, I'm trying to quit."

Individuals in cults have no higher incidence of psychological illness than the general population, but the emergence of immature defense mechanisms blunts healthy functioning and leads to irrational and self-destructive behavior. The article's authors reviewed several immature defenses that cult members utilize during times of physical and psychological stress, and although the authors were not referring to trans-identifying teens in their article, I was struck years later by the similarities I was observing in my teen child during the emergence and evolution of "Ash."

The immature defense mechanism of *splitting* is commonly referred to as "all-or-nothing thinking." Ambivalent (i.e., mixed or contradictory) feelings are not tolerated by an individual, who abandons critical thought and adapts a mentality in which he or she perceives ideas and people as "all good" or "all bad." Ash's trans-identification was constructed around an "us vs. them" mentality. There were those in the know, such as the trans activists, YouTube gurus, and affirming healthcare providers. This constellation of people represented the "us." The "them" category included those who questioned him, accidentally misgendered him, or who used his "dead name" at any time during a conversation. There was an arrogant dismissal of "them" as being so unenlightened or hateful that they weren't worth talking to. "Us" was a more highly evolved population that had surpassed the understanding of "them." It was important to keep the groups separate, to build a wall around "us" to protect its members from "them."

In the world of "us" versus "them," Ash perceived me as one of "them." I had arranged gender affirming care for him, addressed him using the name and pronouns of his choosing, and supported him in countless ways. On the other hand, I had drawn the line at his requests to opt out of PE, use a packer, and move forward with testosterone treatment. From an "all-or-nothing" perspective, that made me completely unlike the moms who let their kids go on cross-sex hormones with few questions asked. I set limits regarding extreme measures, so Ash assigned me to the "them" category despite my overall support. Placing a mom who sets limits in the "them" category was strongly encouraged by the YouTube gurus, Ash's trans peers, and anyone fortunate enough to be considered part of the "us" tribe.

Denial was another immature defense mechanism that I encountered frequently from Ash. Denial avoids the awareness of some uncomfortable truth by disavowing any data that points to it. When we pointed out all the many stereotypical female things Jordan enjoyed during the first decade of her life, Ash responded, "I have no recollection of my childhood." Wow. No recollection whatsoever. Nothing recollected, nothing to consider. A simple sentence wiped out ten years of reality. When I asked Ash if he wanted to join me for a pedicure—an activity we had enjoyed many times in the past—the answer was always no without any contemplation. Ash did not like Disney On Ice, wearing pretty dresses, or glamming it up for a Taylor Swift concert. Why would he? He had never liked those things, or did not allow himself to recall anything from his past that might suggest otherwise. End of story.

Denial can also manifest as disregard of an immediate danger. Ash had no appreciation for how significant it was for a teenager to be on cross-sex hormones. He expressed no overt anxiety about side effects such as sterility, heart disease, increased risk of certain types of cancer, and irreversible changes to his vocal cords. He made statements such as, "I would absolutely love to have a full beard." Even when discussing something as extreme as "top surgery" and "bottom surgery," he approached them with cavalier disregard for the risks, potential complications, permanent disfigurement, and loss of function. There was no respect for the radical nature of these medical procedures, and he refused to entertain the possibility that something could go very badly with permanent, devastating, and life-changing consequences.

A third primitive defense mechanism that I noticed being utilized frequently by Ash and his trans-identifying peers was *projective identification*. Utilizing this defense, an individual projects qualities that are unacceptable to the self onto another person. Ash may have been questioning some of his choices unconsciously, but due to the cult mentality he was unable to ponder those questions on a conscious level. He would then project the questioning onto another individual, who might then question (or be perceived to question) Ash's choices. It is a complex interpersonal dynamic. Ash perceived anyone questioning his transgender narrative as hostile, although it was Ash himself who approached these individuals in an adversarial manner. Any party that he expected to be non-affirming (a religious youth group, for example) was labeled "transphobic" or a "bigot," despite their inclusive language and behavior. In some ways, projective identification is an unconscious effort to elicit an expected response. Cult members expect non-members to be hostile, and almost any response that is elicited is perceived that way. But it is the members themselves that set up this dynamic.

In 2021, Stephen Hassan described a theory on cult mentality that he termed the "BITE Model" of authoritarian control.[10] The application to gender ideology is mine alone, but it is easy to see how these concepts are applicable to a child falsely identifying as transgender.

The BITE Model recognizes four strategies employed by an individual or group to achieve authoritarian control:

- **B**ehavior Control:
    - controlling one's environment and who one associates with
    - living with dependence and obedience
    - restricting/controlling sexuality
    - sleep deprivation

- **I**nformation Control:
    - deliberately withholding and distorting information
    - generating and using propaganda
    - attacking anyone who disagrees

---

10. The BITE model is partially based on the work of Robert Lifton, PhD. In 1963, Lifton called the methodology "thought reform" and described eight methods used to cause mind change. Dr. Lifton did not apply his theory to gender ideology. The application to gender is my own. In part, the BITE model was also based on work by Margaret Thaler Singer, who described six criteria for thought reform.

- **T**hought Control:
  - instilling black/white or us/them thinking
  - changing one's identity and possibly one's name
  - using loaded language and clichés to stop complex thinking
  - teaching thought-stopping techniques to prevent critical thinking
  - allowing only positive thoughts about the dogma
  - rejecting rational analysis and doubt
- **E**motional Control:
  - instilling irrational fear of leaving the group
  - promoting feelings of guilt, shame, and unworthiness
  - showering the cult member with praise and attention
  - threatening friends and family
  - shunning disbelievers
  - convincing members that there is no happiness or peace outside of the group

A cult is defined in various ways depending on the source. The traditional definition is a system of religious worship, especially in reference to its rites and ceremonies. Some sources describe a group bound together by veneration of the same thing, person, or ideal. One of the synonyms that came up during my dictionary search was "clique,"[11] and that conjured the image of teenage girls desperate for belonging.

I am not convinced that the transgender movement is a cult, but there are similarities in the strategies that it uses, particularly when it involves indoctrination of children. The use of immature defense mechanisms by those young and vulnerable recruits says a lot about their level of understanding and independent thought, or lack thereof, in the process.

What we do know is that cults often do not end well for their members. Consider The People's Temple led by the charismatic Jim Jones, and the Southern California–based group Heaven's Gate. Both cults terminated with mass suicide, a tragic reminder of the extreme control these groups exert over the lives of their members.

---

11. Dictionary.com, s.v. "cult," Related Words.

Parker

In the universe of Jordan's transgender idols and heroes, one notable figure reigned supreme. Jordan developed a close relationship with a trans-identified female-to-male teen, who I'll call Parker. They met at a birthday party a few months after Jordan advised us of her own transgender identification. Jordan hadn't known Parker before the party, but certain members of her friend group did, and the invitation to the event had been widely circulated. I had seen it as an opportunity for her to socialize with peers and to possibly establish the beginnings of some additional friendships. I did not know at the time that there would be other trans-identified kids present, although it seems statistically obvious to me now that I have a better understanding of how quickly the transgender contagion was spreading among teenage girls in our community.

On the afternoon of the party, we pulled up to a house decorated with balloons and multicolored streamers. The place seemed inviting and wholesome, and Parker was polite and welcomed Jordan into the home when we arrived. We were greeted by his parents as well, and I lingered for a few minutes in the living room to make small talk with them before I departed. I can't put my finger on why I felt this way, but it struck me even then that something wasn't right. Call it a mother's intuition, a feeling I should've listened to but didn't.

Jordan was enamored with Parker from the beginning. I tried to like him; I really did. He was two years older than Jordan, and although he avoided eye contact and his hair hung in his face like the hairstyle of so many of Jordan's peers, these things alone weren't enough to justify my misgivings. I told myself it wasn't fair the way I distrusted him. Jordan's transgender infatuation was a source of pain for Zack and me. Wasn't it natural for me to be less than enthusiastic about her hanging out with other trans-identified kids? Still, there was something about Parker specifically that unsettled me.

"What do you think of Jordan's friend Parker?" I asked Zack one afternoon. It was an open-ended question, my attempt not to influence his response.

Zack was quiet for a moment before he answered. "I don't know," he said. "There's something about him that I just don't like."

"What do you mean?" I asked.

"He doesn't make eye contact. When he speaks, it's just above a whisper. He seems secretive, furtive. I can't shake the feeling that he's hiding something." Zack paused as he considered this. "I know this is not a kind thing to say about a child, but he sort of ... well ... he gives me the creeps."

"Yes," I agreed. That was it exactly. Parker gave me the creeps.

My open-ended questions to Jordan—"How's Parker? Will you be getting together this weekend?"—were met with suspicion and defensiveness.

"Why do you ask?"

"No reason. You've been seeing a lot of each other lately."

"Parker doesn't care if I'm trans."[12]

Interesting. I hadn't mentioned anything trans-related, although Parker was taking testosterone and seemed to be even more obsessed with LGBTQ issues than Jordan, if that was possible. The effects of testosterone had left Parker with a half-beard—mutton chops to be precise—sharpened facial features, a prominent Adam's apple, and a voice that was just a few decibels above perpetual laryngitis. He did not pass as male, but he did not seem entirely female either. He was something in between, and it was obvious from my conversations with Jordan that she wanted what Parker had, and she wanted it as soon as possible.

"Has Parker ever offered you testosterone?" I asked her.

"No. Of course not."

"Good. If we start to see any evidence of that, your relationship with Parker will be over. I want to be clear about that."

"Mom ..."

"Yes?"

"Nothing."

"Do you want to tell me something?"

"No."

And so it went, this uncomfortable relationship between me and Zack on one side and the two of them on the other.

Parker's parents are kind people, and they seem like loving parents. If they have any concerns about Parker's transition, I have never observed

---

12. Jordan only recently told me that this actually was not true. Parker was very invested in her trans identity.

it or heard about it. They are "super cool" glitter parents,[13] and Jordan had them on a pedestal. In comparison (at least in my child's eyes), Zack and I were from the stone age. We asked questions, pointed out obvious inconsistencies in Jordan's transgender narrative, and refused to blindly facilitate everything our daughter wanted.

I was not one of those parents who went through my child's phone, but on one occasion I glanced at the screen as it awoke on the kitchen countertop where Jordan was charging it. I read it before I could stop myself, an Instagram message from Parker that was indicative of the manipulative undermining I had suspected for months.

("Just blow it off—that's so ignorant. Jesus, your mom and I don't agree on anything.")

As it turned out, our intuition about Jordan's relationship with Parker was accurate. Parker was a predator in all the ways I imagined, exerting his influence not only about transgender ideology but also by demonizing Zack and me in the process. He was verbally and emotionally abusive to Jordan, introduced her to the world of drug and alcohol addiction, and attempted to "groom" her—Jordan's words, not mine—into a narcissistic mirror version of himself. Much of this I learned about later, after he was done with her and the relationship had soured. These are the things Jordan was brave enough to tell me, and I am quite certain there are other things she is not yet ready to discuss.

I do not know if Parker is authentically transgender or not, or how his life will turn out. I have spotted him on a few occasions at school events. His facial hair and other masculinizing features continue to evolve, but he often cross-dresses as a girl: a short, tight skirt; stilettos; a push-up bra beneath a pink top displaying his naked midriff. He is another transgender star at Jordan's school, a litmus test by which we can all prove our allegiance to our school's progressive, open-minded inclusivity.

Despite what Jordan assured me of at the time, Parker was instrumental in driving a wedge between my child and her family. Jordan's

---

13. Parents whom an LGBTQ person might perceive as family, either virtually (receiving support through emails, text messaging, social media, and/or online platforms) or literally (leaving their real family to live with a glitter family). This most commonly occurs when an LGBTQ person's real family has challenged their professed sexual orientation or gender identity. Although glitter families claim to support the identity and well-being of children and teens, they often encourage LGBTQ children and teens to reject and abandon their real families.

disdain for me was a reflection of *his* disdain. She has yet to reveal the full extent of that contempt, but I shudder to think of the awful things Parker convinced her to believe about me. As she continues to recover from the trauma of that relationship, I can only hope she will let those things go. Maybe, one day, so will I.

An Unexpected Casualty

Ripples of our family's struggle were affecting many aspects of my life. I wasn't sleeping well, had difficulty concentrating, and picked at food as if nothing was palatable. I could no longer put my daughter's transgender identification into a box that I could deal with on its own. It shaded everything, invaded my sleep and other relationships, and became the underlying backdrop behind every encounter. One year, as the holiday season was gaining momentum and I was hoping for a bit of joy during what should have been one of the happiest times of year, I stumbled across a painful reminder.

It had been a long and stressful work week, but Friday afternoon had finally arrived. Four-year-old Zoe and I were looking forward to enjoying some mommy-and-me time together, something we had planned the week before. I would pick her up from preschool, and we'd spend the rest of the afternoon in our cozy kitchen baking cookies and doing crafts. There would be cheerful music, matching aprons, easy laughter, and the enticing smell of chocolate chip cookies fresh from the oven. Zoe had tumbled into my life a week before my fortieth birthday, an unexpected gift. She was a bright and inquisitive child, but my younger daughter had been eclipsed by her older sister's transformation, psychological unrest, and all that went with it. This was an attempt to make that better. It was our special time together. This afternoon would be about me and Zoe. I had *two* children, not just one. I didn't want to lose sight of that.

It was delightful to share the warm, familiar space of our kitchen together. I started pulling out things we would need from the cabinets like chocolate chips, flour, and vanilla extract. From our utility craft cupboard, I grabbed paint, paper, moldable clay, Mod Podge, white glue, and a smattering of other art supplies. I turned on some Disney music and we hummed along to tunes like "Hakuna Matata" and "The Bare

Necessities." Zoe brought her step stool to the kitchen counter, and we donned our matching aprons. She stirred ingredients with a big wooden spoon and watched wide-eyed as I cracked eggs into the mixing bowl. We sampled the chocolate chips when I opened the bag, assuring that they were safe for the cookies. Satisfied with our tasting, we poured them into the batter. Each step of the process delighted Zoe, and her shrieks of joy and laughter were infectious. When there was a major flour spill, instead of being upset about the mess, we giggled together as we cleaned it up.

With the cookie sheet loaded with carefully placed balls of dough, I picked it up with mitted hands and placed it gently into the oven. We discussed the importance of being careful with a hot oven. Once the cookies were safely inside (and our hands safely out of harm's way), we both knelt down on our knees and watched through the glass of the oven door as the globs of batter began to bake.

"Having fun mommy," she said, never taking her eyes off the sweet pockets of melting chocolate.

My heart swelled. I put my hand on her tiny shoulder and gave her a hug.

After sampling the cookies and scrubbing the cookie sheets, we went on to paint wooden safari animals, built love bugs from empty toilet paper rolls, and created clay Christmas ornaments in the shape of stars, trees, and sprigs of holly. Zoe brushed up on her painting skills with a purple rhinoceros and an orange elephant. I watched as she hunched over the ornaments, her brush sweeping and dabbing, the glitter falling from her fingertips like snow as she sprinkled it onto the red ribbon she had painted on the holly for her grandma. We would give the ornaments to family members as holiday gifts, we decided. When she was finished and we had washed the paint and glitter from our fingers, we danced in the living room to the lyrics of "Friend Like Me" from *Aladdin*. We talked and laughed without trying.

The drizzly afternoon had morphed into a blustery evening, and I could hear the wind knocking against the sliding glass door that led to the back porch. I lit a fire in the fireplace. While Zoe went downstairs to put on pajamas, I cleaned up the mess and turned on the oven again in preparation to bake the ornaments.

I made a cup of tea while I waited for the oven to heat up, and I sat in front of the fireplace and admired the ornately carved features of the mantel. It had caught my eye when I first viewed the house several years ago. The intricate stone and metalwork weaved a wordless story of mythical animal protectors, kings, and wizards. I fell in love with the house because of it, and I had known—even before seeing the other rooms—that *this* house was *the one*.

I heard the hallmark sounds of my four-year-old ascending the stairs: soft, tentative steps, her hand on the wooden banister for balance. She emerged wearing a fleece sleeper covered in pastel dinosaurs. She'd managed to put it on all by herself except for the top snap, leaving a mint green pterodactyl tail flapping against her neck. She walked by me with a purpose: the oven was ready for our ornaments. I got up and joined her in the kitchen. We dutifully put on our mitts, opened the oven door, and I placed the tray inside while Zoe stood back and watched.

"Juice box?" I offered, and she took it from me before toddling off into my bedroom to watch *The Letter Factory* while I returned to my tea.

Feeling satisfied with the day, I scooped up my laptop and rested it on my thighs.

I'll just take a moment to check email, I thought. *After that, maybe a little Christmas shopping on Amazon.* The ornaments would be ready in about twenty minutes.

Opening my email, I didn't expect such a rapid emotional descent into the mindset I'd managed to avoid all afternoon. I'd received an email from a friend's mom inviting Ash to a party. She had referred to him with mixed pronouns, and expressed uncertainty as to whether Ash could stay for the sleepover portion of the party, since he would be the only "boy" present. Also in my inbox was a "friendly reminder" to complete a science camp enrollment packet in which I would have to address the issue of gender choice for Ash's cabin. Both emails required a response. I had been enjoying the magic of the fireplace only moments before, but it seemed like a long time ago. The majestic ornamental mantel was forgotten, and so was my preschooler.

I considered my answers carefully and tapped away at the keyboard, searching for just the right words. Yes, Ash could attend the party. Whether or not he spent the night was up to the child's mother. The cabin choice for a week-long science camp was a more complicated matter. Should he sleep in the same cabin as the other boys or the other girls?

What about bathrooms and showers? Regardless of the decision, should the other parents be notified? Was a special permission slip required? Was it all too complicated? Should we skip the camp in favor of an activity that did not involve overnight lodging?

I never saw Zoe reenter the room. *The Letter Factory* had ended, replaced by *VeggieTales* and "The Song of the Cebú" —

A shrill scream filled the house, catapulting me from my trance.

(Had she gone back into the kitchen? Did she burn herself? Why hadn't I been watching?!)

I flew into the kitchen expecting a burned hand or worse. What I saw instead was Zoe peering through the glass, viewing the blackened, ruined ornaments she had painted with great care. There was nothing left of the bright colors and dazzling glitter. The purple rhinoceros and orange elephant had been reduced to rotting carcasses. The holly she had decorated for her grandma would never hang from the branch of a Christmas tree.

I turned off the oven. "I'm sorry," I said. I kneeled in front of my daughter and looked her in the eyes.

She stared back at me, her lower lip trembling, the tears spilling down her cheeks. How did she see me, this person she had trusted to get this right?

"We'll have to throw these away," I said, "but we can make new ones. We can start over tomorrow."

She shook her head. "Don't want to," she told me, and she took a step backward, away from me and the smoldering remains of our afternoon together.

She turned and ran toward the bedroom sobbing.

"*Wait, I can fix this*," I wanted to tell her. But I couldn't, not in the ways that really mattered.

Chapter Nine: Calling for Reinforcements

A Heterosexual Mother of Two

Jordan's lack of progress following several months of therapy spurred me to suggest that she discuss the goals of therapy with her therapist. Prior to that, Jordan's understanding of the goals of therapy was limited to "helping with the transition," although she could not articulate exactly what that meant. Like so many terms before it, "helping with the transition" became a vacant and meaningless statement she had learned to parrot from the hordes of social media trans-influencers vying for her attention. Her attempts to explain it further included statements like, "Mom, it's just really hard to be trans," and, "It's really hard to explain," and, "You just can't possibly understand." Precisely *what* was "really hard" was open to conjecture because Jordan was unable to explain it herself, and a goal that could not be explained, quantified, tracked, or measured seemed to me like no goal at all.

Her course of psychotherapy was further hindered by the therapist's refusal to evaluate the self-diagnosis presented by Jordan during their initial session. As I've discussed, critical thought and careful evaluation are essential components of any clinical encounter. Clinicians and therapists should not go along with a patient's self-constructed diagnosis without considering the evidence and deciding for themselves whether the diagnosis is accurate. Not every patient who proclaims that they have a specific condition actually has that condition, and not every patient with a specific condition is treated in exactly the same way. There are many factors to consider. The treatment plan should be tailored to meet the specific needs of the individual. The art of medicine—and the art of psychotherapy, for that matter—cannot and *should not* adhere to a one-size-fits-all approach. Patients are not widgets. Psychotherapists are not robots. Navigating the human mind is delicate and complicated, as it should be. There's a reason why training and experience are so essential.

Jordan came to me with her concerns about eight months after she had started therapy. "Mom, is this normal?" she asked me one afternoon while we were driving home from one of her sessions. "I'm not sure if I should keep going, or maybe I just need to take a break."

"What do you mean?" I asked, and she responded by describing some odd things that were occurring within the context of her therapy sessions. I'll discuss these oddities in a moment. Suffice it to say that Jordan and I explored this for a while, and together we reviewed her progress. Our conversation felt relaxed and natural, an easiness in communication to which we were no longer accustomed. Here it was, I realized: a topic (one of the *only* topics) that my teen did not think I knew absolutely nothing about. I was grateful for the opportunity to connect with her on this. It felt good to be helpful. It was nice to listen and to be heard.

Jordan's therapist had an office on an upper floor in a building in downtown Dante's Watch. It was rare to find a parking spot near the office, so I'd been dropping Jordan off in front of the building before her appointments and then fetching her at the designated time. While I waited, I would get coffee from a local café, browse the bookstore, or do grocery shopping at the nearby Trader Joe's. I had no idea what transpired between drop-off and pick-up, except what Jordan would tell me, which wasn't much. This was okay with me. I consider therapy to be a personal and protected thing, bordering on the sacred. Prior to her reaching out to me regarding the oddities of her sessions, I had not pried into the content of her conversations with her therapist. Now, however, she had come to me with a concern.

"There's just not that much to talk about anymore," she said, and the sessions frequently started late and ended early because of that. She described long silences in which she and the therapist would simply stare at each other, and the periods of talking were filled with idle chit-chat. The long silences—an occasional productive strategy in psychotherapy—did not result in any meaningful insights. Jordan said she didn't know how to use the time and didn't feel that they were exploring any useful therapeutic material. She thought it was her fault that there was nothing to talk about. With her worsening symptoms of depression and anxiety, I wondered why there would be so little to discuss. If Jordan was not spontaneously reporting relevant information, an effective therapist should be asking the right questions.

During her time in therapy, I had not observed the expected improvement in mental health that results from coming out as a transgender person. Her symptoms of depression and anxiety had not improved, her episodes of self-injury continued, and she was experiencing ongoing melancholia, insomnia, and occasional panic attacks. If there was a psychologically beneficial and cathartic side to identifying as transgender, my daughter had not yet encountered it.

But why should I expect therapy to be helping? I asked myself. Whatever psychological conflict had brought Jordan to identify as transgender had yet to be identified and was unlikely to come up during her awkward and abbreviated therapy sessions because there seemed to be so little to discuss. With the only identified goal as "helping with the transition," I doubted there would be further exploration of her emotional situation outside of that context. I take partial responsibility for agreeing to this stent of therapy. I had hoped for something better: personal insight, self-confidence, improved mood, fewer panic attacks, or a reprieve from the cutting behavior, the way she frequently sliced into her body to distract herself from the psychological pain of whatever she was going through.

On a recent vacation I took with Jordan, she wore a bathing suit that revealed the scarring on her thighs from her frequent episodes of cutting: a gnarled and dense tapestry of lines etched into her skin. The sight of it took my breath away, and the part of me that had vowed at the moment of her birth to do everything in my power to protect her from harm sat still and silent in my chest.

"I think I'd like to change therapists," she told me at the end of our discussion, and I looked up at her, blinking away the recollection of all those lines like claw marks in her skin, permanent reminders of all the ways I had failed her. "I think I would be more comfortable if I saw someone different," she said, "like a heterosexual mother of two."

A heterosexual mother of two, I thought, and there it was, a twinge of hope peeking out at me from beneath the wreckage.

Jordan stumbled through her explanation of why she thought a change might be helpful, sifting through her feelings and choosing her words carefully. The difference between this conversation and the scores of conversations that had preceded it was striking. There was a *thinking-out-loud* quality as she continued. Despite the fractured nature of her explanation, I heard my child in there. This was not a memorized recital of internet-acquired talking points. She was telling me of an authentic need.

I wanted to jump up and down with glee, ecstatic to have discovered my child, peeking out at me from her deep dark cave of tortured adolescence. *Yes*, I would find her a heterosexual mother of two, and *yes, I would do it this very minute!* I wanted to get out of the car and dance in the street, my feet barely touching the pavement, a list of possible candidates unfurling behind me like brightly colored ribbons. What I actually did was to sit with patience and compassion, letting her words topple out, as cumbersome and inexpert as they were. I nodded and said "mmm-hmmm" at appropriate times and encouraged her to continue. I made no change in my facial expression. "I'll look into it," I told her.

The statement fascinates me: "a heterosexual mother of two." From her spontaneous yet stuttered explanation, I surmised that Jordan wanted to see someone whom she did not perceive to be struggling with similar issues as she was, and someone who was maternal. I did allow myself to consider the obvious: *Hey, wait a minute. I'm a heterosexual mother of two.* Sometimes that thing you need is right there in front of you. One day you discover it has been there all along.

In the wake of her request, I contacted a colleague who told me she was interested in gender dysphoria, although she had no specialized training and did not consider herself an expert. And yes, by uncanny coincidence, she happened to be a heterosexual mother of two. She agreed to take Jordan on as a therapy patient, and I was relieved that Jordan would no longer be seeing an expert, as I had grown weary of experts and the relentless single-track agenda they all seemed to be pushing. I asked this new therapist about her initial therapeutic goal, and she replied that her goal was to hold space for all that Jordan may be experiencing psychologically, whether that was depressed mood, complicated feelings due to her parents' divorce, the challenges of stepfamilies, impulse control, panic attacks, or gender dysphoria. Or perhaps a phobia of bridges? A fear of spiders? A hatred of fractions or tractors? In short, whatever was psychologically coming up for Jordan would be the focus of therapy, not a predetermined scripted service plan. I was hopeful that this therapy would be helpful, and I did not have the sense of doom I had experienced when she had entered therapy with the previous clinician.

Searching from A to Z

I continued to reach out to every resource I could think of, making a supreme effort not to overlook something that might be helpful, no matter how small and inconsequential it seemed. I was willing to scrape the bottom of the barrel with blood-stained fingernails and endure the agonizing bite of splinters if there was a possibility that I might find something useful. I broadened my search, and turned first to my *A-list* crew: friends and therapists and physicians who had known Jordan since she was a toddler. They had witnessed the abrupt transformation from the little girl to the sullen teen now asking—*demanding*—to be addressed as a boy. My friends were empathic and supportive. They offered us their unconditional love. But this was an unusual and dramatic situation. They had no sound advice to give, scripted or otherwise. They hoped for the best and were available to listen, but there was nothing they could offer in terms of meaningful guidance.

Although I didn't want to, I did finally reach out to the various agencies I had been advised to contact by the gender specialists, such as Gender Spectrum and the Dante's Watch Rainbow Center. I was told to consider them part of my *A list*. After all, they'd been through it too, right?

And oh, how eager they were to assist! The help I found from these groups primarily focused on working through my feelings of grief surrounding the loss of my daughter.

"*It's so hard to lose a daughter, isn't it? We understand that there can be a sense of emptiness and uncertainty about what comes next.*"

I smiled at that. Emptiness and uncertainty, yes. These people had already experienced my struggle and were familiar with my feelings, or so they told me. They were happy to provide me with support through the medical transition of my son, Ash.

"The good news," they advised me, "is there are very few barriers to gender affirming medical care for kids in Dante's Watch."

Yes, I thought. *There are no barriers at all, in fact. It's as easy as swinging through the drive-through at McDonald's.*

Sadly, there was no validation from these groups for what I was really experiencing or the restless terror that was coiled like a rattlesnake in my chest. (*This is all wrong. My thirteen-year-old daughter is talking about having parts of her body surgically removed, and you idiots are rejoicing in the fact that there are very few barriers to getting this done? I need to get her the hell out of this!*)

The *testing-the-water* questions I asked about my authentic emotional experience led to responses that let me know that these groups were not as open-minded and accepting as they claimed. Non-threatening casual conversation starters such as, "In the beginning, did you ever wonder if your kid was really trans?" were met with good-natured statements such as, "Yes, but if there's one thing I've learned, it's that kids don't lie about how they feel."

At this early phase of conversation, the parents seemed happy to be taking me under their wing. They seemed less pleased with my follow-up questions such as, "Yes, kids don't lie about how they feel. But isn't it possible they could be misinterpreting the awkward pain of adolescence and the desire to get away from that with a desire to alter their gender?"

I was met with inquisitive looks and faltering smiles. Then ... a quick return to the talking points. "*It's so hard to lose a daughter, isn't it? We understand that there can be a sense of emptiness and uncertainty about what comes next.*"

There seemed to be a well-rehearsed answer for every question, falling from their mouths like rain. Many of my questions were interrupted with rote responses for what the person *thought* (or perhaps hoped) I was about to ask.[1] There's really nothing one can do in such circumstances

---

1. I find this mode of communication particularly annoying. If one doesn't take the time to listen to the question, how can one offer an appropriate response?
  "Where is the—"
  "Best clinic to find gender affirming treatment for your trans-identified child?"
  "No. Where is the bathroom?"
  "Oh. It's down the hall and to your right."
  "Thank you."
  "You're welcome. When you get back, we can talk about the best clinic to find gen-

but to either get mad or terminate the exchange as quickly as possible. I chose the latter. I was not seeking advice on how to lovingly hold my teen's hand through blissful hormone treatment, a happiness-generating bilateral mastectomy, and long-awaited facial masculinization surgery. But they were there for me, they wanted me to know that. I'd get through this confusing and difficult time with their support.

I'm sure they assumed, consciously or otherwise, that it would just be a matter of time before they could teach me the same meaningless phrases that they too had learned as newbies. I wondered if I would be given flashcards. They would see to it that I could master the same vacant smile, with just a dash of self-righteous judgmental scorn for good measure. I was finding my way. I was learning from the experts.

These groups were not supportive of struggling parents with struggling children. They were supportive of the gender affirming model and gender transition. They were supportive of a very specific brand of socially acceptable parental struggle that was defined by the trans-activist agenda and accepted by the medical community, which was allowing itself to be bullied by the political left. These types of agencies very quickly went from an *A-list* position to a *D-minus*. I needed to find help from other sources.

My significant other—the father of my younger daughter—was completely available to me and on my *A list*. He had known Jordan from a young age and understood my position. He'd observed my pain and knew what I was up against. He steadfastly used he/him/Ash when referring to Jordan, while also agreeing with me that the practice was disingenuous. But of course, I'd warned him of the red balloon, and he was committed to avoiding anything that might precipitate the death of my child. He is a very loving partner, but as anyone who has lived in a stepfamily situation knows, he had very limited power. Like me, he was disturbed that we had Zoe using he/him/Ash. We evaded questions like, "Why did Ash used to be a girl?" and "Why is Ash a boy now?" and "Is Ash a sister or a brother?" Enough time went by, and eventually, sadly, Zoe's questions stopped. The fact that Jordan was once a girl and a big sister was forgotten, those primitive memories evaporating as her toddler brain developed. Ash was just Ash, and Ash was a boy and a brother.

---

der affirming treatment for your trans-identified child."

It was heart-wrenching to watch.

I moved on to my *B list*. Shortly after Jordan changed therapists, I contacted a long-time colleague by email who is a highly regarded gender expert. He lives in another state, and is not someone I spoke to regularly, but I consider him a friend. This man is kind without trying to be, but I had a lot of anxiety about reaching out to him, knowing that it was likely to result in more pain instead of less. Desperation won out. I held a miniscule amount of hope that my friendship with him would prevail, and I would be validated in some minor way. I just wanted him to throw me a bone.

My email went something like this:

"Good morning, Dr. Jones. I wanted to update you on Jordan's progress since we last communicated two years ago. If you recall from our previous correspondence, I had serious doubts about whether Jordan was trans or whether this was something else manifesting as a desire to be accepted into a group of peers with whom she felt comfortable. Over the past two years, Jordan has continued to identify as trans, although I have become increasingly convinced that she is not. Although we've been using male pronouns, addressing her by the name she has chosen (Ash), and supporting her in every way we can think of, her mood and self-injurious behaviors have continued to get progressively worse, and I am concerned that she's spiraling out of control. Now she's talking about hormones and top surgery. I feel that this has gone way too far, but I don't know how to stop it. I'd appreciate any advice you might have to offer."

It's a sad and lonesome thing to send a desperate email to a friend asking for help, only to hear nothing back. I was on pins and needles awaiting his response, but the days dragged on and still … nothing. Why was it taking so long? Maybe he hadn't received my email. Maybe it went to his junk mail folder. Maybe he was on vacation. Or perhaps (I dared to hope) he was calling a friend, a therapist who specialized in the teen trans craze that was currently coursing through our schools and communities like a virus and taking a large percentage of our children with it. The therapist friend would get Jordan out of this, I thought. Or maybe my friend was considering if he himself would be able to work with my daughter via Zoom considering the circumstances. I had put out a call for reinforcements. Help was on the way. (Wasn't it?) All I had to do was to hang on a little bit longer.

The disappointing response came nine days after I hit the SEND button on my laptop. None of my fantasies panned out. His uninteresting advice was to "get through this," all the while affirming my son, Ash. He hoped the pain would eventually go away for me. His exact words:

"My friend, I hope this gets better for you."

He also sent a well-intentioned reminder about the suicide risk of non-affirming behavior. I was growing weary of the admonition that I could somehow control another person's decision to take their life if they truly wanted to. His response was a blow to me. There were no reinforcements on the way. I was hunkered down in the trenches, trying to hold on until help arrived. And the response, crackling over the radio, was this: "Good luck. We hope it all works out for you."

The *A-list* and *B-list* resources came and went. I was moving into *C-list* territory. I contacted the clinic of an acquaintance of mine. We had discussed a few mutual patients through the years, and I was 75 percent sure she would know who I was when I called. She was a kind and empathic clinician, well into her established career, and her practice included medical treatment for transgender individuals. She worked in a very popular clinic in downtown Dante's Watch. Dr. Smith had an excellent reputation and was well-liked by her patients and the community.

By now, I was searching for anyone who would even acknowledge the existence of this up-and-coming trans epidemic, regardless of whether the person could help me or not. (*Can someone please just admit that this is happening? Acknowledge that it's possible so I'll know I haven't gone completely mad. Please. I won't tell anyone. I won't out you. I promise.*) Dr. Smith was seasoned and savvy and someone I expected could easily discern an authentic trans person from someone who was part of the spreading infection. After all, her patients were relying on her to do just that.

A superficially cheerful receptionist answered the phone at Dr. Smith's office.

Receptionist: "Good afternoon, Dr. Smith's office, how may I help you?"

Me: "Hello, this is Dr. Bellot. I was looking to discuss some clinical issues with Dr. Smith about gender dysphoria and obtain her expertise on the matter."

Receptionist: "What is the patient's date of birth?"

Me: "This is not about a patient she's currently treating. I was hoping just to discuss the diagnosis and treatment with her."

Receptionist: "This is very sensitive material. I can't just hand out information about our trans kids. I need to know what patient you're calling about. I don't understand."

Me: "I'm not requesting information about any of your patients. I have some general questions for Dr. Smith that I'd like to discuss, clinician to clinician. May I please speak with her?"

Receptionist: "I don't appreciate being bullied. This is very sensitive material."

(Bullied?)

Me: "Yes, you've mentioned twice the sensitivity of the subject matter. May I please just leave a message for Dr. Smith? She can call me back. Here is my cell phone number."

Receptionist: "Yes of course. And by the way, Dr. Smith goes by they/them now. What was your name again?"

I hung up the phone and sat there, looking out the window. *A list*, *B list*, *C list* ... I hadn't expected to go through them all so quickly. Where did that leave me? I didn't have a *D list*. I was now down to my *Z list*: astrology, tarot card readers, advice I might find scrawled on a bathroom wall. There was no hope there, only quiet desperation. These were things to turn to because nothing else was working. *But what the hell*, I thought. *What harm could it do?*

And so it was that I found myself on the phone one afternoon with a woman who worked as a "supernatural clearer" and resided in upstate New York. Now, I know what you must be thinking: Dr. Bellot has completely lost it. But hear me out. I was desperate. I was beyond desperate. Ordinarily, I don't believe in such things, but a member of my extended family had used this type of paranormal clearing in a dramatic situation that arose in her life, and it had been immediately and completely helpful. Imagine that. What great wonders the world holds in store for us if only we allow ourselves to be filled with wonder. Maybe there was hope in this, after all. I could use a little hope. I was open to a little magic.

Martha, my supernatural clearer, had a very natural, kind, and gentle demeanor, at least by way of FaceTime. She had long dark hair with well-defined streaks of gray that she didn't bother to conceal. There was a picture window in the backdrop of her living room, and through the glass I could see the persistent winter gray of the East Coast sky. For some reason, I spoke with her from my car in the garage. It was not a conscious decision. I had just arrived home from work and instead of going in the house to call her, I called from the garage. There was nobody else home, but this was something I did in secret, something my scientific mind was ashamed of.

If this shame or skepticism slipped into my voice, Martha didn't seem to notice, or was at least kind enough not to mention it. She patiently listened to my whole story from beginning to end. She listened with absolutely no judgment, and she did not offer platitudes or suggestions as to how I might come to terms with the idea that my daughter who I loved with every ounce of my being would soon be asking a surgeon to remove her breasts and, perhaps, to fasten a penis to where her vagina used to be. Martha discussed what she might bring to the table by way of a supernatural clearing, including the possibility that she might be able to offer nothing useful at all. She did not make empty promises or have a big sales pitch for her service. She did not know for sure if she would be helpful, but she thought it might be worth trying. I expressed interest and a desire to proceed.

Once she had my permission to continue, Martha began to describe the process in more detail. She had an aura of serenity about her and was more than capable of holding my emotional volatility. "The first thing," she said, "is to determine what kind of ghost you may have." She described several possible scenarios of why there might be a ghost present in my home and why it might manifest in this specific way, causing so much pain to me and my daughter. "Most people know what a poltergeist is, but that's only one kind of ghost," she told me, and she proceeded to educate me about orbs and other ghostly entities. Amidst her educational monologue, I realized I'd sunk too low in my desperate quest to find someone who might help me. I politely disengaged, but I was grateful to Martha for her genuine kindness and willingness to listen and to believe the things that I was telling her: "My daughter's in trouble. I know in my core that the things she is saying and seeking are not right for her. I need somebody to believe me. I need someone who can help me get her out of it."

Was my mother on my *A list* or my *Z list*? I still don't know, but reaching out to her turned out to be painful for both of us. Imagine a woman who is a loving and dedicated mother. She committed her career to the education of young children in a very poor public school district. She was well-loved by her students and their families and was approached by students years later who recognized her in public and thanked her for affecting their lives so greatly. Although she was adept at motherhood, she was an even more loving and dedicated grandma. To give an example, she dutifully commuted to my house (which was four hours from the town where she resides) every week so that Zoe would not have to go to day care for the first year of her life. Mind you, that year held the worst rain Dante's Watch had seen in decades, and my mother made that commute without question. Every week she would recount the story of her journey, which often involved a major road closure with a lengthy detour in the pouring rain, a landslide, or unforeseen construction. This was not blissful pleasant driving with fluffy clouds above her and hours of ocean views while she sipped on a soymilk latte from Starbucks. This was a four-hour nasty commute, eight hours round trip. It was down-in-the-muck grandma love.

Her days in my home were spent holding my baby, singing to my baby, and praying for my baby. That baby had a congenital abnormality that required a lot of care for the first year of her life. Still, my mother never considered the possibility of not caring for her, of not making the commute, of letting me work things out on my own. If my mother harbored any judgment about my divorce, my having a second child from a new relationship, or any of my other life choices, she never brought it up. She loved me and my two girls in a fierce and uncomplicated way, with a love that only mothers understand.

I should not have asked her for advice about Jordan. My mother is deeply religious, and I anticipated that her advice would come from that perspective. I was angry with God and wasn't willing to hear about His saving grace, but I asked my mother for help and advice anyway, and when she answered in the way that I thought she would, I lashed out at her. What a mean and ungrateful daughter I am. I asked my mother for help and then attacked her for helping me in the only way she knew how. It was a set-up for failure. And the only thing I can say to defend myself is that I had nowhere left to turn, and the realization that it was over—this desperate search for help that was doomed from the beginning—put my back against the wall and my mind and body focused on the fight in front of me. I came out swinging, and the first people I hurt were the ones who didn't deserve it.

Chapter Ten: The Cliff and the Ocean

The Cliff's Edge

The days were steeped in madness: the constant plodding service of the mundane but necessary; the uninspired conversations around work and dinner; the perpetual shuttling of our bodies from one place to the next. Voices jabbered on the radio, in the hospital, over podcasts and restaurant tables and audiobooks. Roads and highways were filled with vehicles while I sat in my car in the driveway and tried to remember whether I was coming or going. My family was sliding—not just Jordan but *all* of us—toward a precipice from which we would soon plunge and would not return whole. We should have been scrambling, digging our heels and fingers into the soil for purchase, clawing at roots and stones half-buried in the earth. We should have been reaching out to each other, forming a human chain, our faces strained and muddied with effort. *If one of us goes, we all go*, I thought, but in the seat next to me was not my daughter but a small slip of paper, a list of things I needed to pick up for dinner. Had I gotten them already? I turned my head to see if there were any bags on the seats and footwells behind me.

I had come to a place where there seemed to be nothing left to do. All the tasks on the to-do list for a parent with a trans kid were already behind me. I had educated myself, obtained consultation from the experts, connected my child with therapists and resources, alerted and educated my friends and family, and reached out to the school. I had taught myself to speak about my child using a new name and pronouns, and I had implored everyone around me to do the same. I'd checked all the boxes, and when I looked down at my list of groceries, for the space of a few seconds the items on the paper were not apples and cereal but that *other* list, the one I'd hoped might make a difference. Attend meeting at Rainbow Center. (Check.) Purchase a binder. (Check.) Research long-term effects of hormone blockers and testosterone on teenage girls. (Check.) Answer my younger daughter's repeated questions about why her sister is now a brother with a different name. (Check.) Address my own agony that she is no longer asking. (Check.)

These days it seemed that I was always in motion but going nowhere, like the dreams I'd had as a child in which I was running in a field of fallen leaves, the soles of my tennis shoes slipping and sliding beneath me. *There's something coming*, I would think as my legs pumped furiously and my heart thudded like a tom-tom in my chest. And even in the midst of those childhood dreams I understood that it was a horrible thing, to be pursued by something just out of sight, to find oneself helpless and alone in the open field.

When I was in high school, amidst *Lord of the Flies*, teenage acne, the quadratic equation, and *The Great Gatsby*—long before I'd encountered the term *gender dysphoria* or allowed myself to imagine that I, with all of my awkwardness and imperfections, would someday be blessed with the wonderful and daunting task of motherhood—I discovered the powerful tool of exercise as a coping mechanism for the many things that plagued me. I credit my high school swim coach. That bad grade in chemistry, the boyfriend who'd suddenly and inexplicably taken an interest in somebody else, the ominous realization that someday soon I would be leaving home: they were still there at the end of an exhausting workout, but I came to realize that what had changed was me. I felt stronger, calmer, emotionally centered and ready to tackle the problems in front of me, or to at least focus on what I could do to make them better. Through the years, I have pursued different forms of exercise, from swimming to martial arts to running. If I work out hard enough, if I push my body as far as it will go and then a little farther until it feels like something might break, I can get out of my head for a while. When I come back, the solution to a problem I've been working on is sometimes right there in front of me. I believe in that other place, where the body takes over and the mind slips behind a thin white curtain and comes out changed. I believe in the therapeutic value of sweating.

As I've settled into a grown-up life of parenting and working and shuttling children around town, walking has become my exercise of choice. It is easy to find great places to walk in Dante's Watch: an ocean bluff trail lined with wildflowers; a dirt path leading into a centuries-old redwood grove replete with wild ginger; a strip of narrow sand with sea-glass treasures waiting to be discovered. Even near the semi-busy city streets, towering oaks and aging eucalyptus trees populate the adjacent fields and local parks. Wildlife from the surrounding forests and hillsides sometimes saunter through the more urban parts of our community. Foxes and skunks have been known to frequent the parking lots of our local coffee shops. At my previous house, a family of quail used to scamper back and forth along the driveway like they owned the place. I've seen four lanes of traffic come to a halt while a herd of deer clip-clopped their way across the intersection. (And *yes*, they were using the crosswalk.)

And so it was that I found myself walking along the coastline north of Dante's Watch one late afternoon. It was my favorite time of day to be outside, the sunlight glistening off the surface of the ocean, the fog thick and nestled tightly against the bluffs, my favorite native grass swaying in the arms of the late-April breeze. I'd been in a dark mood for most of the day, but I could feel that darkness lifting as I parked the car near the trailhead and took to the path.

I had nowhere to go, nothing to prove, but I walked like a woman on a mission, swinging my arms harder than necessary, pitching my body forward as the trail rose in front of me. I made my way past the grasslands and toward the bluff overlooking the water. The soles of my tennis shoes pounded the dirt with an urgent simplicity. The rhythmic tread of my feet became a chant in my head. I walked harder, moved faster, and somewhere along the way it occurred to me that I was crying. It didn't matter. I let the emotion bubble over as my feet picked up speed. Suddenly, I was running: trying to leave the pain behind or running toward a solution, it was impossible to know. Snot and tears left a trail in the wind. My lungs filled with air and then shoved it out, over and over again, until it felt like something was separating inside of me.

The sun had buried itself in the horizon, and the sky was a muddied purple as shades of red, orange, pink, and yellow blended together like the restless churn of the sea below. Here was the Pacific Ocean, stretching out beneath me as I came to a stop along the section of trail that wound its way along the cliff edge. *How had it gotten so late? How long had I been running?* I felt breathless, my lungs smoldering in my chest. The muscles in my legs ached from exertion as I hunched over, my palms flat against my thighs. I looked out at the vastness of the ocean and listened to the sounds of the wild creatures all around me. Waves crashed against the rocks below as black cormorants surveyed the water from their stony perch. On their last hunt of the day, brown pelicans flew in formation above the spray as sandpipers darted back and forth at the water's edge. I was only one of many living things in this moment: an addendum, a sidenote. Life was happening everywhere, alone and together. I tried to take in all of it, to let it filter through me like sand. *Thank you*, I thought, but a gust of wind shoved at me from the open space beyond the cliff, and I took a half-step backward, away from the edge.

I was turning around now, thinking about heading back to my car and my house and the structured order of my civilized little world, when I saw her standing there in the high grass on the other side of the trail, about ten feet in front of me. I had always seen them at a distance, slinking along in the places where the forests meet the fields, their slim and muscled bodies moving silently beneath speckled fur and tufted ears. I had never seen them this close before, without bars or cages between us. The bobcat was not a large animal—about twice the size of a standard house cat—but there was no mistaking it for something domesticated. It let out a low and guttural sound, a growl and a moan and the distant drone of a locomotive twisted together like barbed wire. I took a step backward, then remembered where I was, on the edge of a cliff with a ninety-foot plunge behind me. The bobcat stood its ground, neither retreating nor advancing, and I did the same, with nowhere left to go but down.

I had heard about bobcats attacking people. It was rare, and typically only happened when they were sick or threatened. I wondered if this bobcat was sick, or if its babies were in the tall grass behind it, and the next thing to cross my mind was the things this wild creature might do to protect them. I stood there with my back to the cliff, not knowing what to do. Should I maintain eye contact or look away? Should I try to make myself appear bigger or smaller? Should I make a noise or remain quiet? *If it launches itself at me, I will dive to the side*, I told myself, but I felt frozen and unsure if I was capable of movement.

The bobcat twitched its short tail and took a step toward me. I took a breath, held it, and readied myself for whatever was about to happen. *Fight*, I thought, *be a wild thing*, and I made myself bigger, lifted my shoulders and spread my arms wide. I do not think I was aware of it at the time, but it occurred to me later that I was making a sound as well, something that mimicked the growl of the bobcat but went on longer, a steady *Rrrrrrrrrrr* that slowly tapered, like a motorcycle in the night.

We stared at each other for the pregnant space of several seconds, sizing each other up, on the brink of a fierce and furious encounter that might leave one or both of us dead. I was ready. I would do whatever it took to make it home to my family that night. The bobcat, I imagined, would do the same.

That's when I heard it, a mew from the depths of the grass behind it. The bobcat paused; its head tilted a few degrees to the right.

Go, I thought. *Be with your babies. Let me go and be with mine.*

She studied me a moment longer, then turned and walked into the grass, the green shafts separating ever-so-slightly as she passed, like a velvet curtain that parts just wide enough for the passage of a single body. She glanced back over her shoulder one last time as she disappeared. *You are not a wild thing*, she seemed to have decided. *Where are your claws? Where are your piercing teeth? I could've killed you if I wanted.*

I stood there for a moment, the muscles of my thighs trembling with unspent adrenalin. *Dismissed*, I thought, and I felt like laughing and throwing up at the same time. *Killed by a bobcat*: it sounded ridiculous. And yet, thirty seconds before, it had seemed very plausible, perhaps even the *most likely* outcome. I willed myself to walk with legs I didn't quite trust to keep me upright, retracing my steps along the path as I made my way back to the car. It was true, I realized. I was not a wild thing. I had become weak and civilized. I had forgotten what it was like to be *all in*, to approach every fight like it was the only thing that mattered.

Was I doing that now? I wondered. *Was I approaching this fight over the safety and well-being of my daughter like it was the only thing that mattered?*

Like most mothers, I had nurtured and protected Jordan since the day of conception and had loved her since before she was born. I had felt her stretch her limbs while she was still growing in my belly. I had delivered her from my body and had been immediately and forever changed. We had been together almost every day of her life, and even when we weren't together, I was with her in some small way, cheering her on, hoping for the best, and keeping my eyes peeled for the things that threatened her. When we were apart, she was also with me, reminding me that the world was far bigger than myself and that the universe of emotion was vaster than I'd ever imagined prior to her existence. Who was I before her? The memory of that person was muted and distant.

I am her mother, I thought. More than anyone else, I should be the one protecting her, including if she needs to be protected from herself. *Especially*, I corrected, if she needs to be protected from herself.

I looked down at my clawless fingers and ran my tongue along teeth that were not designed to kill.

Where was my fierceness? Where was my fight? How had I gotten so passive, so willing to follow along with the misguided suggestions of others?

(*The bobcat understands this*, a voice inside of me noted. *She's not attending group therapy sessions or worried about pronouns. You mess with her kittens, momma bobcat is gonna kill you or die trying.*)

I am not a bobcat. I can't just go around killing people.

(*No. But you can get serious. Where is your fierceness? Where is your fight?*)

"What would it mean to get serious?" I asked myself as I opened the door to my car and slipped inside. "What would that look like?" I sat there for a while, rummaging through a collection of extreme responses and the likely and possible outcomes in my head. Here are the ones that didn't involve launching myself at people with splayed claws and murderous teeth:

- We could move away and start a new life in a new town. I considered places where it wasn't so popular and acceptable to be trans, where a trans-identified child didn't become an instant star. I imagined a community where Fourth of July celebrations included festive small-town parades, sparklers, and potluck gatherings in local parks with freshly painted gazebos and cold lemonade. There were downsides, of course. Jordan would resent me for taking her away from her friends and moving her to another part of the country. I could lose her for good. I'd be pulling myself away as well, away from my friends and the rest of my family, perhaps with little in common with my neighbors. I could find myself in court in a custody battle with Zack. He wouldn't move with me willingly.

- Here's another extreme response: I could continue to do exactly what I'd been doing. I could watch Jordan become Ash. I could watch her go through medical transition that landed her somewhere in gender ambiguity. Ash would remain a trans-identified teen, afflicted with self-imposed torture. He would never be fully male, either in body or mind. If or when she detransitioned, she would never be able to reclaim the fullness of her original female body. Ash would be suspended between genders, not reaching mental solace from the changes she endured. She might wake up from the dream someday, recognizing all that has been lost, and I would need to grapple with the fact that I'd allowed it. What would our relationship be like then?

- I could send her to a wilderness camp for the summer. *Take that.* A few months in the Utah desert might do her a bit of good. After fourteen-hour days of hiking with a heavy backpack, eating only protein bars, and drinking warm water from a mildewed bottle, maybe Jordan would come home to her comfortable house with her beautiful bedroom and be thankful. Maybe. But who knows who else would be at that program. Who would she be hiking alongside? Many of the wilderness programs treat teens with behavioral and substance-use disorders. Much of the time the treatment is successful, but Jordan might return home with a new-found interest in methamphetamine, or would possibly be more oppositional than she'd been before? And still without gratitude ...

- Jordan could attend a boarding school. That would put some intensive structure in her life. But why would I expect *that* school to be any less encouraging of a trans-identified student than a school in Dante's Watch? With the breadth of what the schools allowed (*Enabled? Encouraged?*), she might come home fully medically transitioned, with nobody at the school thinking to notify me. Not to mention my daughter would be away from me for nine months a year. I would miss her. She would miss me. And she needed me. No matter how much she pushed me away, I mustn't lose sight of that.

- We could send her to a private Christian school close to home. Having experienced the lack of boundaries in the public school system, it was appealing to have clear guidelines for life and to instill the unconditional love that Jesus taught and modeled. But Jordan might rebel. She could come to hate me, her dad, and her sister. Zoe would lose the sibling who she adored. The possibilities for how Jordan's rebellion might manifest were endless.

- I could say no. No special names or pronouns. No more talk of being transgender or wanting medical and surgical transition. This option gave me pause. Why hadn't I done that from the beginning? Oh, yes, there was the red balloon. The dead daughter thing. I had almost forgotten.[1]

Shifting: Sadness to Anger

It's funny how a near-death experience with a bobcat on the edge of a cliff sometimes changes one's perspective. Despite our brief adversarial encounter (*Were we ever really adversaries, or more like kindred spirits who gave each other a bit of a fright?*), I took away something from the experience that stuck with me long after the adrenaline faded from my system. "Here is my fierceness! Here is my fight!" became my rallying cry, at least for a while, as grief and sadness took a back seat to anger and frustration.

Anger is like fast food. It tastes good going down and then you regret it for the rest of the day. Here are the things I was angry about, and I apologize for all of them because nobody is at their best when they're on a rant. Feel free to skip to the next section if you want. I'll catch up with you there once I've gotten this out of my system.

- Over the course of our struggle, I've come to see the "gender experts" as less well-intentioned than I initially imagined them to be. The

---

[1]. The suicide warning has become such a prominent tool in convincing parents and others of the importance of embracing the gender affirming model that it is important to point out that the DSM-V *does not* state that suicide risk or attempts necessarily lessen with gender transition. After sex reassignment, an individual's psychological adjustment may vary, and suicide risk may persist.

ones we encountered were not exactly a thoughtful bunch, and I doubt they have a clear understanding of what they are dealing with. Self-righteous elitism? They have that down pretty well. A false perception that they are far more enlightened than the rest of us? Sure. A commitment to stick to their talking points and to shame detractors by labeling them transphobic, bigoted, hateful, right-wing, unenlightened, or just plain stupid and uninformed? You betcha. But willingness to question their previous suppositions and to approach this complex issue with humility, open-mindedness, and a healthy respect for evidence-based medicine? Not so much.

In short, they pretend to know a lot about something that few people know a lot about. Scratch beneath the surface, and you'll find politics, social agendas, and the kind of quick-to-demonize reflexive hysteria so often shared by people who feel threatened by those who have the audacity to question them. Their arrogance and insecurity compromise them, limiting their ability to provide objective guidance to struggling children and their families. They become bullies, although they are seldom aware of it. For those on the receiving end, it leads to skepticism and distrust of the experts when we need them the most. People have lost faith in the medical and scientific communities. I don't blame them. As a member of those communities, I have come to realize that the irony of this rampant public disillusionment is that we have done it to ourselves.

- As medicine and science begin to topple under the weight of their own biased perspectives, the institution of journalism has fallen along with them. These days it is hard to get the plain and simple facts. It is all about the headline, the sound bite, the left or right spin on a pool ball that ricochets around the table oblivious of the consequences of the reckless havoc of its own trajectory. Sensationalized news stories tell us how we should feel and why, while the details of *what actually happened* are trimmed to the bare minimum and lie on the floor like abandoned party favors. This undermines our ability to discuss the issues rationally. We can't talk about the pros and cons of gender affirming care because we're all too angry to communicate in a respectful way and to listen to each other.

- In today's society, everyone is advertising for their cause. Pride flags used to be about celebrating human diversity and showing support for the LGBTQ community. As a long-time social liberal, I waved them myself during our town's annual Pride Parade. Now they seem to be everywhere: at the coffee shop, the library, posted every ten feet along the walls of our school classrooms and hallways. A business without a Pride flag or some highly visible sign about equity and inclusion is immediately suspect. ("I noticed you don't have a Pride flag in your lobby. Aren't you supportive of the LGBTQQIP2SA+ community?" – "Well, yes, I am. But this is a funeral home.")

- Why is it necessary for people to thrust their sexual orientation and gender identity out in public? ("Does anybody really care that you identify as pansexual queer nonbinary? You're the town librarian, for God's sake!") Politicians proudly proclaim the gender and sexual identities of their children as evidence of their own progressive social inclusivity. Now we have the first openly bisexual governor in the country, but how is that *my* business? Is it germane to her ability to do the job? Do I care? Should anyone care? I have no doubt we've had *many* bisexual politicians before her who have not thrust their sexual preferences into the universe. It's amazing we were able to function in such an informational vacuum.

- For almost two centuries, women have tirelessly endeavored to make progress for gender equality[2] and equal rights. Why now must we decide that a girl who outperforms boys in multiple areas must be "gender nonconforming?" Why can't she simply be a smart, independent girl with an interest in activities that do not fit traditional stereotypes? Why can't a boy with an interest in figure skating and the color purple just be a boy with an interest in figure skating and the color purple? Why suddenly must he be gender expansive, or gender fluid, or gay, or a girl?

    Although I wasn't around to ask them, I can't imagine that the suffragettes had this in mind. Women who had the audacity to stand

---

2. If gender is merely a self-identification or a whim, we are not really talking about gender. We are talking about sex in the genetic sense of the word.

up for equal rights regardless of sex (*equal* rights, not *special* rights) endured the risk of sexual assault, involuntary psychiatric hospitalization, forced tube feeding, and even death, all while demonstrating bravery in the face of adversity. They were willing to risk all of this so that women could vote or join the workforce in an occupation of their choosing. What might they say about an intelligent girl with many natural gifts, including her athletic ability and an aptitude for geometry and mechanical drawing? I speculate that they would not think she is crossing gender stereotypes. She is a gifted and talented young woman. That is to be expected.

- Things have been getting worse for women. We live in a country where a mediocre male athlete can shatter all kinds of athletic records previously set by women, as long as that male athlete proclaims themselves to be trans. It's not a matter of excluding trans individuals from sports. It's a matter of basic human anatomy and sexual dimorphism. Simply put, men's bodies are built differently than women's bodies. On average, men have more muscle mass, longer limbs, greater upper body strength, larger bones, and superior lung capacity. These differences allow men to be naturally stronger and faster than women. (Women, on the other hand, are less prone to bonk our heads while attempting stupid things. For women, therefore, the use of helmets during our daily activities is optional.) And no, not *every* man is stronger and faster than *every* woman, but the physical advantages of being genetically male are numerous. If they weren't, there would be no need to separate men and women in college and professional sports. There would not be women's basketball teams and men's basketball teams; there would just be basketball. (If we insist on being blind to the inherent athletic advantages of having an XY genotype, let's encourage women to be NFL running backs and see where that gets us.) Now, suddenly, it's considered hateful and transphobic to insist that an athlete with a male body (regardless of how they identify) compete against other athletes with male bodies. How demoralizing and disrespectful to female athletes who have dedicated their careers to athletic excellence. How dangerous this can be for women competing in contact sports with genetic males. How many lethal or catastrophic injuries must they suffer before we put an end to this madness?

- I am frustrated by people's desire to label themselves with pronouns when no clarification is needed. ("That's Arnold Schwarzenegger. He uses he/him/Terminator pronouns, just in case you were wondering.")

There. I've said a few things that will undoubtedly get me in trouble. I should stop now. I've done enough damage already. But ... while I'm at it ...

- I would like to say that I am mildly annoyed (*really?*), okay, just a smidgen resentful (*is that right?*), fine, I am absolutely furious (*oh, now you've really done it*) with the trans activists for targeting our children and using them as pawns in the incessant push of their broader political agenda. At the same time, the trans activists have proven themselves quite adept at indoctrinating adults to behave like well-trained dogs rather than responsible protectors of the youngest and most vulnerable among us.

- Most egregiously (at least in my mind), I am horror struck at the mental health community and its lack of adequate response to the transgender craze. Are we not clinicians who make diagnoses based on clinical criteria?[3] Since when do we accept patients' self-diagnoses as unquestionably true? Psychiatrists should be the leaders in the field of mental illness and should be setting the tone. Obviously, we aren't doing it. Maybe it's because anyone bold enough to question the current state-sanctioned practice of blindly greenlighting all medical and surgical transition procedures for children runs the very real risk of being either reprimanded by the Medical Board of

---

3. The DSM-V goes out of its way to say that other clinical entities *must* be considered and ruled out prior to making a diagnosis of gender dysphoria. Such entities include things as simple as nonconformity to gender roles (such as "tomboyism" in girls), transvestitism (cross-dressing for the purpose of sexual arousal without questioning one's gender identity), and body dysmorphic disorder (the perception that one's body is abnormal without questioning one's gender identity). The clinical diagnosis of gender dysphoria *must* be limited to those individuals whose distress and impairment meet the specified criteria.

California or losing one's state license to practice medicine altogether. We are forced to choose: protect our children or do whatever we must to cover our own professional asses. Sadly, most of us in the mental health community have chosen the latter.

Shifting: Anger to Love

Anger was a necessary phase on my journey through the transgender sea, but it did not feel good to me. I'd grown tired of feeling sad and helpless, and it was empowering to put sadness to bed early so I could hang out with anger on my back porch for a while, the two of us smoking cigars and drinking whisky until the crack of dawn. But alas, all such nights eventually come to an end. I woke up with a hangover and a mouth like cotton, a hickey on my neck, and the stale stench of cigar smoke still lingering on my hair and clothing.

Over the next few weeks, I continued to try on the idea that I might be wrong and that everyone else was right about Jordan being transgender. Always second-guessing myself I was, as I spent my days in the shadow of that notorious red balloon that forever hovered over my shoulder. I attempted to file Jordan's destructive problem away for a while. I had another child who needed mothering and love, and it was important to tend to her. I had patients in my private practice who I needed to properly assess and diagnose (somebody had to), and they deserved my time and attention. I could no longer let Jordan's problem also be *my* primary problem and the central driving force of my life. At some point, I had to move on.

These were the things I told myself, but even during those self-admonishing lectures, I knew that it was impossible to let go of my daughter. I was angry with Jordan for putting me through this, but being angry with a child I loved was not sustainable. Chronic exhaustion set in. I felt joyless and had trouble sleeping. My sense of agency over my life had dwindled to nothing. I was upset and emotionally labile most of the time. I tried to preserve what I could. I went to work every day and fulfilled my obligations. I paid my mortgage and dutifully exercised when I could. I took vitamins and went grocery shopping. I felt perpetually vacant.

On a Wednesday afternoon in mid-July, things caught up with me. I left work early because I was simply too tired to continue. I didn't have space in my schedule for rest, recuperation, or innovative thought, so the space created itself. "I just need to rest for a while," I promised myself, "then back to work." Lying on top of my blue bedspread with a heather-gray fleece blanket pulled over my thinning frame, I closed my eyes and drifted. I was racing along the trail that brought me to the bluff overlooking the ocean, the sun hunkered low on the horizon as brown pelicans glided in formation just above the water. I was sitting next to my daughter as the gender specialist discussed all the many ways we could turn my child's body into something different. I was pushing Jordan on a swing at our local park, her small five-year-old form so light and delicate against the sky. I was watching the labor and delivery nurse as she adjusted the rate of Pitocin that slid through the thin plastic tubing and into my arm. "Your contractions are getting stronger. Are you feeling that? This baby is coming."

I opened my eyes in a cavern, the subterranean air cold and damp against my skin. A thin shaft of moonlight descended from above, and I moved toward it, my hands extended in front of me, my naked feet inching along the jagged and uneven terrain. It was so dark that I touched it before I could see it: a frayed rope that had been fashioned into a makeshift ladder and hung like seaweed from the aperture above. I put a foot on one of its rungs, shifted my weight onto it, and heard the thing tighten and groan as I began to ascend.

I kept climbing, half-expecting it to snap and send me plunging back into the darkness. The rope held, and I emerged through the opening onto a beach where the surf ebbed and crashed against the shore as sandpipers darted back and forth at the water's edge. *I've been here before*, I thought, but I was on my hands and knees now, the sand wet against my skin. I looked up to see Jordan sitting alone beneath the moonlight. She was facing the ocean, her knees pulled tight against her chest. Long brown hair cascaded over her shoulders and down the back of her shirt. She hadn't worn it that way since sixth grade, and in the soft light I could see that she looked very much the way she had back then: her body younger and draped with a few extra pounds; her left cheek stippled with pimples; a preteen girl on the brink of the most awkward and difficult decade of her life. She hadn't spotted me yet, and she rocked back and forth as she stared out at the ocean, that great and horrible thing just a few yards in front of her.

I got to my feet and walked across the open beach, the surf pounding in my ears, the night sky timeless and infinite above us. I sat down next to her, our bodies connecting but separate, that eternal dance of mother and child.

"I love you," I said. "I will never leave you."

She sighed and leaned into me like the memory of a dream we had almost forgotten.

Chapter Eleven: Recruitment

Now We're Talking

I emerged from my dream that afternoon with a sense of purpose. I had been stuck on the side of the road for too long already, spinning my wheels in the mud of my fear and frustration. I needed help to get my daughter out of this, and convincing Zack that it was the right thing to do became my top priority. How to accomplish that was the pressing question, and I reached back to my medical training for the answers.

Years ago, during residency training, I learned an important lesson. At its simplest and most basic level, it comes down to this: "The patient will be up in five minutes." That's five minutes—one, two, three, four, five—and it's hard to believe that five minutes would make much of a difference one way or another; but believe me, it does. In the heat of the battle, five minutes changes everything, and deploying those words—"The patient will be up in five minutes"—changes the fundamental nature of the conversation.

Medical residency is notorious for its long and arduous hours, and during those years one's patience is short, time is precious, emotions are raw, and family is often forgotten or neglected. For a resident in training, the hierarchy of priorities goes something like this:

1. Don't get fired.
2. Do whatever is necessary to avoid getting chewed out by your superiors.
3. Remember that pretty much everyone is your superior.

4. Stay on the good side of nurses.
5. Try not to kill anyone.
6. Sleep when you can.
7. Eat when you can.
8. When you do eventually kill or injure someone due to your own incompetence (it happens to every resident), don't let anyone see you cry.
9. If you find the time, try to learn something.
10. Remind yourself that things will someday—*hopefully*—get better.

Regardless of one's intended specialty, the first year of residency is spent rotating through many different units in the hospital. During my two-month rotation in obstetrics, I delivered 126 babies. The following month, I was doing pediatric ambulatory care. Then it was on to the intensive care unit where I was managing code blues.

Along the way, we learned "clinical pearls." (See #9 in the hierarchy of priorities: If you find the time, try to learn something.) Clinical pearls are small nuggets of fact, truth, or wisdom in medicine. They stand out against the backdrop of all the other things to learn and remember, like small pearls glistening in the murky depths of the vast sea of medical knowledge. Instructors cast these pearls into the water, one at a time. We dive for them, try to catch as many as we can in our outstretched hands, realizing that we cannot catch them all. Sometimes we share them with each other, and in this way a clinical pearl develops a life of its own, passed down from generation to generation, making its way across the country and across the planet. Ask any doctor the meaning of "One view is no view," and they will tell you that a single X-ray is not enough. You must look at things from more than one angle. If you limit yourself to a single X-ray (or a single point of view that you rely on completely and without question), you're apt to miss something. One view is no view. It's an important lesson, something we seem to have forgotten with the rush-to-treatment-without-thought-or-hesitation gender affirming model.

Here's another pearl that I learned in the ICU: "In a cardiac arrest, the first pulse to check is your own." Unless one deals with it every day, managing a medical emergency is a very stressful experience. Not every patient can be saved, but the most effective and well-run resuscitations are performed by people who are calm, efficient, thoughtful, and methodical. If the team is panicking, yelling, running around, and not working together, the chance of saving the patient drops precipitously. I learned this during my first night in the ICU when a patient who'd been admitted earlier that day suddenly developed difficulty breathing, his oxygen levels plummeting from 94 percent to the mid-70s in the space of a few minutes.

I ran through the possibilities in my head—pneumonia, heart attack, blood clot, collapsed lung, fluid overload—and the terrifying realization occurred to me that this patient might need to be intubated. It was something I hadn't done before—putting a breathing tube into a patient's trachea—and I knew that I could kill him if I didn't do it right. The nurses were all looking at me, awaiting orders, but I was sweating, my heart like a jackhammer in my chest.

"What's the problem?" a voice asked. I turned to find the supervising doctor standing in the doorway.

Thank God, I thought, *he hasn't left yet*. I could've hugged him, or perhaps strangled him. What was he *thinking* leaving me alone like this? I didn't know what I was doing. I wasn't prepared to handle a situation of his magnitude.

"His … um … pulse ox is dropping," I told him. "I don't know why. I think he … might need to be intubated."

"Okay," he said. "Good luck with that. He's over 400 pounds, so it's going to be difficult."

My attending physician turned to go.

"*Wait*," I said. "Can you help me? I haven't done this before. Please, I … don't know what to do."

He paused, looked back at me. "Is he on oxygen?"

"Yes," I said. "We switched him to a mask a few minutes ago. It's not helping. He's getting worse instead of better."

"You should check that," he said, and he walked away, leaving me standing there to figure out the rest of it.

I followed the tubing with my eyes. The oxygen had become disconnected from the wall. We'd been covering his mouth and nose with a plastic mask, but no oxygen was flowing. My patient didn't need to be intubated; he needed his oxygen tubing to be plugged back into the wall. I reached over, plugged it in, and the patient's breathing returned to normal.

"Thank you," I said, plopping down next to my attending a few minutes later. I opened the patient's chart and began documenting what had happened.

"Thank yourself," he told me. "You saved him."

"I panicked. I should've checked the oxygen. I assumed it was something worse."

"Don't panic and don't rush," he said. "Assess the situation. Take your time and do things right the first time."

I nodded.

"Slow is smooth and smooth is fast," he said. "In order to be fast and not make mistakes, you must go slow. Will you remember that?"

"Yes," I said. It sounded like a clinical pearl.

"Well," he said, "I'm heading home for the night. I think you've got the rest of this."

He stood up, stretched, and left me sitting there with my clinical pearl. It was the beginning of a busy night, and it wasn't long before I was needed by another patient, and another patient after that. I thought about time a lot that night, how slow is smooth and smooth is fast, and although I was inexperienced, painfully slow, and far from smooth in the care that I provided, it was reassuring to know that it was okay to go slow, to assess the situation, and to make every effort to do things right the first time.

A month later, I was done with the ICU, and I forgot about time for a while after that. I was in the thick of it by then, the days coming and going and blending together. I slogged through it, and it wasn't until my emergency medicine rotation that the next really good clinical pearl landed in my lap.

I trained in inner-city Philadelphia, and the emergency room was hopping twenty-four hours per day. Shifts were busy and patients were sick. We darted around like rabbits, putting out fires, being pulled in a thousand different directions at once. My attending physician that night was Dr. Raposa, a tall and confident man, slightly balding, who wore a long white lab coat. He had a deep voice and had a way of interacting with people that resulted in his desires being carried out. I thought of him as the medical version of Darth Vader, although much less nefarious. As his resident storm troopers, we had both a healthy fear and a great respect for Dr. Raposa. We stayed out of his way, watched him, and learned.

Late nights in the ER were inherently fraught with conflict due to sick patients and tired, overworked staff. It was not infrequent for the following scenario to arise. An ER resident evaluates a patient—let's say, for chest pain—and makes the decision that the patient requires admission to the internal medicine floor to rule out the possibility of a heart attack. An internal medicine resident, who does not want to be paged at 3 a.m. to come to the ER and admit a patient, arrives grumpy and exhausted. He evaluates the patient and decides that the chest pain is reproducible when he pushes on the chest and is therefore related to a muscle strain and not a heart attack. (This is convenient for the internal medicine resident because it means he does not need to admit the patient.) He advises the ER resident that the patient can be discharged home with outpatient follow-up with his primary care physician. The ER resident disagrees, and a "spirited discussion" ensues. The internal medicine resident ultimately decides that it will take more energy to argue than to admit the patient, and admission orders are finally written, reluctantly so.

This exact scenario happened one night. After the internal medicine resident left the ER, the nurse had to call up to the medical floor to give the nurse-to-nurse report. It was me, the nurse, and my attending, Dr. Raposa, sitting at the desk when the nurse made the call and spoke with the floor nurse on the speaker phone. Dr. Raposa and I couldn't help but overhear the conversation as the ER nurse attempted to give her report to the nurse upstairs on the med/surg floor.

ER nurse: "I have a chest pain patient who is being admitted to Bed 2026, and I would like to give report."

Floor nurse: "I'm about to go on break."

ER nurse: "Well, I'd like to get this patient upstairs before I go home for the night."

Floor nurse: "We just had two other admissions, and we still have several nurses who need to go on break. You know, according to union policy, we must incorporate three breaks into our eight-hour shift, so somebody has to go on break as soon as they clock in. It's a lot of work for me to have to provide break coverage for all the other nurses. This admission may have to wait until shift change in three hours. Besides, I heard that this is a soft admission, and the patient doesn't really need to be here. Can't you guys just discharge the patient?"

ER Nurse: "No, we cannot discharge the patient. He may be having a heart attack and needs to be admitted. But I suppose we can keep the patient in the ER for three more hours to accommodate your nurses' break schedules. I'll sign the case out to the next ER nurse when I leave, and I'll let that nurse know she cannot be the one to take her break as soon as she clocks in. After all, this is a chest pain patient, and he may be having a heart attack."

They hang up.

Dr. Raposa: "Nope. We're not waiting three hours for the patient to be admitted. Watch and learn."

He picks up the phone and calls the charge nurse of the admission unit.

Dr. Raposa: "Hi. We have a chest pain patient down in the ER who needs admission, and we need to give report."

Charge Nurse: "Yes, the nurse already called, and we will consider admitting the patient next shift. We've still got a lot of breaks that need to happen before we can all leave for the night. Besides, it sounds like a really soft admit. Can't you guys just discharge th…."

Dr. Raposa (cutting her off): "No. The patient is being admitted. He'll be up in five minutes."

Charge nurse: "No, no, no. We can't take him in five minutes. The room needs to be cleaned and we're out of blankets. We need at least a half hour."

Dr. Raposa: "Great. The patient will be up in a half hour."

He picks up the receiver and hands it to the ER nurse.

Dr. Raposa: "You can give report now."

The ER nurse takes the receiver. She mouths the words, "Thank you," and begins to give report.

Dr. Raposa (looking at me): "That, my friend, is how we go from a three-hour wait to thirty minutes. You don't plead, you don't argue. You announce that the patient will be up in five minutes. And now, you see, we're finally talking."

Five minutes, I thought, and I stored it away, another clinical pearl that would serve me well in life as much as it did in medicine.

There are times when pleading and bargaining and appealing to basic human decency fail to get me anywhere. In most cases, I decide to let it go. After all, one must pick one's battles. When it's important, however, I remember the pearl that Dr. Raposa handed me that night in the ER at 3 a.m. in inner-city Philly. "The patient will be up in five minutes." It resets the conversation and brings the issue to an immediate state of renegotiation. Five minutes cannot be postponed or ignored. It can't be put on the agenda for next month's meeting. It's an 800-pound gorilla standing in the doorway who must be dealt with.

At some point during our transgender adventure, I decided it might be helpful to send Jordan to a private school where she could start fresh and make new friends. I saw it as an opportunity for her to climb out of the trans-identity rut that she had dug for herself. I needed to convince both Zack and Jordan that it was a good idea, and so I began with a well-thought-out email in which I outlined the potential benefits of changing schools, the research I'd done on local options, and the reasons why a private school might be beneficial. I described the three private schools I'd investigated, provided information on pros, cons, cost of tuition, location, and anything unique about each of the schools. I spent hours putting the information together and framing it in a way that I thought would be appealing to the two of them.

Off the email went, and I followed it up with several text messages and phone calls, suggesting that we meet over coffee to discuss the possibility. I might as well have been talking to myself. When pressed about it, Jordan's father seemed to recollect the communications only vaguely, and the idea was quickly written off, as if he was swatting at a gnat that had just now materialized in front of him.

And then I remembered Dr. Raposa and his unique pearl.

Text message to Zack: "After giving it some thought, I've decided to enroll Jordan in the private school we talked about. I really think it's the best option. We're required to submit a deposit for the first semester, so I'll be writing a check from our joint account that we use for her expenses."

Guess what? Immediate response! Angry, yes. Furious, absolutely. But, hey: suddenly, we were finally talking!

Zack "convinced me" not to enroll her that day (not that I'd intended to do so), but he went with me to tour the school later that same week. This approach yielded a discussion on the same day. He saw that I might act without his approval and, *finally*, he was giving this private school idea his full attention. I was not willing to wait three hours for the patient to be admitted. The patient would be up in five minutes.

I used this technique and others to get Zack's attention, help, and support when I needed it the most and wasn't getting through to him in other ways. The tactics were effective, although I didn't feel good about using them, and I was both saddened and a little resentful that I had to. Still, I was fighting for the life and well-being of our daughter—we *both* were, I reminded myself—and the strategies allowed me to tap into Zack's best show of true love for Jordan, which was there all along.

There were setbacks and frustrations, countless times when I felt that it was not working, that we had gone off the rails and were heading for disaster. It was a desperate and lonely time for me. I'd entered the woods looking for my daughter, but I had to find Zack as well, and convincing him that we needed to intervene was harder than I'd expected. *I can't do this without him*, I thought, and so I worked the problem, tried not to panic, and told myself that in a cardiac arrest, the first pulse to check is your own.

Alone and Together in the Forest

How do I tell this part of the story? There were so many conversations between me and Jordan's father. I feel like I did most of the talking, and occasionally he listened. Zack was less convinced than I was that we needed to do something. He'd adopted the rationale that it didn't matter if Jordan's transgender identity was real, manufactured, or just a social fad. The safest thing, he thought—especially with the red balloon hanging over us—was to support her current gender identity and to see how things progressed, which is what we did for a while. But there was the recurrent cutting to consider, her social withdrawal, worsening mood, and psychological deterioration. Jordan wanted to start testosterone as soon as possible, and she talked about the surgeries she would get when she turned eighteen. It was clear to me that we were losing her and that she was losing herself. In a few years, she would be off to college. If we hadn't turned things around by then, she would move forward with all of it, and I was quite certain that she would someday deeply regret it.

Zack had a busy work schedule, a new marriage, and a more *laissez-faire* approach to parenting in general. I suspect that he aligned himself more with Jordan than he did with me. I don't know whether he didn't notice that she was getting worse or preferred not to see it because it meant that he would have to confront her.

I continued to try to get through to him, but I came to see my recruitment of Zack as a battlefield. I'd get him to agree to something, advancing on one front, only to take heavy losses somewhere else. It was demoralizing. I didn't want to fight with him. I needed us to be allies.

I had made some gains with Jordan by shifting my attitude from sadness and anger to love, and I decided that this was the approach that I needed to take with Zack. He was a good father. He loved me once; he loved her still. I had to tap into that. I had to remind him of the past to connect with him in the present. I changed tactics, and the discussions we had were more pleasant and less confrontational. I was turning the ship—*slowly, slowly*—and I tried not to focus on the rocks ahead.

It wouldn't be practical for me to tell you about every conversation. Instead, I will tell you a story about a woman whose daughter gets lost in the woods. The search for her daughter pulls this woman deeper and deeper into the forest until she too is lost. Instead of finding her daughter, she comes across her daughter's father, but he is just as lost as the woman. To make matters worse, he is disoriented with fatigue and dehydration, and he keeps insisting that the things they come across are their daughter when they clearly are not. "This tree is not our daughter," the woman tells him, a bit frustrated that she must explain this to him, "but the way its limbs sway in the breeze *reminds* me of the way she used to dance in our living room. Do you remember that?"

"Yes, yes," he says, "although I can't remember the music."

"It went like this," the woman says, and she hums a little bit of it as they move together through the woods.

"This giant mushroom is not our daughter," she tells him when he insists that it is, "but the top of it makes a roof like the ones you used to make out of pillows when the two of you built your forts. Do you remember that, the way she served you make-believe tea in those little plastic cups while you sat on the floor beneath the canopy of blankets and pillows with stuffed animals all around you?"

"*I remember,*" he says, and his face brightens as they walk onward.

The act of remembering allows them to remember other things, like the time they went hiking and had to remove their shoes before crossing the wide and shallow stream in the woods, the way the sun pressed down on their shoulders and glinted off the pebbles lying just beneath the water. "She always liked that stream," the child's father comments. "If there is a stream in these woods, I bet she would go there."

And so, they set out in search of a stream, and eventually they find one. It's not as wide as the one they used to cross in those other woods, but it's *wide enough*, and the child's parents follow it until they get to a small clearing, a spot where the sun presses down on their shoulders like it did on that other day when it was the three of them as a family.

"She's not here," the woman says, her heart aching with sadness and disappointment.

"Perhaps she will come here soon," he tells her. "Perhaps she will find us instead of the other way around."

They decide to cross the stream together, their shoes and socks held high in their hands. When they get to the other side, they sit down along the bank and rest for a while.

"I miss her," he says. "I hope that she finds us."

The woman nods. The sand is soft and dry beneath her. She reaches down, scoops it into her hand, and watches as it spills through her fingers.

Our daughter did not find us in those woods. She too had forgotten about the pillow forts, the tea and crumpets, the way she used to sway and dance in our living room, the feel of the cold and rushing water around her ankles. Finding Jordan and bringing her back to us took more than simple remembering. But I did find Zack, and I helped him remember our daughter in a thousand simple and important ways. Sometimes we fought. Sometimes we argued about all the ways a mushroom was not our daughter. Sometimes I hummed to him as we walked and walked, the light growing dimmer, the sticker bushes scratching at our legs.

Eventually, I brought him out of those woods. I brought *us* out. It was the first step, and it was critical to the success of everything that came later. I recruited Zack to help me bring our daughter back to us. I do not know if I could have done it without him. Time was growing short. The forest is worse at night. If we hadn't found each other, if we hadn't done this together, I do not know how long or how deep we might have wandered.

Chapter Twelve: The Intervention

Confronting the Red Balloon

Before I discuss the intervention that helped us reclaim our daughter, I want to talk for a moment about the red balloon. It had been hovering over us for so long, threatening like a petulant child to explode if we didn't respond in the way that it wanted.

"*Would you rather have a healthy son or a dead daughter?*"

The rhetorical question had been posed out loud so many times by so many people that it followed me everywhere. I thought about it in the shower, at work, during my evening walks, and while I lay awake at night, staring into the darkness.

"Would you rather have a healthy son or a dead daughter?" the barista asked, smiling at me from behind the counter of my favorite coffee shop.

"Excuse me?" I glanced around, startled by the question.

"Would you like room for cream and sugar?" she repeated, and I let the breath slide out of me, the world dimming for a few seconds before it snapped into focus.

I muttered an answer, found an out-of-the-way place along the wall, and waited for my coffee. I was having a rough day, the kind of day where you wake up irritable and then crack your shin on the bed frame on your way to the bathroom. Maybe I was just scared. Zack had swung by the house earlier in the day to pick up Jordan. After much wandering in the forest, he had come around at last. We were planning an intervention for this evening.

"... doesn't care about the red balloon ..."

"... let children be who they want to be ..."

"... safest thing ..."

I put a hand to my forehead. People were talking all around me. How much of it was only in my imagination?

"... been medicating kids for decades ..."

"... son or a dead daughter ..."

"... recognize the huge risk that she's taking. If it were my kid, I wouldn't be doing that."

I was sweating, hyperventilating. *Relax*, I told myself, but there didn't seem to be enough air in the room. I abandoned my coffee, crossed the lounge, and pushed my way through the doors and out into the parking lot. Standing in the open air, I struggled to catch my breath. Even out here I could hear them judging me, shaking their heads as they peered out the window. I found my car, dropped into the driver's seat of the Beetle, and closed the door.

"Shit, shit!" I erupted, gripping the steering wheel with both hands and squeezing it as hard as I could. *What the hell were we doing?! Why were we messing with the red balloon?* I closed my eyes, gritted my teeth. "It's okay," I told myself. "You haven't done anything yet."

Oh, but we would. It was only a matter of hours.

It took me ten minutes to get control of myself. "Things will go well," I announced, but I wasn't sure of that, *couldn't* be sure of that. What if she decided to run away? What if she tried to hurt herself?

"Would you rather have a healthy son or a dead daughter?"

I looked up. There was the balloon in the rearview mirror, swollen and angry, wedged into the back seat behind me.

"Go to hell," I told it. "I am not afraid of you. You do not control me or my family."

I turned around in my seat to face it. I had never seen it this red before. Its top was pressed flat against the roof's interior.

"It's an outlandish question," I told it. "A healthy son or a dead daughter? *Shut up* with that. I don't have a son, and I could lose my daughter either way. What if she transitions, realizes too late that she's made a terrible mistake, and kills herself because of it? What then?"

The balloon simply sat there, like a bloated tick that's taken on too much blood but refuses to let go, its body stretching and stretching ...

"Suicide is tragic, but it's a personal decision," I continued. "Ultimately, I have no control over another person's decision to take his or her life, and neither do you. *Of course*, I would rather have a healthy son than a dead daughter, but those are not my only two options."

I sighed. I was talking to an imaginary balloon. I had officially lost it. Still, here it was, taking up space in the back of my car.

I turned my head and looked out the passenger-side window. I could see the metal chairs and bistro table where we had gathered as a family on that cold spring day three years ago. They sat empty now, abandoned and forgotten along the side of the building. So much had happened since then. How had things gotten out of control so quickly?

"The gender affirming model has *not* saved her; it has made her worse," I said. "I have no doubt that continuing down that road will eventually destroy her." I glanced at the balloon in the seat behind me. "But perhaps there is another path. By no longer following the gender affirming model, we may be giving her permission to reclaim herself. As a result, her psychological pain and suicide risk might decrease. Do you think that's possible? Can we save her without losing her?"

The balloon was silent in the seat behind me, but it seemed less ominous and a bit smaller than it was before. I reached back and poked it gently with my finger. It yielded and shifted away from me, but nothing else happened. It was a cheap thing, I realized, made of red latex and filled with helium. Its nylon cord was dirty and tattered. There was something sad about it, like a carnival prop that had been left behind after the tents had been dismantled and the show had moved on to the next town. It smelled like stale popcorn and candy apples. Why had I been so afraid of it for so very long? Why had it held sway over all our decisions?

My Beetle is a convertible. I turned around, stuck the key in the ignition, reached up, and held the switch with my finger. The windows slid down an inch or two, and then the top folded back on itself until there was nothing but open sky above me. I did not see the balloon float away, but when I looked in the rearview mirror the back seat was empty. I took in a deep breath, filled my lungs with fresh air and something that felt like hope. I was still afraid of the potential consequences of this evening's intervention, but the fear was manageable.

I closed my eyes, heard the *click-click-click* of the roller coaster chain as it pulled me up the hill.

Welcome to The Cyclone, I thought. *Please keep your hands and feet inside the vehicle at all times. The ride is about to begin.*

"Okay," I said, "here we go." I opened my hands, let go of the metal bar in front of me, and a moment later, the world was in motion.

The Art of Remembering

Here's the way it happened: Two weeks before, Zack had gone to visit his parents on the East Coast. His mother was ill. It was the kind of illness that waxes and wanes but inevitably worsens over the years, and the visit had not been a joyous one. I remember the first time I met his parents, how they had welcomed me to their home and fed me dinner. They had an old dog who was very sweet but also incontinent. When the dog took a dump on the floor during dinner, Zack's father tried to distract me while simultaneously tending to the mishap. That was my first impression of him, his kind and indomitable spirit, his willingness to do what needed to be done. We bonded over that (as much as one can bond with another person over dog shit), and I have had a deep affection for his family ever since.

"How are things going?" I texted my former husband during his trip back East during the summer of 2021.

"I don't know. She's almost ready," Zack responded, and I could imagine them sitting around her bedside, keeping his mother as comfortable as possible, waiting for the inevitable. It was the reason he had gone out there, to be with his father and siblings during those final days. His mother couldn't communicate. She had stopped eating and drinking more than a week earlier. Her arms were contracted and pulled inward against her emaciated body. It made me cry to think of her that way. I let it come, the tears coursing down my cheeks and falling from my face onto the screen of my cell phone, making the letters large and blurry.

"Last night I stood in the kitchen after everyone had gone to bed," Zack texted. "I was looking at the pictures on the refrigerator. There are so many of Jordan when she was younger."

"Send me some," I responded, and he did, taking photos with his phone and texting them to me one after another.

Long hair. Fancy dresses. French braids. A picture of Jordan wearing a tiara. Here were the things our daughter claimed she could no longer remember, the things she pretended hadn't happened.

"I'm going to show these to Jordan," Zack texted. "I want her to see them."

I paused for a moment, my fingers hovering above my phone's electronic keyboard. "She hasn't forgotten," I typed. "She's just waiting for permission to remember."

The phone was silent for a while. I sat there looking at it, wondering if he was focused on other things. It's one of the oddities of electronic conversations. They begin and end abruptly. How do you know when the discussion is over?

I put my phone on the table, got up, and went to the kitchen to make myself a cup of coffee. There were plates and utensils in the sink. I rinsed them off and loaded them into the dishwasher. Fifteen minutes later, I returned to the living room to find his message against the black backdrop of the screen.

"I'm going to talk to her when I get back."

"The intervention?" I typed.

"Yeah. I'm going to show her these pictures to help her remember."

"Okay," I said, and I hit send.

I stood there for a while, the phone in my hand. We had talked about this, the best way forward. After hundreds of conversations, numerous arguments, countless hours of research, multiple therapists, and an internal struggle the likes of which I can never fully convey, Zack and I had finally come to an agreement that it was time to intervene. I wanted to do it together, but Zack had objected to that, pointing out that it might feel to Jordan like we were ganging up on her.

"She'll receive it better from me if it's just the two of us," he said, and I knew he was right.

The years of mindless affirmation and enabling of our daughter's self-destructive behavior were coming to an end. She was not a boy trapped in a girl's body. She was not he, him, they, or them. She was the most important person in both of our lives, a bright and wonderful fifteen-year-old girl named Jordan. If we were going to lose her, it would be on *those* terms, not to the lie that was steadily consuming her.

"I'm so sorry about your mother," I told Zack when he returned to

California a week later. "I feel such a deep sense of sadness about her passing."

"Thank you."

"You should take some time. I know you must be struggling."

He looked down at the stone pavers in my driveway. He was here to pick up our daughter.

"My sister put together a slide show of my mother's life," he told me. "There were all these pictures she found in my father's basement: photos of my mom as a child, the neighborhood where she grew up, the swimming pool where she and my father met, pictures of her graduating from college, of the two of them getting married, old Polaroids of when she was pregnant with me and my brother and sister…"

He trailed off, the muscles of his jaw clenching and relaxing.

"There were birthdays and dinner parties, a cross-country road trip we took one summer to the Grand Canyon, a week of skiing in West Virginia with our neighbors. There were pictures of Jordan when she was a baby, my mom holding her on the night she was born. Jordan was so little back then. Do you remember how tiny she looked in the car seat on the day we brought her home from the hospital?"

Zack smiled, and when he looked up his eyes were distant, focused somewhere in the middle, between then and now.

"You know what I realized," he asked, "when I was looking at all those pictures?"

I shook my head.

"My mother was happy. She lived a happy life. Her friends and family: that was everything. It was the unifying theme. Sitting there watching it as one memory after another appeared on the screen in front of us, it was like she was talking to us: me, my brother, my sister, my father. 'You were all part of this,' she seemed to be saying. 'Thank you. This is what you gave me.'"

I nodded. I was crying again. I couldn't help it.

"I'm going to talk to her—Jordan—tonight."

"Tonight? Are you sure?"

"I'm ready," he said. "I'm going to show her the pictures that I took from the refrigerator. I'm going to remind her of those days, how once she was happy and now she is lost."

I opened my mouth to say something, but the front door opened behind me and our daughter descended the steps to the driveway. "Hey," she said, stepping into her father's hug. "I'm sorry about Grandma."

"Thanks," he said. "I'm sorry she had to go through that. She's in a better place now. I believe in that."

"Yeah," she said, "me too." She took a step back and tilted her head toward the truck. "Come on," she said. "I wanna tell you about something."

I exchanged looks with her father. "Better go," I told him.

He smiled, nodded, and followed her to the truck.

"Good luck," I whispered, but they were in the truck by then, and neither of them heard me.

Zack and Jordan

I asked Zack to write about this part, our intervention with our daughter. I've done some light editing to capture the tone of that evening, but this is what he wrote:

> I stuck to the plan. That's the hardest part, isn't it? We picked up dinner at an Italian restaurant and ate in the truck. She didn't know it was coming, the things I was about to say to her. I was afraid, the food turning over in my stomach. Suddenly, I didn't want to do it.
>
> When we were finished eating, I was ready with the photos. I talked to her about my mom, how important Jordan was to her, how she had held her and sang to her on the night Jordan was born. I scrolled through the photos, one after the other, the years of Jordan's life and personality unfolding along the way. The evidence was right there in front of us, the parts of herself she had locked away, the things she claimed to no longer remember.
>
> I told her that I missed her, that we loved her, and that we would always fight for her. I told her that it wasn't working, this whole gender identity transformation experiment. She had transformed herself into someone we didn't recognize. She was hiding, and she had lost herself in the process.
>
> I pointed out that a parent's job is not to agree with their child in all things. A parent's job is to teach and protect their child as best they can, even when it's hard. Especially when it's hard.

"Mom and I are changing course," I told her. "Your name is Jordan and that's the name we will use from now on. Your pronouns are she and her. If you want to continue at your current school, we expect you to comply with the spirit of this intervention. No more talk about being trans. No more he/him/Ash. We are prepared to do whatever it takes to make this happen. If it means switching schools or moving to another state, so be it."

"Why are you doing this?" she asked me.

"Because we love you, and we will not watch you destroy yourself. You are the most important person in our lives. We refuse to give up on you."

She wouldn't look at me. "I want to go home," she said.

"Okay," I said, and I started the truck and headed home.

I lied awake for hours, wondering if I had done the right thing. I considered gathering up all the knives from the kitchen and keeping them in my locked bedroom. In the end, I didn't do it. There are always more knives in the world, I reasoned. I can't follow her around for the rest of her days. How she responds to this is up to her.

I awoke in a sweat around 1 a.m. Perhaps it was the sound of the door as she closed it or the quick tread of her footsteps on the stairs. Maybe it was just the silence of the house, how there was one less person than there was supposed to be.

I got up, went to her bedroom, and found it empty. *It's happened*, I thought, but I didn't know what *it* was. Not yet anyway.

I got dressed in a matter of seconds, ran down the stairs, and checked the rest of the rooms. There was no sign of her, so I grabbed the keys, started the truck, and went in search for her.

The neighborhood was dark and still, the moon just a sliver in the sky.

I drove through the streets hoping to catch sight of her, telling myself that I wasn't too late, that nothing bad had happened already. The truck's headlights illuminated front yards and driveways, homes in which no one was missing. I pulled to the side of the road, turned off the ignition, and listened for her through the open windows. *Should I call the police*, I wondered, *set out on foot, or make another pass through the neighborhood?*

I restarted the engine, put it in Drive, and expanded my search, rolling through the surrounding neighborhoods before circling back through my own. Even the familiar houses looked ominous and brooding, alien versions of the ones I had seen so many times in the daylight.

On the fourth pass I saw her sitting on the front steps of our house. I pulled the truck into the driveway, killed the motor and headlights, got out of the vehicle, and sat down next to her on the steps.

"What are you doing out here?" I asked her.

"Sitting," she said. "I couldn't sleep."

I leaned back, put my elbows on the step behind me. "I couldn't find you. I was worried."

"I went for a walk," she told me. "Sometimes it's easier for me to think that way."

I nodded. "What were you thinking about?"

"Next steps … where to go from here."

"What did you decide?"

"Nothing," she said, and we sat there for a while after that, neither of us speaking. The night breeze kicked up a notch. The leaves whispered to each other in the yard.

She sighed, stood up, and ascended the steps to the front door. I sat there for a few minutes longer, taking in the night. A neighbor's cat appeared from the shadows, proceeded along the fence that divided the two properties, and disappeared once again into the darkness.

The next morning, Jordan took a shower and got dressed. I met her downstairs in the kitchen. On the drive to one of her last days of summer art class, we stopped at the bagel shop for breakfast, our usual ritual. Neither of us spoke about our conversation from the night before.

"Have a good day," I told her when I dropped her off at the studio.

"You too," she said, and that was that.

Chapter Thirteen: The Aftermath

Circling from Above

I awoke in the morning knowing that something had changed with my daughter. I was scheduled to work at the hospital that day, so I got up, took a shower, and went through my morning ritual as I prepared myself for work. I waited until 9 a.m. to call Zack, knowing he would've dropped off Jordan by then. "How did it go?" I asked him, and he recounted the details in much the same way as he has told them in the previous chapter.

"Our conversation was short, but"—he paused for a moment, and I could hear the faint sound of sirens in the background—"it was a long night. She decided to go for a walk at one in the morning. I woke up, couldn't find her in the house, and had to go looking."

"That's scary," I said. "I'm sorry you had to go through that."

"Yeah, well ... that was it for me. I haven't slept since then."

The sirens faded. Someone else's emergency.

"And this morning?" I asked. "How did she seem?"

"She seemed fine," he said. "We stopped on our way to art class for bagels and cream cheese."

"Bagels and cream cheese," I said.

"Right."

I shook my head. It seemed too simple, too easy. There was another side to this. I just didn't know what it was yet.

I hung up with Zack, but I spent the rest of the morning bracing myself for whatever would come next. It wasn't long before I found out. Jordan's demeanor on the morning following the intervention had been a hiatus. Perhaps she had simply been in a state of shock. She spent the next week recovering, planning, and getting herself ready. There was a battle looming. She was gathering ammunition, assembling her troops. She took to the air and circled above me, casting the shadow of her outstretched wings on the ground at my feet.

Sometimes the best you can do as a parent is to endure the beating that your child has in store for you and to love them anyway. In psychotherapy, we refer to this as the therapeutic art of "holding." The term "holding" refers to a concept introduced by D. W. Winnicott[1] that involves being emotionally present in order to recognize and understand what a patient (or, in the case of parenting, what a child) is feeling. The therapist (or parent) provides a safe and accepting "holding environment" for anger, frustration, and intense emotional states. The therapist or parent is not defensive or dismissive, and they do not try to redirect the conversation. This allows the patient or child to feel heard. It conveys the message that their feelings are both real and important.

There are, of course, huge differences between being a therapist and being a parent. In therapy, holding a patient's anger, frustration, and emotional outbursts is easier because the professional relationship is clear. As a parent, it's much harder to remain emotionally neutral. It's easy to become frustrated, hurt, or angry yourself. It's hard not to fight back, even if you know it's not the right thing to do.

In the battle that followed, the shots came frequently and from every direction:

"You just don't get it."

"My name is Ash."

"I've always known this about myself."

"I will correct you when you misgender me. Every. Single. Time."

---

1. D. Winnicott, "Transitional Objects and Transitional Phenomena," *International Journal of Psychoanalysis* 34 (1953): 89–97; D. W. Winnicott, D. W., *Collected Papers: Through Paediatrics to Psycho-Analysis* (London: Tavistock Publications, 1958); D. Winnicott, "The Theory of the Parent-Child Relationship," *International Journal of Psychoanalysis* 41 (1960): 585–595.

"I hope you know what you're doing."

"That house of trust we built together: it's gone."

She responded with tears, arguments, and sniping. Thinly veiled threats of self-injury abounded. She fluctuated between knowing she had no choice in the matter and returning to the same familiar ideology that she'd been clinging to for years. It was as if we had broken into her room one night and pulled her from the clutches of a cult, and she lashed out at us because of it.[2] We were in the trenches now, and I hunkered down and took it. This was a war of attrition. We would wait this out. It was not going to be over in a day.

I admit that I was scared. I wondered, like Zack, whether I should hide all the knives that were in my house. This had been a dramatic intervention, and the outcome was anything but certain. The only thing I *was* sure of was that we had finally corrected something we had been doing wrong for a very long time. Our support and enabling approach to her demanded gender identity had yielded only ongoing melancholia and isolation from her family. The gender affirming strategy had provided no relief for our daughter.

"I no longer have the support of my immediate family," she told me one evening, and I recognized the phrasing immediately as something she was mimicking from a YouTube video that I had watched during her early days of attempted gender transformation.[3]

I did my best to maintain course. It was not helpful that Zack was called away to be out of town for two weeks following the intervention. It was bad timing, and the result was that most of Jordan's grenades of fury were lobbed at me. Then again, maybe it would've been the same if

---

2. The literature on cults gives widely varying amounts of time as to how long it takes for one to recover from being indoctrinated into a cult. Some figures give time spans from six months to up to seven years, and of course the word "recovery" is loosely defined. It could be argued that one never fully recovers from time spent in a cult. It is worth noting that those who had interventions respond more favorably than those who walk away or who are cast out of the cult.

3. "Leftover cult language" is a documented aftereffect of having been a member of a cult. The use of loaded language is used to control someone's thinking while in the cult and hinders communication with others after the person departs. The words persist, although the sense of elitism and solidarity the person associates with the words is absent.

Zack had been present. I am the target of my daughter's wrath, while Zack is the object of her perpetual adoration. It is our family dynamic, something I have come to expect. Even on the sunniest days, it can often feel like winter.

"Welcome, Eagles!"

The new school year was almost upon us, and we approached Jordan's high school orientation day with a mix of excitement and trepidation. Imagine a mid-August morning filled with potential. The day would be hot, but the hour is early enough for the temperature to still be pleasant. Envision a mother with a fresh cup of piping hot coffee in the Volkswagen's cup holder, driving her child to the local high school, humming along with a familiar song on the radio. Now imagine that the air is electric with nervous enthusiasm as soon-to-be ninth graders mill around their new campus. Visualize teenagers happily reconnecting after a summer vacation of sports camps, family vacations, sleeping in, and lazy days by the community pool drinking ice-cold cans of Dr. Pepper while snacking on Bottle Caps and Doritos. Some kids look at the football field and running track with their parents. They talk about the sport teams they will try out for, and their conversations buzz with anticipation and just a flicker of anxiety. Other children tentatively walk through the newly updated performing arts center, wondering aloud to their mothers if they should try out for the school play. The mothers smile the gift of reassurance and give an almost imperceptible nod: a small gesture, but enough to release the teen from insecurity. This is the beginning of high school, something to be relished and remembered. It is the birth of a new era, the next movement in the dance of child and parent, the art of discovering and letting go.

Now that you're imagining this scene—the butterflies flitting across the dew-speckled grass, the sun glinting off the metal flagpole at the entrance to the building—kindly imagine the massive foot of a gigantic gorilla descending upon the entire scene and smashing it to smithereens. That was the kind of day we were in for: the gorilla, not the butterflies. This was a wholesome, joyous, family movie in which zombies would unexpectedly erupt from the ground halfway through the first act. "I didn't see *that* coming," you might say, munching on handfuls of lightly buttered popcorn, and believe me, I hadn't been expecting it either.

Let me start by telling you an important piece of background information. Without being solicited, the school counselor had contacted me during the summer before high school to ask if Jordan went by Ash and to clarify preferred pronouns. Apparently, someone at the junior high school had taken it upon themselves to convey this information to the high school. Considering our intervention, I updated the counselor that our daughter would be going by her birth name of Jordan with female pronouns. I stressed that it was *very important* that this change was *officially* in place with the school before the orientation. I was assured that it would be.

But, as one might predict, it was not. Exit butterflies. Enter gorilla. In the aftermath of that horrible day, I wondered why the school had been *so efficient* in changing Jordan's name and gender to false ones but so inept at changing them back.[4]

The new-student orientation was arranged so that students were required to walk about the campus accomplishing various tasks, such as receiving their books, being instructed on how to obtain a library card, getting their PE clothes, learning how to obtain a school lunch, being assigned a locker, signing the obligatory paper that they had read the handbook and understood the school rules, and so forth. During that process, they would explore the buildings and grounds and get a grasp of the lay of the land. It was a clever way to orient incoming ninth graders, allowing them to become comfortable with their new environment. Each station consisted of one or two parent volunteers or teachers, and a large sign with a bright canopy alerted students as to what would be accomplished at that station. (One canopy donned the obligatory Pride flag, although it was unrelated to the task at hand.) There was also a handful of upperclassmen roaming about the campus, assisting the incoming freshmen with the process of orientation and providing friendly

---

4. Here we are, more than three years out of this nightmare, and I am still having to sporadically correct names and pronouns that pop up with the random, senseless zeal of whack-a-moles within the school system. I find it infuriating, especially the school system's *these-things-are-hard-to-correct* attitude when I bring it to their attention time and time again. The reverse situation (misgendering a child who has announced themselves as trans) is not tolerated.

encouragement so that the new students would feel good about being there.

As we pulled into the parking lot, a navy-blue banner greeted us with, "*Welcome, Eagles!*" My daughter had been sulking around the house and lobbing her grenades of fury at me for almost a week, and I was suddenly struck with a feeling of dread as we passed through the gates. Was it premonition, or were we both just a little nervous? I made a joke to ease the tension. She scowled at me. I shut my mouth and nosed the Beetle into a spot.

Jordan was out of the car before I turned off the ignition, and she marched across the parking lot in an irritable huff. I hustled after her, but I lost sight of her in the crowd, and she made it to the first station way ahead of me. In my peripheral vision, I could see parents and teenagers all around me, smiling and conversing excitedly about the prospect of high school. I understood that their lives were not perfect either, but I felt jealous of the experience others appeared to be having. They were starring in that made-for-TV after-school special. Jordan and I were starring in a different kind of movie: a zombie apocalypse in which the mother is bitten in the opening scene and transforms into a grotesque flesh-eating monstrosity.

"That woman's waving at you," Jordan said as I reached the first station. I turned and saw a familiar face, and I raised my hand in response. Jordan took advantage of the distraction and was off in a flash toward the next station. I dropped my hand and the trace of smile on my face and trotted after her.

Maybe I should've stopped and returned to the car. Maybe I should've allowed my daughter to do this without me. But I had taken the day off to be with her, and people in zombie apocalypse movies aren't particularly good at making obvious, commonsense decisions. They cock their heads, listen to the sound of snarling coming from the old, abandoned warehouse, and say, "I wonder what that could be. I think I will go investigate."

I'd missed the first station, but I caught up with her at the second. I braced myself, wondering if the proper name would be listed for my child. As predicted, the name listed was Ash (either an error or a purposeful *screw you* from the school system toward the mother who had the audacity to attempt to reverse the process of gender transformation; it was hard to know for sure). I tried to correct it with the volunteer at the table while Jordan tended to another matter, but as the morning rolled on it was like bailing water from the *Titanic* as the ship sank faster and faster. Jordan eventually became wise to what I was doing. She glared at me with eyes like daggers, and I felt it more than saw it, the blades slicing into me from the bushes. I staggered after her, wounded and bleeding.

At some point, I went to the school office to discuss with the counselor what was happening. With the chaos of the day, however, I could not get in to see her. The receptionist gave me a puzzled look from behind her trendy cat-eyed spectacles when I told her the reason for my visit. In hindsight, I wonder if the counselor might have been more available to a parent with a different issue to discuss. If I wanted to discuss my trans child and the new pronouns and name they were requesting, for example, perhaps I would not have been rebuffed so quickly. Instead, I was told, "She's occupied with other things on such a busy day. We hope that you understand."

It was perhaps the fourth station when Jordan turned on me, and we argued about the name and pronouns that the school had assigned her. Other parents, either embarrassed for me or appalled by my unsupportive, non-gender affirming, Stone Age behavior, pretended to look away. Jordan stormed off to the next station. I was missing a leg now, cut off below the knee, and I crawled after her, leaving a trail of blood in my wake. She became progressively angrier, more irritable, and more emotionally labile from one station to the next. Every station was a fight, an argument, a heated exchange between our young heroine and her vile oppressor. I dragged myself along the ground from station to station. My right arm was gone as well, and one of my eyes had somehow fallen out of its socket and hung precariously from its stalk along the side of my cheek.

A mother volunteer at one of the tables finally approached me quietly and explained, "This form is only about expired library books. What precise name is on the form doesn't matter too much. And it looks like you have a good kid. I don't think he'll return library books late. The worst thing that will happen is you'll have to pay for a library book that Ash doesn't return."

I looked up at her in silence, my one good eye squinting into the sun. Her face was full of compassion, but the words she had chosen told me that she thought I was the one embarrassing myself. Jordan looked smug, standing behind her. "Ackhhh," I said, my head throbbing, my swollen tongue gray and sizzling in the mid-day heat.

Eventually, they had to drag me out of there. I had become an inert thing, motionless and baking on the concrete walkway. Parents and their children either navigated around me or simply stepped over me on their way to the stations. Crows landed in close proximity to where I was lying, eyeing me with their black orbs and hungry beaks. A small child—*Where was his mother?*—hunkered down in curiosity and started poking at me with a stick.

They stuffed me in the car, put my severed appendages in the trunk, and we drove home in silence. Jordan disappeared into her room as soon as we made it home. She hadn't answered me when I'd asked if she wanted to ride home with the top down.

After this fiasco, I contacted the school principal and explained the situation with Jordan and the circumstances during orientation. I let him know that despite our "best efforts," the school counselor and I had not been successful in making the situation right. I implored him to make the corrections. We had worked too hard to be sabotaged in this manner. I didn't want her being addressed as Ash or changing for PE class in the boy's locker room.

In his best school administrator's tone, the principal reassured me that everything would be fine. He informed me that all the bathrooms were gender neutral and that students could use the locker room congruent with their professed gender identity. Jordan would be listed by her legal name on the class roll sheets (although he offered no explanation as to why that had not happened prior to orientation), but teachers would honor name requests regardless of the circumstances, including gender identity related reasons. I was told that although they'd like to support us, "There's only so much we can do."[5]

---

5. I was disappointed by the things I was hearing, but I had gotten used to being disappointed by the school system, and there didn't seem to be much use in arguing. It's not their fault really. The school districts take direction from the state, and they have been forced to drink the Kool-Aid thrust upon them by the absurd notions of the California Department of Education (CDE). Throw in a few lawsuits from disgruntled children and their gender affirming supporters, and fearful administrators are among the first in line to fill their cups with the sugary, red drink. In California, there is very little a principal can do in the face of a child proclaiming to be transgender and insisting on the

In the weeks following our intervention, Jordan seemed encapsulated in a shell of anger. I imagined what lay beneath that anger: a churning sea of loneliness, sadness, grief, resentment, relief, confusion, hopelessness, and hopefulness. Jordan barely looked at me during those days, and she ignored her younger sister when approached, leaving Zoe hurt and dismissed by the older sibling she admired and adored.

I imagined Jordan in her dark bedroom, turning to YouTube to understand her emotional experience. She would be looking for solutions to this new problem: the *parental* problem. The gurus would be there for her. TikTok is loyal. They understood how she felt and would be ready to offer advice. Her parents did not understand her and were ruining her life. Perhaps she would find herself in a chat room with other kids who did not have the support of their immediate families either. I wondered what kinds of solutions would be offered, but I already knew.[6] By now I had a pretty good idea about what I was up against. I could hear them whispering to my daughter from the electronic ether. *Return to us. Get rid of your family. We will take care of you. Always.*

Gathering the Flock

The future is forever in motion, constructed and disassembled by the things we do in the present. Would I choose to stand by while Jordan sat in isolation with the door closed, filling her time seeking advice from a fake, online glitter family? Would I shrug my shoulders and echo the school principal's philosophy—"There's only so much I can do"—while my child was pulled farther and farther from the people who loved her the most? I had seen that future already, had lived it for years, and I was determined that we would not go down that path again.

---

full-service, everything-the-way-you-want-it treatment. Either roll out the red carpet or be replaced by someone who will. When school officials say, "There's only so much we can do," they really do mean it. At best, the CDE has set forth misguided rules to follow. At worst, the motivations of the CDE may involve such things as advancing the "progressive" propaganda of trans activists, public school teachers' unions, and a host of special interest groups. In my opinion, the politicization of the issue by the public school system is obscene, and children and their families suffer the consequences.

6. Free Mom Hugs advertises on their Facebook page, "If your parents aren't accepting of your identity, I'm your mom now."

I found myself thinking about that beach in my dream where I sat next to a younger version of my daughter and put my arm around her as she rocked, both of us staring out at the ocean. She had leaned into me in that dream, and I reflected on the words someone had recently said to me: "Your attachment is all you have to get her out of this."

What does she need right now? I wondered, and it was right there in front of me. *She needs me. She needs her family. She needs to be reminded that there are people who truly love her.*

I contemplated ways to make that happen. I could find ways to show her that I loved her, but this was bigger than just me. I needed to send up the bat signal and call in the reserves. I needed to gather the flock. *Her* flock. Would they respond when I called them? Would they know what to do? It's a scary thing, asking for help, allowing yourself to be that vulnerable. Could I handle the pain of silence or excuses? *"We'd love to be there, but it's such a busy time right now. Maybe next year when things slow down a bit ..."*

I called them anyway: my parents, brother, aunt, uncle, and cousin. "An emergency three-day weekend," I told them. "I need help with Jordan." It was hard to articulate what I meant by "help," but they had been through enough of this to know or at least intuit what she needed.

We decided to meet at my parents' cabin near the lake. Jordan expressed no interest in going, but she understood that she had no choice in the matter. She put together a haphazard bag of belongings, threw it into the back of the car, donned a dark hoodie, and covered her ears with headphones that would remain in place throughout the entire three-hour car ride. She declined snacks when we stopped. "I'm not hungry," she mumbled to nobody in particular. When Zoe pointed out that she could plug her headphones into the DVD player and watch *Shrek* with her, Jordan made brief eye contact with her sister and shook her head.

We arrived at our destination in a vehicle of silence. By now, it was late August, and the mountain air was fresh and crisp. Thick pine trees towered above us, and the late-season wildflowers were still hanging in there. Orange poppies and purple-blue lupine welcomed us. We pulled into the driveway to find three deer in the front yard, munching on their roadside salads. They eyed us furtively as a family of chickadees bustled near the hedges.

Our flock was there too. *Every* person who had seen my bat signal showed up. They came without ego or expectations. I was so grateful.

When we entered the cabin, my dad was putting DVDs on a shelf. He greeted Jordan warmly and pulled her in for a long hug against his enormous body. He showed her all the movies he had brought, including some of her personal favorites like *Titanic* and *The Notebook*. Jordan wordlessly observed me unpack my air popper, nutritional yeast, and cans of Diet Coke in the kitchen. My mom, her normal cheerfulness toned down to a serene kindness, had stacked up some board games and puzzles and told Jordan how excited she was to spend time with her for the next couple of days. Although her gaze was mostly downcast, I saw something change in my child's eyes. There was no space for emotional isolation and brooding here. This would be a time of love and family gathering. I wondered if she would choose to accept it.

A short time later, Aunt Phyllis walked up the front steps with several grocery bags filled with homemade baked goods, while shouting, "Jordan, I brought your favorite: homemade chocolate mint brownies. I brought some vanilla ice cream too—to cut the sweetness!" Uncle Frank, a brilliant but quiet man, followed behind her with his soft and engaging smile. He used Jordan's name frequently and casually when he spoke, taking some of the sting out of me using it when I addressed her. Uncle Frank slipped me a bottle of wine on his way in, his way of saying, "We've got this. You can relax now and trust that things are going to be okay." I loved him for that, the weight of the last few years lifting a bit from my shoulders.

Cousin Kate arrived a short time later, bubbling over with infectious excitement. She carted in what appeared to be an oversized fisherman's tackle box, although its exterior had been colored a deep and vibrant purple. "I brought my craft kit," she announced. "We will *not* be bored this weekend!" Jordan pretended to have no interest, but as soon as Kate started taking out her beads, brightly colored fabric, glue gun, and a pair of jeans for ripping, Jordan wandered over and started opening some of the compartments. She discovered a BeDazzler and jeans that were just her size. Jordan smiled, dropping her guard for a moment. A brief flicker of enthusiasm was there and then gone again in the space of a second.

Not being one to loudly announce his arrival, my brother slid in quietly later in the day, two rescue dogs in tow. He'd been surprised by my invitation to join us, not sure how he could contribute much of anything to this unique situation. He silently hugged Jordan, and then they sat together on the floor with Frodo and Goliath while the beasts put their heads into her lap and wiggled with joy. I later saw my brother slip a take-out bag in the fridge that contained Jordan's favorite sushi roll and miso soup. His understated expression of love was invaluable.

During that long weekend, Jordan swam in the lake, walked under the trees, baked chocolate chip cookies (an old family recipe) and a tres leches cake (a new recipe), and helped solve a murder mystery puzzle. (It's definitely a team effort to complete a thousand-piece puzzle that comes with no picture of the completed project.) There was no Wi-Fi. She made minestrone soup with my mother using orecchiette pasta, which Jordan selected. They both wore aprons. We played Scattergories late into the night and had some good laughs (does the term "Assless Chaps" count as a word beginning with the letter A?). Nobody allowed her to push us away, and nobody let her feel for even a moment that she was not absolutely loved for her entire being.

By Sunday, she had softened—a small but noticeable change—and the flock departed from their communal roost, each of us leaving stronger and more emotionally fortified than we had been when we'd first arrived.

Taking Flight

And so began freshman year. Jordan walked to school every morning and returned every afternoon. I didn't know what transpired during the school day or whether she was following our instructions about using her birth name and female pronouns. She assured us that she was complying. The outcome of not complying would be to start fresh at a new school where nobody knew she had ever identified as transgender. I could not rely on the school to tell me anything, so I didn't bother asking. Jordan's behavior was not perfect. There were times when she was angry and resentful, but those episodes were less intense and became less frequent once she fell into the rhythm of school.

Many months prior to the beginning of high school, prior to conceiving of the intervention in its full form, I had bought tickets to a concert that was scheduled to occur in late September. The band was a long-time favorite of mine, and Jordan had grown up listening to them. She enjoyed the music, and during a simpler time, she had told me that certain songs resonated with her and made her feel connected with things on a deeper level. When I'd purchased tickets to the concert, we had both been excited about attending the show, reminiscing about the music that we had listened to together.

Now that we were post-intervention, I wasn't sure if Jordan would still want to go to the concert with me. We weren't the best of friends these days, and her enthusiasm for anything positive that pertained to me was at an all-time low. Still, I heard that persistent echo, *"Your attachment is all you have to get her out of this,"* and the thing my daughter had once said to me: "*I need a heterosexual mother of two.*"

I was relieved to be hearing other things in my mind besides, "Would you rather have a healthy son or a dead daughter?" The narrative was changing. The story of my family was still in motion.

Whether she wanted to attend the concert or not, Jordan assumed that we were going. During the long drive, she texted friends and made a few comments about how she didn't remember the songs anymore, that the band was a thing of her past. "I have almost no memories of my childhood," she told me, that stale and loaded language from another era.

Never mind, I told myself. We had arrived.

The outdoor venue was a beautiful place, replete with sunshine, warmth, fresh air, and an energy of love and acceptance. I had purchased food from Trader Joe's that I knew she would enjoy: tofu spring rolls with peanut sauce, the chocolate Joe-Joe's cookies she was so fond of, organic fresh apricots, and iced oat milk lattes. She did not acknowledge the spread of food or express any gratitude to me for getting her favorites, although she did eat hungrily, which I took as a good sign. During the occasional suspended moments when the vibe between us felt almost normal, I took a few selfies of the two of us on the open lawn.

The opener finished and the headliner began. The sun was low on the horizon, the stage lights came up, and the music was just as I remembered. Jordan's phone was put away, something she did without prompting. It never reappeared that night because something better had taken its place. More snacks were eaten and Izze drinks were consumed. It turned out that Jordan *did* remember the songs, every single word of them, and her lips moved to the lyrics. She quietly sang as she gently rocked back and forth in her seat to the familiar melodies. I pretended not to notice, but she lost herself more and more in the music as the evening continued. By the end of the night, she was standing on her seat, singing and dancing, her arms held high above her head. The band saved a few of their most well-known and beloved songs for the end of the show. Jordan belted out the lyrics as if she was the one holding the guitar and standing at the microphone.

I closed my eyes and listened to the sound of her voice. This was the same person whose small hands had wrapped their tiny fingers around the metal pole of a carousel horse as we rode in circles to the music. She had helped me paint and decorate her childhood bedroom, transforming the space into a magical aquarium, its blue walls sparkling with glitter and speckled with life-size fish and a purple octopus. "Look, Mommy, a starfish," she said, pointing into the water, and I realized we were at the beach now, her pantlegs rolled up to her knees in the tidepool. There were hermit crabs too, something wonderous and not to be afraid of. She took a step forward, faltered, and started to fall. "*I've got you*," I said, reaching out to steady her, but she took no notice, studying the water with the rapt attention of a four-year-old.

I opened my eyes as the concert ended, the notes fading into the night but still echoing in my head, like a child asking for "*five more minutes*" before heading home from the beach, the carousel, the ebbing joy of the day's adventure. We drove home with the top down and the night sky swirling above us.

Over the following weeks and months, things began to change for my daughter, so slowly that at first it was almost imperceptible. The anger lessened. The harshness began to dissipate. She began to watch Netflix episodes from the living room rather than the solitude of her bedroom. She wrote items on the grocery list that I left posted in the kitchen, adding occasional humor to her itemized requests: (1) Red apples; (2) Vanilla yogurt; (3) Unicorns. She made eye contact when she spoke to me, and it lingered longer than it had in a very long time. She initiated baking projects. I came home one afternoon to find a homemade blueberry muffin and an ice-cold glass of soy milk on my desk.

During these early positive changes, a friendship dissolved between Parker and Jordan. Their parting was melodramatic and painful for my daughter, but over the months that followed she made her peace with it. Parker was invested in Ash, not Jordan. He belonged to a part of her life that was fading now. During times of personal growth, we are sometimes forced to leave behind those who are hell-bent on holding us back.

Small things gave way to bigger changes. One day it occurred to me that Jordan now looked forward to going to school. She set her alarm, got out of bed, and launched into her school-day preparations with an air of enthusiasm on most mornings. This was a big difference from her resistance and grumpiness during previous years, and getting her out the door was no longer a fight. She'd heard about the upcoming school play and wanted to be involved. Instead of a traditional foreign language, she opted to take Italian at the local community college, and she loved it. I did not need to prompt her to do homework or organize her school materials. She rediscovered her natural zeal for learning and a sense of agency that was new for her. As her freshman year progressed, she was getting straight A's. She kept some of the same friends, many of whom are in the LGBTQ community, and she made some new friends. At some point that year, the transgender flag that had been prominently displayed on her wall came down, although I had not instructed her to remove it.

Then much bigger changes came. On my birthday, she got out her ukelele and serenaded me with, "Hey, Soul Sister," which is one of my favorites. Occasionally, I heard her sing in the shower, something I'd not heard her do since fifth grade. The melancholia and anxiety that had intensified for three years lessened and did not return. For the first time in quite a while, I no longer felt that she was on the cusp of self-injury, and I was able to let go of my persistent, relentless fear of it. Jordan became kind to her younger sister, seemingly without trying. She painted a magical mural on Zoe's bedroom wall that was brightly colored and consisted of toadstools, butterflies, and fairy houses. Together, they decided that Zoe's room was enchanted, which led to giggling, wide-eyed wonder, and connection. Their relationship blossomed. Zoe delighted in having a sister. Even at her young age, she sensed that something nefarious had left our lives. None of the feared consequences of parental non-affirming behavior came to pass. To sum it up, Jordan was doing great.

Chapter Fourteen: Reflections

What I Wish I'd Noticed

"It came as such a shock," is a frequent comment I hear from parents of trans-identified kids. "There were no signs of this."

I nod. It's the first clue that their child is most likely not transgender.

Parents want to tell their story, and the conversation inevitably turns to a recounting of the child's life and the lack of any evidence of gender dysphoria prior to the turbulent years of adolescence. Like me, they recount the tea parties, the lacy dresses adorned with rhinestones, the pig tails tied with pink ribbons, and the preference at a young age for same-sex friends. They don't recall any spontaneous utterances of, "I wish I were a boy," or wanting to wear boys' clothes for a season to "just try it out." Parents scrutinize themselves, asking the self-damning questions, "How did I miss this? What were the clues that I failed to notice?"

The answer is probably that there *were* no clues, since there was nothing unusual to notice.[1]

Assuming that the answer is nothing, a better question for the parent of a trans-identified adolescent with no prior history of gender dysphoria is, "What should I notice now?"

Reflecting on the time following Jordan's coming out, there were

---

1. There are, of course, a small percentage of children who *are* transgender, and the discovery of this for both the child and their parents may start early and *makes sense* when a name is finally put to it. My comments in this chapter do not apply to those children and their families. Those parents need a different book. I've mentioned one of them in the next footnote.

things that I noticed but didn't pay enough attention to. There were many reasons for this: my own indoctrination into the gender affirming model during medical school, the social landscape of my community, my political leanings, the lack of support from Zack, the advice of the gender specialists from whom we sought evaluation and assistance, and ... *oh yeah*, the ever-present red balloon. These observations should have screamed out to me that Jordan did not have gender dysphoria, but I dismissed them and focused instead on the background noise of everything else. And what about my parental instinct, that *profound knowing* in my core that something wasn't right? I was told to write that off as grief. "Being the parent of a trans teen can be a difficult adjustment, after all."

The following are my personal observations of Jordan and many of her trans-identified peers. They are also consistent with traits of many trans-identified young adults who I have treated in my clinical practice. (You might recall my discussion of patients Dex and Con from chapter seven). Take a deep look at your kid and ask yourself if any of these characteristics are consistent with your own observations:

1. After declaring herself as trans, Jordan was unwilling to *even consider* the possibility that she was a cisgender girl. There was no openness toward self-reflection, thoughtful discussion, or curious exploration regarding the subject. She was unwilling to consider the possibility that this could be anything else.
2. Very little, if anything, about my daughter's story fit a typical transgender narrative.[2]
3. Jordan's sudden transgender identification emerged during a time of extreme social stress (the beginning of middle school). LGBTQ affiliation offered a prepackaged group of friends and social acceptance. In a different community, she might have joined a gang or a different clique for similar reasons. During times of stress and uncertainty, children are in desperate search for a safe harbor. Belonging to a self-identified group is the fastest way to get there.
4. Jordan adamantly separated herself from anything that predated the

---

2. To discern this, you will first need to familiarize yourself with the prototype of an authentic transgender narrative. My favorite book in this regard is *True Selves: Understanding Transsexualism—For Families, Friends, Coworkers, and Helping Professionals*, by Mildred L. Brown and Chloe Ann Rounsley.

time of her coming out. ("I have no memories of my childhood.") I did not associate this with trans identification at the time, but I later came to realize that the same tactics are part of a cult mentality. There is a change of name, appearance, and identity. Often a new birthdate is established. All ties to the past are severed. There is no "before." There is only the "after."
5. Jordan spoke with frank disgust and fear that people would "misgender me" or use her "dead name." When the wrong name or pronouns were accidently used by people who knew her well and had not yet grown accustomed to using a new name and pronouns, the mistakes were not perceived as unintended slips but rather mortifying personal attacks from which she might not recover.
6. Her answers to my questions regarding her new identity were mindless and well-practiced, as if she had been coached on what to say. (This was, of course, exactly what was happening.) She could not articulate things differently and returned to the same verbiage with every conversation.
7. Her defensiveness and intolerance to being questioned about her trans identification were impressive. I was reminded of the adage, "Truth does not mind being questioned. A lie does not like being challenged."
8. If the topic of detransitioning was ever mentioned in our conversations, it was always met with, "I'm never detransitioning." Her approach to transgender identity was all or nothing.
9. Words such as "always" and "never" were generously used, when in fact those words are rarely accurate.
10. Her mood and anxiety became *worse* after coming out.

What I Wish I'd Done

There are so many things I wish I'd done differently. The first list I created for this section was an exercise in self-flagellation that spanned several pages. Every misstep I listed made me think of another. Eventually, I realized that lamenting *everything* I did wrong wasn't productive, and it wouldn't help the reader either. We come to every challenge as we exist: flawed and imperfect. Your imperfections are different than mine, and your journey will be different too. Instead, I tried to focus on a short but manageable list of regrets, and I humbly suggest that you do the same. Applaud yourself for being brave enough to ask the questions that you're asking, and for being persistent enough to make it this far. Here is a list of regrets worth contemplating:

1. I wish I'd been more aware and involved with what Jordan was doing on her iPhone and computer. What websites was she visiting? What videos was she viewing? What is TikTok exactly? How many social media accounts does she have? She was way too young to be given the latitude I gave her with electronics. I mistakenly assumed that because I had played a few video games when I was younger, she was doing her generation's version of the same thing. I was wrong. Social media is an entirely different animal. I didn't understand the risks of it then, but I do now. I had no idea how nasty it could be.[3]
2. I wish I had recognized that even though she was no longer a young child, my daughter needed me during her teenage years. It was important that I continued to be her primary attachment.[4] Too much peer influence led to nowhere good. As a teenager, she tended to blow me off, something I equated with "normal adolescence." I allowed her to push me away. Because she had the appearance of being confident and independent, I assumed that she was.
3. I wish I had paid more attention to the obvious signs that things were not going well. I was too deferential to the medical community and gender specialists. I knew the truth, if only in my heart. I should have acted on it sooner. How powerful might that have been? How much suffering could have been avoided?
4. I wish I'd allowed myself the time and luxury of finding a proper therapist from the start.
5. I wish I had trusted my instincts, listened to my heart, and said no from the beginning. No new name or pronouns. No new identity to

---

3. See the section "Parents on Online Influences: Porn, Anime, and Social Media" in Josie A. and Dina S., eds., *Parents with Inconvenient Truths about Trans: Tales from the Home Front in the Fight to Save Our Kids* (Durham, NC: Pitchstone Publishing, 2023).
4. Please read *Hold onto Your Kids*, by Gordon Neufeld and Gabor Maté. I recommend this book to any parent, whether your child identifies as transgender or otherwise.

hide behind. Let's cut the bullshit and figure out what's really going on.
6. I wish … I had said no from the beginning.

Moving Forward

Next comes the difficult task of formulating advice for the parents of trans-identified teens. If you are the parent of a trans-identified teen with no prior history of gender dysphoria, the advice I give is from one parent to another. It is not medical advice. I trust you can get plenty of expert opinions on your own, and probably already have. And this advice is not for everyone. Each kid is different, so take what you need and leave the rest.

- **Limit access to the internet and devices.**
  Some transgender gurus found on YouTube and other internet sites are authentic transgender individuals trying to do the right thing, although the internet also has its share of predators. Either way, many of these messengers and teen influencers are not giving your child advice that will lead them to a better place. The vast majority are not psychiatrists, psychologists, or medical professionals. If you would not trust a random YouTube influencer to prescribe your diabetes medication, remove your appendix, or oversee a family member's chemotherapy regimen, you shouldn't trust them to deliver appropriate medical and psychological advice to your struggling teen. The potential for long-term damage and brainwashing is profound. If you think you have a pretty good idea about what your teenager is viewing on the internet, you're probably wrong.

  Put your child's laptop (that they claim they need for homework) in a public place, such as in the living room or on the kitchen table. (Letting your child sit with devices in their bedroom is *so 2021*.) Install parental protection software. There are many options and levels to choose from. Keep an updated file with their logins and passwords. Make sure your child knows that you'll be periodically checking the things that they're doing on the internet. Do not log in every day and read everything. That's stalking and disrespectful. Do "spot checks" when you sense something is amiss. It's for your child's protection, and it is not negotiable. You have both the right and the responsibility to check their devices for things that will hurt them.

If you decide to give your child a smartphone (there are compelling reasons why you might decide not to do this), limit the amount of time that your child is allowed to use it. Something like an hour a day is best. Be firm. They'll be extremely annoyed with you for doing this, but it will save you and your kid plenty of heartache and headache down the road. They probably won't thank you for this intervention until they're a parent, if ever. So, buck up. Parenting rarely leads to immediate gratification.[5]

- **Internalize this concept: Your child needs you.**
  Do not allow them to push you away. Now is the time to draw from the attachment you have with your son or daughter. Do fun things together as much as possible. Continue to lay down good memories. (You can't afford not to.) Go on dates. Make space for time together that is suspended outside of the dynamic that has been created by gender ideology. Do things together every day that provide an opportunity for your child to talk to you about whatever comes to mind. (Activities that don't require the burden of eye contact work well. Doing art together, riding in the car, baking, going on a hike, and folding laundry are good examples.) Tell yourself every day that they need you. Say it out loud. Remind yourself that the parenting gig is far from over, even though your child acts like it is. You've been around, and you know better.

- **Give yourself space to examine your real feelings.**
  Keep a journal. Let everything flow without inhibition. This is the only space where you can explore thoughts in their pure form without them being tainted by inadequate description, misunderstanding, or agenda (yours or someone else's). Even if you are in therapy,

---

5. As I experienced, these interventions are much more difficult if your child lives in two homes, but you need to make it work. Find the other parent in that forest. Put aside your differences and swallow your pride. Whether you now loathe each other, remain friendly, or wish you'd never parted, this is your child we're talking about. You've both loved her since before she was born.

it's still important to keep a journal. Sharing your feelings in the safe space of a confidential psychotherapy office can be powerful. Still, the things you say to a therapist are often self-edited, even if it's only by unconscious omission. A therapist might slightly misunderstand you and reframe your statements, which you come to accept as your truth. Your mind and your private writing are the only places that you can look at your thoughts and feelings as they naturally occur. You can examine them in safety, explore them uninterrupted from all angles and from beginning to end, without having to share your space. You can rage if you want to. You can admit things to yourself that you might not feel comfortable admitting to your therapist. That can lead to personal discovery, growth, development, and catharsis. It might shed light on the one pure truth in your life that leads you out of the wilderness.

- **Find a proper therapist for your child.**
  I wish there was an easy way to do this. Bad therapy can be far worse than no therapy, so take your time. Therapists vary widely in their degree of skill and humility, and you need one with both. The garden variety gender specialist will quickly introduce the red balloon during that first appointment, and they will then proceed to entrench your child further in his or her false identity. Internet searches for those treating gender-questioning adolescents will not lead to a therapist to whom I would feel comfortable taking my child. Look for *actual* gender specialists as I defined them in chapter three. Some helpful resources may include Therapy First, Genspect.org, and InspiredTeenTherapy.com.[6] You must interview the therapist prior to your child meeting them. Ask the potential therapist questions such as:

  · "Do you implement the gender affirming model for all patients?"
  · "How do you diagnose gender dysphoria?"

---

[6]. Beyond Trans (beyondtrans.org) has a directory of therapists and other useful services for people who may feel distressed or ambivalent about transition. 4th Wave Now (4thwavenow.com) is a community of people who question the medicalization of gender-atypical youth, which may be useful in connecting with other parents in a similar situation who have obtained a good therapist for their child. Both websites are informative.

- "What do you do if you get a gender case that you're not certain about?"
- "What percentage of teens who present to your practice do you diagnose with gender dysphoria?"
- "Are you knowledgeable in the treatment of trauma, anxiety, and depression?"

Ask the last question because these are far more likely to be the things that plague your child. A therapist who answers these questions properly will not take your child's self-diagnosis as accurate from the start. If it turns out that your child *is* trans, these therapists will be able to discern that after careful evaluation over multiple sessions. Please dispense with the notion that the therapist will take your insurance. Free yourself from that requirement. You will make the money happen, and it will be worth every penny.

- **Get your kid involved in activities outside of the LGBTQ community.**
  Even though you won't be disclosing your motivations for doing this, your child probably won't want to do any of the things you sign them up for. Get them involved anyway. It will allow them to develop interests that encourage other areas of their brain to fire, and they'll be exposed to people who think differently. Although they probably won't admit it, your child will soon develop insight into how small the world is for someone preoccupied with LGBTQ issues. I signed Jordan up for an art class, music lessons, sent her to a church youth group, and she studied abroad one summer. All were out of her comfort zone and exposed her to peers she would not have met otherwise. It's not necessary or even realistic to eliminate *all* their LGBTQ contacts, but connecting your child with a larger world is the first step in pulling them out of the hole they have dug for themselves.

- **Consider saying no to your child's professed trans identity.**
  This is a tough one, especially for parents who care deeply (as most parents do) about the health and well-being of their child. There is a natural tendency to support our children in all things. "I love you just the way you are," I used to tell Jordan during her early childhood

years, and it remains true to this day. If I believed or even suspected that my child was a boy trapped in a girl's body, I would've embraced it. The child comes first, not the agenda.

The problem I faced was that the things Jordan was telling me weren't true. How did I know for sure? I've tried to explain it in this book, but the bottom line was that I knew my child. We had walked the path of her life together. I wasn't a transphobic bigot refusing to believe in the possibility that my child could be trans. I held the door wide open and inspected it. I asked myself, "Am I *absolutely certain* that she is not trans?" It was a critical question, and I considered it deeply. In the end, the answer was yes, I was certain, which brought us to the intervention.

I don't know your child, but you do. Here are some possibilities and approaches to consider:

- Your kid comes out as trans and you think, *Yes, of course; it all makes sense now.* In this case, there's a decent chance that your child is authentically transgender. Love and support them. Be gender affirming. Unless they're incredibly well-adjusted, you will probably need to get them into therapy since the road ahead can still be rocky, even if their gender identity is clear.
- Your kid comes out as trans and you think, *I'm not sure, but maybe. It's at least partially consistent with the things I've noticed over the years.* In this case, you'll want to explore it further. Do the hard work of working with them to figure it out. Find a proper therapist (see my comments above on choosing one) and get that started. Consider implementing the gender affirming model and assess your child's response. Pay close attention to your inner voice. Trust in the fact that you know your child best: better than their friends, their therapist, their school counselor, the social media influencers, and the gender specialist from that well-respected academic institution. If you're on the fence, give it some time. The gender affirming model will lead to positive changes in your child's mood, confidence, and overall happiness. Or perhaps it won't. Perhaps you will need to switch gears somewhere along the way. I can't tell you if or when that time will come, but it will become more obvious as things unfold.

- Your kid comes out as trans and you think, *Where the hell is this coming from? This isn't consistent with what I know about my child at all.* And so, dear parents, what will you do? Either follow your child into the darkness or find a way to pull them out of it before you lose them forever. Chances are, you know what route to take, although the path is hazardous and riddled with obstacles. Maybe it's the scariest thing you will ever do. By now you've most likely had at least one expert float you the red balloon and place the string delicately in your hand. You've heard the rhetorical question, "Would you rather have a healthy son or a dead daughter?" I suspect that, up until now, you've been clenching that string pretty tightly, as I did.

  How do you manage your fear of the red balloon or the very real possibility that it could explode? That's a hard question for a parent to answer, but what I *can* say is that what you are holding is nothing more than a string, and that string is attached to fear. The decisions we make out of fear are not our best decisions. We may come to regret the things we could've done but didn't. How long will you hold that string? How long will you allow it to dictate every decision you make? What would happen if you let it go?

  Here is the question reimagined: "Would you rather have a suffering child who clings to a false trans identity, or the opportunity to reclaim your child and save them from a lifetime of regret?"

  You unclench your hand ... and feel the string sliding through it. You watch as the balloon drifts away in the breeze, never to be seen again. Maybe it ends up tangled in the branches of a tree, the way so many balloons do. Perhaps the fate of the red balloon is trite and uninteresting, its paralyzing effect lifting as you loosen your grip. Let it go. It's not something you can carry forever.

- **Forgive yourself, no matter the outcome.**
  The hardest part about all of this is not knowing how things will turn out. It's been like that from the beginning, from the moment you realized that a new life was coming in the form of a child. You

dared to imagine the best while fearing the worst. You agonized over decisions both made and avoided. You tried to keep them safe from the things that would hurt them, and yet they fell anyway, skinning their knees and hitting their delicate heads but managing to survive because it was never possible to protect them from everything. Still, you blame yourself, for the times you weren't there or the things you should've done but didn't. Let it go. Show up now when they need you the most. Be present as much as possible. Know when to fight for them and when to trust that you have done everything you can and that they must take it from there. You are an important part of this equation, but its success or failure does not rest on you alone. Trust in God or whatever higher power you believe in. Forgive yourself for not being perfect. Find a way to move forward.

Transitions

At the time of the writing of this book, I don't know what the future holds for Jordan. She turned eighteen six months ago, and she continues to thrive with no signs of resurgence of the trans identity. Still, she remains at risk. I allow the comments that she makes, the clothing she buys, and the future she describes for herself to reassure me. Nothing about her way of being heralds a male identity or a plan for transition. There is no indication that she is living the uncomfortable existence of a male trapped in a teen girl's body. It is obvious to me that she is doing better, and these positive changes are validating. I am only sorry that it took me so long to find the right way to help her.

The trans flag that once hung on the wall in Jordan's bedroom came down several years ago (her decision, not mine). Where it once resided, a lesbian flag hung in its place for several months until that too disappeared. Is my daughter a lesbian? I don't know. Chances are, she doesn't know either. As of now, she remains part of the LGBTQ community, and I think it's important to mention that many detransitioners and desisters identify as homosexual once they no longer identify as trans.[7]

---

7. James Cantor, "Do Trans- Kids Stay Trans- When They Grow Up?" *Sexology Today*, January 11, 2016; T. D. Steensma et al., "Gender Variance in Childhood and Sexual Orientation in Adulthood: A Prospective Study," *Journal of Sexual Medicine* 10 , no. 11

There is some irony to this. Individuals who reverse course following medical and surgical transition have sustained permanent or semi-permanent anatomic and physiologic changes that they no longer desire. Since detransitioners often go on to identify as gay or lesbian, it can be extrapolated that members of the LGBTQ community are the ones most likely to be harmed by the current aggressive push for the medical and surgical transition of children prior to the age of consent and against the wishes of their parents. Hence, one part of the community becomes injured by the other.

Jordan went from T to L in the LGBTQ acronym, although she has also taken a recent interest in boys, suggesting a possible move from L to B. It doesn't faze me, this jumping around from one orientation to the next. Being a lesbian or bisexual doesn't involve the medical and surgical mutilation of one's body. She does not incur the health risks of hormone blockers, testosterone, and multiple complicated surgeries. Her ability to bear children is preserved. These are reversible identifications, ones she can move into or out of with the ease of simply changing her mind. Jumping through the letters of the LGBTQ acronym also confirms what I already knew. Jordan is far less certain about who she is and where she is going than she once seemed. The cement of her identity and sexual development has not yet hardened. Thank God we didn't allow her to launch herself into medical transition when she and the gender specialists were clamoring for it.

Unlike her now-defunct trans identification, Jordan's exploration of her sexual orientation has not been destructive to her family relationships. As her mother, I don't care about her sexual orientation, or more correctly, I care only that it makes her happy and allows her to live an authentic life. If her authentic life involves romantic relationships with women, she has my full support.[8] I am still the person who supports equal rights for LGBTQ individuals, although I have lost interest in attending Pride parades and waving my flag.

Here's something else I have noticed. I have not seen the reemergence of the "alter ego" that arrived when Jordan became Ash: the dark

---

(2013): 2723–2733.
8. And let's not lose sight of an important fact. If Jordan identified as a transgender man and I thought he was leading an authentic life in doing so, Ash would have my full support.

melancholia, the defensiveness, the isolation from family, and the single-minded obsession with all things trans. Jordan recently thanked me for supporting her in exploring her lesbian identity. There's a key word there: exploring. That word never came up while she identified as trans. If you recall from chapter two, "This is me letting you know."

As a family, we try to avoid vast amounts of open-ended time that will lead to unnecessary social media engagement or excessive time spent with peers. I am proud to have relatives who work with an animal rescue, and Jordan will be going to work on the rescue for part of Christmas Break. I have amazing parents who are willing and want to take her to their house or their vacation home as often as she would like. Zack has family on the East Coast who I know would love a visit from Jordan at any point. During breaks from school, I sign her up for structured activities such as volunteer work or pottery courses at the community college. She recently got a part-time job. These are all things that limit peer involvement outside of school and extracurricular functions. I try to surround her with those who are gender affirming in the true sense of the term.

A Reminder

Sometimes I allow myself to enjoy the gratitude of Jordan being out of this and the relief it has brought to my family. I feel I've earned that bit of peace. In doing so, it is easy to forget how many children are still in the middle of it and the large number of families who continue to suffer. It is a journey fraught with peril. People get lost along the way. A resolution with a good outcome is anything but certain.

Toward the end of the writing of this book, I was working in the hospital one afternoon when I was called to see "Scout," a bright, mild-mannered 24-year-old female-to-male transgender individual who had been admitted to the hospital following a suicide attempt.

As I entered the room, Scout seemed relieved to see me. He'd heard I was coming and was waiting to tell someone of his pain and to discuss his options moving forward. He reported to me that he had socially transitioned from a female to a male five years ago. He had a long history of anxiety and depression, both of which predated his social transition.

He suffered from chronic symptoms of melancholia, sleep disturbance, lack of interest in typically enjoyable activities, panic attacks, a chronic sense of loneliness, and an unstable sense of self. Scout had the support of his immediate family. His social transition from a female to male identity had resulted in no change in his symptoms.

Scout had been referred by his tele-therapist to a gender expert who had recommended hormone blockers and testosterone shortly thereafter. The sharpening of Scout's facial features and the reduction of his hip circumference were welcome changes. The acne and beard were not. Medical transition brought worsening mood symptoms. He had pointed this out to his doctor, wondering aloud if his increased depression could be due to the testosterone, since mood disturbance is a common side effect of this medication.[9] He was advised not to be overly concerned. These things take time, his doctor reassured him. It was best to be patient.

After a couple of years on testosterone with worsening psychological symptoms, Scout revisited his concerns with his doctor. There was no reevaluation of the diagnosis, despite Scout's symptoms, narrative, and poor response to treatment being inconsistent with gender dysphoria. It was recommended that he continue the current therapy and that he move forward with surgical gender transition. Top surgery was scheduled. Six weeks prior to my meeting him, Scout underwent a bilateral mastectomy. There were no medical complications from the surgery, and it was considered a "success" according to his medical providers.

Scout explained to me that he had been waiting for a sense of relief and euphoria following his top surgery. It never came. On the day of his suicide attempt, it dawned on Scout that a part of his body was permanently gone. There would be no coming back from this.

We processed what had happened. Although he felt despondent following his surgical transition, I pointed out that he was not out of options. There were ways to detransition if he wanted to, but the decision was up to him. At the very least, it was something to consider.

Scout was polite but clung to his transgender identity. I hope he tucked the discussion away in his brain where he could access it later if he needed it. As I left the room, I wondered if Scout's doctor would be

---

9. Sirpi Nackeeran et al., "Testosterone Therapy Is Associated With Depression, Suicidality And Intentional Self-Harm: Analysis of A National Federated Database," *Journal of Sexual Medicine* 19, no. 6 (2022): 933–939.

undeterred in keeping his patient on this track despite clear evidence that it was killing him. Perhaps, following a suicide attempt, it was time to reevaluate the diagnosis and treatment. I wanted to believe that his doctor might reconsider his approach to the things that were torturing Scout and had brought him to this moment of life-threatening crisis. What was the likelihood that this would happen?

I thought a lot about Scout that evening, the pieces of our conversation rising and falling in my mind as I crossed the parking lot and headed home. He had talked about his supportive parents, and I wondered what they might be thinking in this moment. They had followed the advice of the gender experts, but the outcome was not a healthy son or a dead daughter. Scout's parents have an unhealthy child, and I fear that his future is bleak without an appropriate intervention.

Chapter Fifteen: The Future

I sit in my car in the school parking lot as I write this, the laptop perched on a backpack in front of me. It's 10:55 p.m. and the night presses dark and cold against the glass. The school's spring play opens in less than a week. Jordan's rehearsal is running late. It's crunch time, "hell week"; that's what they call it.

I've shut off the engine to save on gas, and a shudder rolls through me as a chill settles into the compartment. The rain is coming down now. I can hear its drumming patter on the rooftop above me. Beyond the windshield, I can barely make out the shape of the building. It's disorienting, waiting for her to emerge. I could be anywhere, or nowhere at all.

I want to tell you what will happen, how things will play out from here. It's important, but I don't know where to start. I've been looking back at this for so long. In all of that remembering, I have forgotten how hard it is to see the path ahead.

The future is never as clear as we would like it to be. Have I made the right decisions? What shall become of my family and yours? What new insights and discoveries will change our current way of thinking? How shall we begin the critical task of fixing the many things that are broken?

A Community of Detransitioners

One consequence of charging full steam ahead toward the medical and surgical transition of young people is the mounting number of individuals who have been there and back.

A recent survey of 237 detransitioners[1] found that 92 percent of those surveyed were genetic females. Respondents reported significant difficulty getting the help they needed for detransition. While 51 percent received help and advice from an LGBTQ organization regarding medical and surgical transition, only 13 percent received guidance from such organizations related to their desire to detransition. Patients reported difficulty finding a gender specialist or medical provider who was willing or able to provide accurate information on stopping or changing hormone treatments. They also reported difficulty finding a specialist who was willing or able to address complications related to surgeries or medical transition, or who could provide information and access to reversal procedures. Respondents had the most difficulty finding help for their psychological needs. Learning to cope with gender dysphoria, feelings of regret, internalized homophobia, physical and social changes related to detransition, rejection from the LGBTQ community, and the psychological aftermath of leaving a manipulative group were all cited as needs that went unaddressed in the wake of detransitioning.

A common theme from respondents was a sense that it was difficult to talk about detransition within LGBTQ spaces and among trans friends. Many expressed a feeling of rejection and loss of support related to their decision to detransition. They described difficulty finding a detransition-friendly therapist and said the detransition experience was isolating.[2] Some emphasized support they received from family and friends, as well as online detrans groups and lesbian and feminist organizations. Women helping other women. One might wonder, or at least I do, what happened to the glitter families promising judgement-free acceptance now that these individuals were struggling and needed their support.

Brave girls and women have put their stories on the internet about their experiences with detransition. I am comforted to read about other loving parents who made mistakes like the ones I did. The stories are especially heartbreaking when coming from women who have gone through detransition themselves. Their tales are eerily alike and remi-

---

1. Vandenbussche, "Detransition Related Needs and Support."
2. I recently suggested to a community organization that they promote detransition awareness as part of their Pride Celebration. The suggestion was immediately dismissed. No questions were asked as to why I thought that might be helpful.

niscent of Jordan's own experiences. They describe a painful adolescence (whose wasn't?) intercepted by the promise of emotional relief by transitioning out of the uncomfortable body of an adolescent girl. These women universally speak of the "coaching" they received: what to memorize to tell doctors and therapists to convince them to prescribe the desired medications. "We didn't discuss all the implications of medical intervention—psychological, social, physical, sexual, occupational, financial, and legal—which the Standard of Care directs the mental health professionals to discuss," a young woman recalls. "What the Standard of Care describes, and the care people get before getting cleared for hormones and surgery, are miles apart."[3]

In the same article, one detransitioner tells the story of looking in the mirror when she was trying to pass as a boy. What she saw was, "My baggy uncomfortable clothes; my damaged, short hair; and my depressed looking face. It didn't make me feel any better, I was still miserable, and I still hated myself."

Another detransitioner puts it like this: "I'm a real live 22-year-old woman with a scarred chest and a broken voice and a five o'clock shadow because I couldn't face the idea of growing up to be a woman."

"Transitioning made my mental health much, much worse. Not better," says another detransitioner. "It was a 'f--k you' to the hurting child inside of me. It was telling her that she didn't matter. It was telling her that I hated her and wanted to annihilate her. It was an act of war against myself."[4]

With 87 percent of detransitioners expressing a need to hear about others' experiences, there lies an opportunity for new communities to

---

3. Jesse Singal, "When Children Say They're Trans," *The Atlantic*, July/August 2018; World Professional Association for Transgender Health, "Standards of Care for the Health of Transgender and Gender Diverse People, Version 7." Chapter 16 (entitled *Reproductive Health*) notes, "Many transgender...people will want to have children. Because feminizing/masculinizing hormone therapy limits fertility, it is desirable for patients to make decisions concerning fertility before starting hormone therapy... Cases are known of people who received hormone therapy and genital surgery and later regretted their inability to parent genetically related children. Health care professionals...should discuss reproductive options with patients prior to initiation of these medical treatments for gender dysphoria. These discussions should occur even if patients are not interested in these issues at the time of treatment, which may be more common for younger patients."
4. Mary Margaret Olohan, *Detrans: True Stories of Escaping the Gender Ideology Cult* (Washington, DC: Regnery Publishing, 2024).

form. This is already happening with groups such as DeTrans Alliance Canada, Beyond Trans, the Detransition Advocacy Network, and the Pique Resilience Project,[5] to name a few.

Detransitioners are often in desperate need of professional help from psychiatrists, therapists, and non-psychiatric physicians. The current dearth of resources is appalling, especially considering the hordes of medical providers who were eager to usher them down the path of medical and surgical transition in the first place. I predict that a combination of treatments will be necessary for detransitioning women, including medications to treat symptoms of depression, anxiety, and post-traumatic stress disorder, as well as hormone and surgical treatments to mitigate some of the loss and injuries resulting from previous medications and surgeries associated with the urgent rush to transition. Psychotherapy may be required in a variety of formats, including individual psychotherapy, group therapy, art therapy, and potentially eye movement desensitization and reprocessing (EMDR), which is a specialized therapy used to treat post-traumatic stress disorder. I foresee the possibility of treatment programs opening where detransitioners could access all these services on either a residential or intensive outpatient basis. Given the fact that this is a developing field currently in its infancy, there is a need for clinicians who feel a personal calling to help these individuals on their path toward wellness and recovery.

The Invisibles

I've discussed at length the physical, emotional, and psychological injuries incurred by children swept up in the transgender pandemic. The pain to those children and their families is monumental, the outcomes devastating. The extent of such damage can never be erased; it can only be examined and dealt with in retrospect. The best we can hope for is partial repair of the individual and their families. Many will never recover.

---

5. Although the Pique Resilience Project is no longer an active group, it was my personal favorite. Founded by four detransitioned and desisted women, they told their stories and provided information and support to others. I highly recommend listening to their short-lived podcast, *Danger Ramen,* which you can access on YouTube and SoundCloud. The narrative of their experiences is both humorous and compassionate.

There is another small group of victims of the transgender pandemic: authentically transgender children themselves. What will happen to the small number of children in my community or in *any* community who've had authentic gender dysphoria from a very young age and need treatment and services to help them make sense of it? Will they receive the careful and thoughtful counseling they require, or will they continue to be drowned out by the cacophony of other voices clamoring for attention? Will they be pushed toward medical and surgical transition before they are ready? Will they be seen as "just another trans kid" by people on both sides of the political spectrum, who either embrace them with overzealous fanfare or dismiss them with eyerolling annoyance? After hearing personal accounts from so many detransitioners, will these authentically transgender children become scared and dissuaded from exploring their own gender identities? Will they have trouble finding healthy peers and mentors to bond with and look up to? What is the chance of such a child's success and happiness in a society that has become so polarized by the issue?

Change

How heavy are the things we carry? It depends on how long we carry them and the sacrifices we must make to avoid letting them go.

What would it look like for us to change? I see several options for where it could start:

- **Parents and providers must demand an evidence-based approach to the treatment of children with expressed gender dysphoria.**
  Although the term "evidence-based medicine" was introduced in the early 1990s, the scientific approach to the practice of medicine dates back several hundred years. The belief that medical treatments should be guided by the best available evidence from scientific testing, clinical trials, and systemic reviews of the literature is so ingrained in the training of today's medical practitioners that we often assume that the evidence in support of a given treatment or intervention is more robust than it is. It is our duty to review the data, to test hypotheses, to question prevailing wisdom, and to ask ourselves

whether the conclusions reached by our predecessors are strongly supported by the evidence. We don't know as much as we think we know, and "expert opinion" without rigorous scientific testing is like sprinting in the dark.

In April 2024, British pediatrician and former President of the Royal College of Paediatrics and Child Health, Dr. Hilary Cass, published the most extensive evidence-based review of pediatric transgender care to date.[6] Commissioned by England's National Health Service, "The Independent Review of Gender Identity Services for Children and Young People" (or, as it is commonly known, the Cass Review) assessed data from 131 publications describing characteristics of children and young people (abbreviated CYP) referred to gender services, 53 publications on masculinizing or feminizing hormone interventions, 50 papers on medical interventions to suppress puberty, 10 papers on psychosocial support interventions for children, 23 guidelines or position statements for CYP gender services, 24 papers reporting care pathways for CYP referred to gender services, 11 papers on the impact of social transition in relation to gender for CYP, survey data from 15 CYP gender services in 8 countries, and information from 113,269 children and young people across 18 countries.

In an interim report published in March 2022, the Cass Review noted that "in 2014 the number of referrals started to grow exponentially in the UK, with a higher number of birth-registered females presenting in early teenage years." This led to the creation of the Gender Identity Development Service (GIDS), which did not follow the usual practices and control measures applied to new treatments. Lack of adequate data collection, infrequent physician attendance at multidisciplinary meetings, and poor psychological support for children with comorbidities were all cited as areas of concern. The interim report also noted that general practitioners and non-GIDS staff often felt "under pressure to adopt an unquestioning affirmative approach"[7] to children who were uncertain of their

---

6. Hilary Cass, *Independent Review of Gender Identity Services for Children and Young People* (April 2024), cass.independent-review.uk/home/publications/final-report/.
7. Hilary Cass, *Independent Review of Gender Identity Services for Children and Young People: Interim Report* (March 2022), 17.

gender identity, "overshadowing" provider concerns about the poor mental health of their patients.

Excerpts from the 388-page final report, published two years later, include the following findings:

- "There is lack of high-quality research assessing the outcomes of hormone interventions in adolescents with gender dysphoria/incongruence, and few studies that undertake long-term follow-up. No conclusions can be drawn about the effect on gender dysphoria, body satisfaction, psychosocial health, cognitive development, or fertility." (p. 33)
- "It has been suggested that hormone treatment reduces the elevated risk of death by suicide in this population, but the evidence found did not support this conclusion." (p. 33)
- "The 'watchful waiting' approach continued in the UK until 2011, when puberty blockers were trialed under a research protocol; the 'early intervention study'. ... the UK's preliminary findings did not demonstrate improvement in psychological wellbeing, and in fact some birth-registered females had a worsening of 'internalizing' problems (depression, anxiety) based on parental report." (p. 70)
- "There were no statistically significant changes reported in gender dysphoria or mental health outcome measures whilst on puberty blockers, and 98% proceeded to masculinizing or feminizing hormones." (p. 71)
- "A subsequent re-analysis of the early intervention study ... found that 37-70% experience no reliable change in distress across time points, 15-34% deteriorate and 9-29% reliably improve." (p. 71)
- "The percentage of people treated with hormones who subsequently detransition remains unknown due to the lack of long-term follow-up studies, although there is suggestion that numbers are increasing." (p. 33)
- "Every case considered for medical treatment should be discussed at a national multi-disciplinary team ..." (p. 35)
- "All children should be offered fertility counseling and preservation prior to going onto a medical pathway." (p. 35)

Reaction to the Cass Review has been swift. England's National Health Service discontinued the routine use of puberty blocking medications, closed the Gender Identity Development Service, and replaced it with several regional centers for "the assessment, diagnosis and treatment of children and young people presenting with gender incongruence." NHS Scotland has paused the practice of prescribing puberty blockers to children referred to its gender clinic.

In the weeks that followed release of the final report, Dr. Cass received threatening emails and expressed frustration regarding rampant online disinformation pertaining to the report. Such efforts to bully and undermine the careful and responsible approach of evidence-based medicine continue and have become the common tools of ideologues with no interest in protecting the health and wellness of our children. I would like to think we have all become better at dismissing these tactics as the desperate efforts of people who have nothing meaningful to contribute to the conversation. The loudest and most antagonistic voices are seldom the ones we should be listening to.

The Cass Review's thoughtful, well-researched, non-politicized findings should be mandatory reading for parents of children with expressed gender dysphoria and for any provider who treats these children in their practice.

- **The medical community must be willing to postpone medical and surgical transition until a diagnosis is clear.**
Most medical providers are committed to acting in the best interest of their patients. Contrary to some critics, I do not agree that the push for medical and surgical transition of children and young adults is financially motivated by greedy clinicians looking to profit. I am not so naïve to think that money is not part of the equation, but it's a small part, and clinicians who do this mostly for money are the rare outliers. In the United States and many other countries, most physicians have plenty of work—*too much* work—that needs to be done. We are not waiting for the phone to ring, trying to drum up business. If anything, we are already stretched too thin. It is our sense of duty that pushes us forward, and we want to do what's right for our patients.

"Doing the right thing" means different things to different people. In the treatment of trans-identifying teens, it has become murky and increasingly dictated by politics and agendas. People have become deeply opinionated without taking the time to understand things deeply. The climate must change such that rigorous scientific debate is not only tolerated but encouraged. Physicians should be allowed to voice concerns and express their opinions in public and professional forums. Personal attacks and disciplinary actions by employers and state medical boards against medical providers who have the audacity to bring reasonable concerns to the table leads to an environment in which it becomes too risky to advocate for the health and safety of our patients. That's dangerous health care that runs counter to everything we hold dear about the profession.

For our part, medical providers involved in the treatment of transgender adolescents should take the time to gain a deeper understanding of the dynamics of adolescent psychology and the social factors that can affect and skew trends in gender identity. We must adhere to diagnostic criteria and reject the ridiculous notion of accepting a child's self-diagnosis as the final and most accurate diagnosis. When in doubt, we must be willing to postpone medical and surgical transition until the diagnosis is clear.

Ideally, the medical community would embrace this commonsense approach. Where common sense, professional ethics, and due diligence fail, a few lawsuits might do the trick.[8] Either way, pushing a political agenda at the expense of children or avoiding proper informed consent because the proposed treatments are too complicated, "icky," or scary to talk about is ethically and legally indefensible.[9]

- **The mental health community must not accept every patient's self-made diagnosis as accurate.**

---

[8]. "Legal Action May Change Transgender Care in America," *The Economist*, May 7, 2023; Keira Bell, "My Story," *Persuasion*, April 7, 2021.

[9]. Themis Resource Fund is an independent, nonprofit, nonpartisan organization that connects detransitioners with attorneys and helps them fund litigation to seek compensation for injuries sustained from affirmative gender treatment. See www.themisresourcefund.org.

What shall become of the mental health providers who claim expertise in "treating trans teens"? Will they remain subservient to the whims of children, taking every patient's self-made diagnosis as an unquestionable truth? Will they take the time to understand the diagnostic criteria and dare to perform analyses of their own? Will they come to a point, as if awakening from a dream, in which they realize that not all children claiming to be trans require the exact same approach? Is there any space in our practice for careful independent thought, or is that just one more thing to be labeled "transphobic"?

I hope things will change for the better. It is such important work, and we have been asleep at the wheel for way too long. It's time to wake up, take control, and pay attention to what is happening.[10]

- **Significant steps must be taken toward reducing or eliminating social media access to children and adolescents.**
  According to the U.S. Surgeon General's 2023 Advisory "Social Media and Youth Mental Health,"[11] up to 95 percent of adolescents ages 13–17 and 40 percent of children ages 8–12 report using a social media platform, with more than a third of adolescents saying they use social media "almost constantly."[12] The advisory notes that "the current body of evidence indicates that while social media may have benefits for some children and adolescents, there are ample indicators that social media can also have a profound risk of harm to the mental health and well-being of children and adolescents."

---

10. I used to be proud of my home state of California, but we are headed in the wrong direction. Under a proposed amendment to California AB 957, which was easily passed by both the California State Senate and California State Assembly, parents who do not affirm their child's requested gender identity could have lost custody of their child. Fortunately, the amendment was vetoed by Governor Newsom, which was a surprise to me given the governor's ultra-liberal political agenda. Had Newsom signed the bill, psychotherapists would have played an instrumental role in having children removed from loving homes.
11. U.S. Surgeon General's 2023 Advisory, "Social Media and Youth Mental Health" www.hhs.gov/sites/default/files/sg-youth-mental-health-social-media-advisory.pdf.
12. Emily A. Vogels, Risa Gelles-Watnick, and Navid Massarat, "Teens, Social Media and Technology 2022," Pew Research Center (August 10, 2022), www.pewresearch.org/internet/2022/08/10/teens-social-media-and-technology-2022/.

A longitudinal cohort study of 6,595 U.S. adolescents aged 12–15 found that adolescents who spent more than three hours per day on social media faced double the risk of experiencing poor mental health outcomes including symptoms of depression and anxiety.[13] When asked about the impact of social media on their body image, nearly half (46 percent) of adolescents aged 13–17 said social media makes them feel worse, 40 percent said it makes them feel neither better nor worse, and only 14 percent said it makes them feel better.[14] Adolescent girls and transgender youth are disproportionately impacted by online harassment and abuse.[15, 16, 17, 18] In a nationally representative survey of girls aged 11–15, one-third or more say they feel "addicted" to a social media platform and nearly 6-in-10 adolescent girls say they've been contacted by a stranger through a social media platform in a way that made them feel uncomfortable.[19]

In light of these findings, there is a need for social media companies to monitor their content more closely and to take significant steps toward reducing or eliminating social media access to children and adolescents. Where Big Tech falters, state or federal governments sometimes intervene. In 2023, the Utah State Legislature passed SB 152 and HB 311, which would have imple-

---

13. K. E. Riehm et al., "Associations Between Time Spent Using Social Media and Internalizing and Externalizing Problems Among US Youth," *JAMA Psychiatry* 76, no. 12 (2019): 1266–1273.
14. D. S. Bickham et al., "Adolescent Media Use: Attitudes, Effects, and Online Experiences," Boston Children's Digital Wellness Lab (August 2022), digitalwellnesslab.org/wp-content/uploads/Pulse-Survey_Adolescent-Attitudes-Effects-and-Experiences.pdf.
15. J. Wolak et al., "Sextortion of Minors: Characteristics and Dynamics," *Journal of Adolescent Health* 62, no. 1 (2018): 72–79.
16. Federal Bureau of Investigations National Press Office, "FBI and Partners Issue National Public Safety Alert on Financial Sextortion Schemes," December 19, 2022, www.fbi.gov/news/press-releases/fbi-and-partners-issue-national-public-safety-alert-on-financial-sextortion-schemess.
17. D. Finkelhor, H. A. Turner, and D. Colburn, "Which Dynamics Make Online Child Sexual Abuse and Cyberstalking More Emotionally Impactful: Perpetrator Identity and Images?" *Child Abuse and Neglect* 137 (2023): 106020.
18. D. Finkelhor, H. Turner, and D. Colburn, "Prevalence of Online Sexual Offenses Against Children in the US," *JAMA Network Open* 5, no. 10 (2022): e2234471.
19. J. Nesi, S. Mann, and M. B. Robb, "Teens and Mental Health: How Girls Really Feel about Social Media," (San Francisco: Common Sense, 2023), www.commonsensemedia.org/sites/default/files/research/report/ how-girls-really-feel-about-social-media-researchreport_ final_1.pdf.

mented conditions for social media companies providing service in Utah.[20] Although the bills were repealed and replaced following complaints about the constitutionality of the bills, they called on companies to:

- verify the age of a Utah adult seeking to maintain or open a social media account;
- get the consent of a parent or guardian for Utah users under age 18;
- allow parents or guardians full access to their child's account;
- create a default curfew setting (10:30 p.m. to 6:30 a.m.) that blocks overnight access to the accounts of minors ;
- protect minor accounts from unapproved direct messaging;
- and block minor accounts from search results.

In addition, the bills stated that social media companies:

- cannot collect a minor's data;
- cannot target minor's social media accounts for advertising;
- and cannot target minor's social media accounts with addictive designs or features.

Would children and adolescents have found a way around some of these safeguards? Undoubtedly. The bills were not perfect even if their constitutionality was not in question. But such a legislative effort does represent a meaningful change in how the state views and approaches social media platforms and their effect on young, developing minds.

Utah is not the only state taking issue with the ways that social media companies target children. In a recently filed lawsuit,[21] attorneys general from thirty-three states sued social media giant Meta (formerly Facebook) for violating federal children's online privacy

---

20. In 2024, the Utah State Legislature voted to repeal and replace the Utah Social Media Regulation Act with HB 465 and SB 194, the Utah Minor Protection in Social Media Act. For more on that legislation and the latest developments related to Utah's efforts to protect minors online, see Utah Protecting Minors Online, socialmedia.utah.gov.
21. Case 4:23-cv-05448, filed on October 24, 2023, in a San Francisco federal court.

law and state consumer protection laws. An excerpt from page 1 of the complaint states:

> Meta has harnessed powerful and unprecedented technologies to entice, engage, and ultimately ensnare youth and teens. Its motive is profit, and in seeking to maximize its financial gains, Meta has repeatedly misled the public about the substantial dangers of its Social Media Platforms. It has concealed the ways in which these Platforms exploit and manipulate its most vulnerable consumers: teenagers and children.

On the same day, attorneys general from eight other states and the District of Columbia filed their own lawsuits against Meta, alleging that its practices violate state consumer protection laws.

If successful, these lawsuits could force Meta to change how it designs and markets its social media platforms to the public. The legal strategy has drawn comparisons to lawsuits filed against the tobacco industry in the 1990s, which led to hundreds of billions of dollars in damages and changed the way that tobacco is marketed.

These early legal battles underscore what parents have known for years. Social media is addictive. It is toxic to the mental and psychological health of our children. Knowing this, we must ask ourselves: why would we put it in their hands, and what can we do to limit its effects?

- **Schools must return to working in partnership with parents.**
  I remember a time—it seems like not so long ago—when I felt like my child, her school, and Zack and I were all equal collaborators in Jordan's education and social development. It was elementary school, I admit, a time when parents were openly encouraged to be present and involved in the activities of the school and its young students. I knew Jordan's teachers by name, and they knew me. Sometimes we chatted when I stopped by to pick up Jordan at the end of the day. We trusted each other. I had a strong sense that we were working together toward a common goal.

  All of that ended when Jordan began middle school. Suddenly, parents were asked to drop their children off at the front gate and *not* to enter campus. *Safety*, I thought. With so many school shootings, maybe fewer people coming and going was better.

It wasn't just the campus itself, though. If we had questions about the curriculum, homework, or how Jordan was doing in school, we were told to ask our child. It was such an abrupt change from the previous six years that it took some getting used to. *No matter*, I thought. The school was teaching my child to problem solve and to become more independent.

There were limits, of course, to how much a sixth grader could navigate. *Will there still be parent-teacher conferences?* I wondered. The answer was no. All communication was by email, and it was general stuff (no school next Friday; winter break starts on December 20) and nothing specific about my daughter. I remember my own middle school and high school education, and this felt different, a conscious decision to remove parents from the equation. At first it perplexed me (like the "new math" that baffles me still), but as time went on it felt like they were hiding something. I know that sounds paranoid and a little crazy, and I told myself this at the time. Still, it bothered me. I wanted us to be a team again, not separate islands refusing to communicate. Things were tough for my daughter in middle school. There were a lot of tears—Jordan's and mine—and we could've used a close partnership with the place where she spent so much time.

As Jordan latched on to her trans identity, I needed the school more than ever. Instead, the curtain of silence closed more tightly around her. My questions went unanswered, not just by my daughter but by the school as well. Somewhere along the line, her teachers, guidance counselor, and principal had decided that I was the enemy, or so it seemed, and I was developing the same feeling about them. The distance between us widened. At times, it seemed like they were intentionally sabotaging my efforts to help my daughter.[22] Perhaps

---

22. The National Education Association (NEA), the largest teachers' union in the United States, has partnered with the Human Rights Campaign (HRC), an LGBTQ+ activist group. HRC identifies one of its platinum sponsors as Pfizer pharmaceuticals, the manufacturer of one of the most widely prescribed testosterone medications in the United States. How is this not a conflict of interest? Why is this tolerated? To put things in perspective, physicians are prohibited by law from accepting even the smallest of gifts—a free pen, for example—from a drug company. Shouldn't we expect teachers to do the same?

I should've moved her to a different school, but Jordan and Zack pleaded with me not to do that. Jordan had developed friends at her school, a precious commodity in any phase of life but in middle school most of all. And where would she go? This was supposed to be one of the *best* schools in our community. Would a private school be any better?

If I could sit down with them now, I would ask the teachers, counselors, and administrators, "What happened to the way we used to be?" Why do so many public-school faculty seem to assume the worst about parents from the beginning? Why do they create a space in which there *is no space* for the parents of the children they are teaching? Parents *want* to play a role in our child's social and academic development. We *should* be part of this process—not helicopter parents, just partners. What can be done to repair that? What can be done to bring us back together?

- **Parents deserve greater trust and latitude in deciding what's best for their children.**
  The medical care of transgender adolescents is a touchy subject. People get pulled onto the battleground by their political views, experiences, and beliefs. There's very little appetite for listening, growth, healing, thoughtful conversation, or social progress. Instead, it's a place for fighting. Our attention is focused on doing as much damage as possible to our perceived opponents.

  I have no doubt that a multitude of groups and individuals will vehemently disagree with the opinions and insights that I've discussed in these pages. They will debate the facts and admonish my conclusions and recommendations. They will find small errors and point to them as reasons why the larger message cannot be trusted. This book will be labeled "hate speech" by some and will be banned from certain libraries and other platforms. Many will attempt to discredit my concerns by attacking me directly through slander and false claims. ("You realize she's actually a pedophile communist robot born on Neptune and trying to overthrow the government, don't you?") A few desperate and misguided souls will resort to bullying and threats of violence against me and my family. It is for these reasons why I have altered the names of people and places in this book, including my own. The primary goal is to protect my child and the privacy of those who I have mentioned in this book. I recognize that the best way to do that was to remain silent. But what about *your* child? What about the hundreds of thousands of children and families who are still suffering?

Adolescence is a difficult and confusing time. Children are impulsive and impatient. They are prone to following their peers, wherever it takes them. They have difficulty imagining a future in which they might want something different than what they want *right now*. As adults and parents, it is our job to look at things with a more careful lens. Often, it is our job to say no when we feel that our children are about to do something that could hurt them. *No*, they cannot stick a metal fork into the electrical outlet. *No*, they cannot run around on the roof of the house or eat *all* the candy in the Halloween basket during a single night. Maybe one day they will become an electrician, or a roofer, or a culinary expert in Halloween candy, and it will be okay for them to do those things. Until then, it is our job to protect them. Why should this be controversial? Why should we remain locked in battle instead of trusting parents to do what's right for their children?

Tomorrow

Today is almost over, and I am settling down for the night. I have washed my face, brushed my teeth, and donned my PJs. It is an evening routine I learned from my mother when I was small and depended on her to teach me the basics of how to care for myself. She did a good job, providing me with what I needed but not always what I wanted. It embarrasses me now that I used to rage against her, throwing tantrums and hurling angry words when I disagreed with her decisions. She loved me anyway, and I am so grateful that she did. Thank you, Mom, for being strong and kind and willing to do the hard work of parenting when things got rough. Thank you for not giving up on me, and for not allowing me to give up on myself.

The sheets are cool and welcoming as I slip into bed and wait for them to grow warm against my body. I am tired from the activities of the day, the goals I accomplished and the things I did not. It occurs to me that I could've done better, that I took some of my time for granted and wasted it on negative thoughts and unimportant distractions. Perhaps tomorrow will be different and I will be a better version of myself. I believe in that potential in all of us, that we can rise above our differences and find ways to move forward. We are intelligent and empathic creatures, and we have come too far to give up on each other now. We can get there. It's important that we do.

Epilogue

Here we are, at both the end and the beginning. I don't know what the future holds for Jordan, although I hope she continues to explore the world around her and finds ways to live an authentic and meaningful life. She will be heading off to college soon, but she is always with me, even as the distance between us becomes greater.

My experiences from recent years have reminded me of the agency that I have over my own life, whether I choose to claim it or not. There are *always* choices, and the choices I make will guide my future. I choose to pray for my children daily and to keep my heart and mind open to all possibilities. I recognize that I am usually the only thing standing between me and what I want to do or the way I want to feel. No matter how messy things seem in the moment, God is always there in the middle of everything. It is my choice to acknowledge that.

Not so long ago, our lives were different. I worked the oars of our tiny rowboat as the waves crashed against the hull. It was just Jordan and me back then, the sky dark and volatile above us. I could taste the salty spray of the water against my face, the metallic tang of fear and adrenaline. The wood groaned beneath us, threatening to splinter in half and divide us in two. How had we gotten so far from the shore? How would we find our way home?

The waters are calmer now, and I row with a mix of relief and uncertainty. I can see the shoreline, the small harbor where Jordan once played as a child. We cannot go back there, and so we search for a different place, a spot along the coastline that she must choose for herself. I will drop her off there and hope for the best. It will not be my place, but hers.

I will make the trip home without her, and although she may sometimes visit me, our relationship can never truly return to how it was when she was younger.

Did I know this was coming? I suppose that I did. It started with a home pregnancy test, an ultrasound, the birth of a child who relied on me for everything. Every day she got a little bit stronger and more self-reliant. "I can do it myself," she used to tell me, and I knew that eventually the day would come when that was true.

She sits on the wooden seat of the rowboat and looks out across the water. The sea calls to her, and I realize that the fear is still with me: that she might cast herself overboard—*even now*, so close to the shore—and disappear forever beneath the surface. I am grateful to have found her, to have wrestled her away from this thing that almost destroyed her, but her continued recovery is more tenuous than I would like to believe. My hands tighten on the oars, I clench my teeth, and the fear settles like a restless animal in my chest.

The sun is behind me, and the right side of Jordan's face is lost in shadow. The breeze ruffles her hair, lifting a dark lock and setting it down again along her temple. I am reminded of the depth of my love for her. I take a deep breath and try to capture this moment in my memory. *What are you thinking*, I want to ask her, but I don't. She will tell me when she is ready. Instead, I lean back and pull at the oars. We have a little time left, just the two of us, and I want to enjoy it.

Glossary of Terms

Autogynephilia: Derived from the Ancient Greek terms αὐτός (*autós*, "self") + γυνή (*gunḗ*, "woman") + φιλία (*philía*, "love"), or "Love of oneself as a woman." It is listed in the DSM-5 as a specifier for the diagnosis of transvestic disorder, in which a person has recurrent and intense sexual arousal from cross-dressing. (*See* Transvestic Disorder.) With the autogynephilia specifier, the person is sexually aroused by thoughts or images of himself as female. According to the DSM-5, "Autogynephilic fantasies and behaviors may focus on the idea of exhibiting female physiological functions (e.g., lactation, menstruation), engaging in stereotypically female behavior (e.g., knitting), or possessing female anatomy (e.g., breasts)." This is a distinct and separate diagnosis from gender dysphoria.

Binder: A constrictive wrap that goes around the torso and is designed to flatten breasts and make them less noticeable under clothing. Binders are commonly used in presurgical transgender men (anatomically female individuals who identify as men) as part of social transition from female to male. The use of binders has several potential side effects, including back or rib pain, shortness of breath during exertional activities or at rest, skin rash or fungal infections, impaired breast development, pneumonia, and broken ribs.

Bottom Surgery: A term that encompasses a variety of complex surgical procedures. For an individual desiring surgical transformation from male to female anatomy, **vaginoplasty** describes the surgical creation of a vagina and the surgical removal or reconfiguration of the penis, scrotum, and testicles. The skin of the penis and scrotum are often used to create a vaginal canal and vulva (mons, labia, clitoris, and urethral opening). For an individual desiring surgical transformation from female to male anatomy, **phalloplasty** describes the surgical creation of a phallus from donor site tissue (skin and soft tissue from the patient's forearm, thigh, or back). Removal of the ovaries, uterus, and vagina are commonly performed. Both surgeries involve many potential complications, including bleeding, infection, necrosis of the transplanted genitals, urethral stricture (scarring and narrowing of the urethra causing inability to urinate), and urinary fistula (an abnormal passageway from the bladder to the bowel or skin of the abdomen). Healing time for either procedure is extensive (months). A less invasive option for female-to-male surgical transition is a **metoidoplasty**, which involves cutting ligaments around the clitoris and using hormones to enlarge the clitoris to create a "microphallus." Neither phalloplasty nor metoidoplasty result in the ability to achieve an erection.

Cisgender: A person whose gender identity corresponds with the gender they were identified as having at birth.

CisHet: An individual who identifies as both cisgender and heterosexual. The term is frequently used in a derogatory manner by trans rights activists or some members of the LGBTQ community to describe a "privileged" group (compared to a group with a marginalized identity such as transgender or homosexual).

Cross-Dressing: Wearing clothing of the opposite sex. Although individuals with autogynephilia, transvestic disorder, or gender dysphoria may cross-dress, cross-dressing is not synonymous with any of these conditions. There are a variety of reasons why an individual might cross-dress. In the movie *Yentl*, Barbara Streisand posed as a boy so she could receive an education in Talmudic Law, which was forbidden for women in Poland in 1904. In *Mrs. Doubtfire*, Robin Williams presented as a female housekeeper in an attempt to spend more time with his children, who he desperately missed following his marital separation. A non-transvestite man might cross-dress as a woman to be allowed into women's spaces, such as female locker rooms, bathrooms, or dressing rooms. The reasons for doing so might include a sense of entitlement, feeling powerful or exerting control over women, or experiencing sexual arousal from being present in a space where women are naked or undressing. The key distinction is that sexual arousal is not obtained from the cross-dressing act itself. It is important to note that none of these examples involve individuals with gender dysphoria. It is therefore reasonable that women might be uncomfortable with the presence of a biological male in these spaces, regardless of the person's expressed gender identification.

Dead Name (noun): The birth name, given by a child's parent(s), to an individual who later identifies as transgender and changes his or her name to something different as part of their gender identity social transition.

Dead Name (verb): To refer to an individual using a person's birth name instead of the new name that the individual has selected for themselves.

Desist: To cease to proceed or act. In gender identity terminology, to desist is to revert (prior to any medical or surgical gender-related treatments) to a gender identity consistent with a person's birth gender.

Desister: An individual who previously identified as transgender who reverts to a gender identity consistent with his or her birth gender prior to any medical or surgical gender-related treatments.

Detransition: Cessation or reversal of a gender transition that included medical and/or surgical treatments.

Detransitioner: An individual who ceases or attempts to reverse gender transition that included medical and/or surgical treatments.

Diagnostic and Statistical Manual (DSM): The handbook used by healthcare professionals in the United States and much of the world as the authoritative guide to the diagnosis of psychiatric disorders. The DSM contains descriptions, symptoms, and other criteria for diagnosing psychiatric disorders. The current edition is DSM-5.

Dutch Protocol for the Treatment of Children with Gender Dysphoria: Based on a series of small case studies from the Netherlands from 1998 to 2011, the Dutch protocol utilized puberty-blocking medication for the treatment of a subset of adolescent patients with gender dysphoria who met the following strict inclusion criteria: (1) minimum age of 12 years; (2) history of life-long gender dysphoria that increased during puberty; (3) psychologically stable without serious comorbid psychiatric disorders that could interfere with the diagnostic process; and (4) having family support. During puberty suppression, there was no change in body dysphoria, although behavioral and emotional problems decreased, and general function improved. All patients received regular sessions with a psychologist or psychiatrist during the study, making it difficult to ascertain whether the outcomes were due to puberty blockers, access to regular sessions with a mental health specialist, or both. The Dutch protocol claimed that puberty suppression is reversible and could be used as a diagnostic tool. Both claims have been widely refuted.[1]

Facial Feminization: A multistep procedure consisting of multiple surgeries designed to make a person appear more feminine. The most common surgeries include changing the hairline and surgically contouring the forehead, nose, jawline, and Adam's apple. Cheek implants, lip reshaping, and lip lifts can also be used.

Facial Masculinization: A multistep procedure consisting of multiple surgeries designed to make a person appear more masculine. The most common surgeries include forehead lengthening and augmentation, cheek augmentation, reshaping the nose and chin, jaw augmentation, and thyroid cartilage enhancement to construct an Adam's apple.

Feminizing Hormones: A group of hormones including estrogen, progesterone, and androgen blockers. Side effects can include (but are not limited to) changes in cholesterol that can affect cardiovascular health; increased serum potassium levels with the potential to affect cardiac conduction; hypercoagulability with increased risk of stroke; anemia; in-

---

1. M. Biggs, "The Dutch Protocol for Juvenile Transsexuals: Origins and Evidence," *Journal of Sex and Marital Therapy* 49, no. 4 (2023): 348–368.

creased risk of certain types of cancer; changes in sex drive and sexual functioning; and changes in mood and anxiety.

Gender Affirming Model: A therapeutic stance that focuses on affirming one's chosen gender identity and not repairing it. This may include using a requested name or pronouns corresponding with the gender a person identifies as (or, in many cases, chooses) and having the individual use the restroom or locker room of the identified (or chosen) gender identity. It may involve medical interventions such as hormones, hormone blockers, and various surgeries or cosmetic procedures that render an individual to look and feel like the gender that individual identifies as (or chooses). The reader will notice that on occasion I put "gender affirming" in quotes. Given the low prevalence of authentic gender dysphoria (as defined by DSM criteria), it should be noted that for most children with a self-diagnosis of gender dysphoria, the gender affirming model perpetuates a false gender identity and does not affirm an individual's actual gender.

Gender Dysphoria: A medical diagnosis (as defined by DSM criteria) that refers to psychological distress that results from an incongruence between one's chromosomal and anatomic gender at birth and one's gender identity. Gender dysphoria may begin in childhood, but some individuals do not experience it until later.

Gender Expansive: A term used to describe a gender identity or behavior that is broader than the commonly held definitions of gender and gender expression in one or more aspects of a person's life.

Gender Expert/Specialist: The definition of a "gender expert" or "gender specialist" has been defined in a variety of ways and differs vastly depending on the source. In my experience, a gender expert or specialist is anyone advertising or proclaiming to be one. I have defined my ideal version of a gender specialist in "The Gender Specialists" section of chapter three. None of my experiences with gender specialists yielded encounters with individuals whose clinical approach came close to this ideal definition. I use the terms gender expert and gender specialist interchangeably throughout this book.

Gender Nonconforming: A person whose behavior or appearance does not conform to prevailing cultural and social expectations about what is appropriate for his or her gender.

Genital Nullification Surgery ("Nullo" or "Eunuch Procedure"): A surgery that removes all genitalia, leaving the patient with a small hole through which to urinate but no genitals. A double mastectomy with removal of the nipples can also be performed, leaving the individual with a "blank chest" (except for the long bilateral surgical scars). There are numerous clinics in the United States and throughout the world offering these surgeries.

Genspect: An international organization that includes professionals, trans people, detransitioners, and parent groups who advocate for a non-medicalized approach to gender diversity. It is an excellent resource for parents of trans-identified teens. As of April 30, 2024, Genspect now offers Continuing Medical Education (CME) to doctors who are interested in learning about evidence-based non-medicalized approaches to the treatment of patients with gender-related distress.[2]

Glitter Family: An organization or group of individuals whom an LGBTQ person might perceive or utilize as an adoptive family, either virtually (receiving support through emails, text messaging, social media, and/or online platforms) or literally (leaving their real family to live with a glitter family). This most commonly occurs when an LGBTQ person's real family has challenged or rejected their professed sexual orientation or gender identity. Although glitter families claim to support the identity and well-being of children and teens, they often encourage LGBTQ children and teens to reject and abandon their real families. Some schools and teachers collude with glitter families to indoctrinate

---

2. Genspect's recent addition of CME is a promising step toward offering medical providers accredited, evidence-based education that provides alternatives to the gender affirming model. A position statement from its website notes, "We believe that there are many routes that may lead to the development of distress over an individual's gender. Equally, there are just as many routes out of such distress. That's why we would like to see a wider range of treatment options and more evidence-based approaches to gender-questioning children and young people." "Our Position," Genspect, genspect.org/our-position.

young students to leave their real parents. A popular poster displayed in some schools includes the text, "If your parents aren't accepting of your identity, I'm your mom now."

LGBTQ: In this book, I use this acronym to represent a wide variety of individuals that include non-heterosexual and non-cisgender people. For the sake of brevity, I have kept the letters limited to LGBTQ or LGBTQ+. I recognize that these letters alone do not encompass all possible sexual preferences or gender identifications. Lettering is far too simplistic to capture the breadth of such a complicated human condition, but my intention is to include anyone who feels they may fit into this community.

Love Bombing: The action or practice of lavishing an individual with attention or affection, especially to influence or manipulate the person. Teens who newly declare themselves to be transgender will experience love bombing from a wide community of individuals. This is also a tactic sometimes used by cults to recruit new members.

Masculinizing Hormones: A group of hormones including testosterone (also known as "T") and estrogen blockers. Testosterone is available in multiple forms and can be given at a variety of doses and frequencies. Side effects can include (but are not limited to) changes in cholesterol and an increase in red blood cell production that can exacerbate cardiovascular conditions and increase risk of heart attack, stroke, and life-threatening pulmonary embolism; changes in sex drive and sexual functioning; worsening of acne; changes in mood, aggression, and anxiety; vocal cord changes leading to permanent deepening of the voice; increased growth of facial and body hair; increased risk of certain types of cancer; and infertility. Some effects are reversible if testosterone is discontinued, although some are not.

Medical Transition: Medical treatments designed to alter the appearance, voice, and/or functioning of an individual's body to align the individual with a gender identity that is different from their birth gender. Medical transition most commonly involves the use of hormones and/or hormone blockers, although other cosmetic procedures (e.g., laser hair removal) might also be utilized. Although gender reassignment surgeries could be considered a type of medical transition, I have used the term "surgical transition" in this book to denote surgical treatments.

Metoidoplasty: *See* Bottom Surgery.

Misgender: Referring to a person using a word such as a pronoun that does not correctly reflect the person's gender identity (i.e., a female-to-male transgender individual might say, "That person misgendered me," if he is referred to as she/her.)

Nonbinary: A gender identity that does not conform to the traditional two binary genders (male or female). Nonbinary individuals often request to be referred to using the plural pronouns they/them. Nonbinary gender identity is not a medical diagnosis and is not included in the DSM-5. It is important to understand that although this term has become widely used, it is a lay term and is described differently depending on the source. There are no objective diagnostic criteria. Although not synonyms, the term "gender fluid" has been used to describe individuals on this spectrum.

Packer: This is a realistic or semi-realistic appearing penis made from material such as silicone or even something as simple as a rolled-up sock. A packer is placed beneath clothing to create a genital bulge in the clothing to simulate the presence of a penis, allowing a female-to-male transgender individual to feel more confident in their male gender portrayal. Packing can be part of social transition.

Pediatric and Adolescent Gender Dysphoria Working Group: A former group (active from 2018-2020) whose website provided a platform for international discussion where clinicians and researchers could explore the evidence for different models of treatment for gender dysphoria. Rigorous scientific debate was possible due to the absence of a political agenda. Following numerous online attacks and labeling of the group as "an alliance of anti-transgender activists," the group has dissolved. Former members of the group have been openly criticized online, including a psychotherapist who uses exploratory psychotherapy rather than unquestioning gender affirmation. The psychotherapist has been accused by trans activists of being, "a key figure in anti-transgender extremism."[3]

Parents with Inconvenient Truths about Trans (PITT): PITT is a space for parents who have been impacted by gender ideology to share their uncensored stories, experiences, and thoughts, while remaining anonymous to protect themselves and their families. The objective is to support members and to inform the public about the devastating impact of gender ideology on families through accounts of personal experiences. They believe that when people understand the realities and implications of the gender affirming model in all its forms, people will join in ending the medicalization of gender identity for children, teens, and young people.

Phalloplasty: *See* Bottom Surgery.

Pronouns: Linguistic designations tied to gender that are used for referring to someone in the third person. Examples include he/him/his, she/her/hers, they/them/theirs, ze/zir/zirs, xe/xim/xirs. Combinations of these pronouns such as he/they have become popular and have led to increased gender confusion, rather than less.

Social Transition: Presenting in public as a newly identified gender. Social transition can include changes in hairstyle or types of clothing; packing (use of a penile prosthesis under clothing); tucking (pushing the testes into the inguinal canal by use of a tight garment called a gaff); binding (flattening the breasts by use of a tight chest garment called a binder); use of breast, hip, or buttock prostheses under clothing; announcing one's new gender identity to friends, family, classmates, and coworkers; or changing legal documents to reflect a chosen name, gender, or pronoun.

Stand to Pee (STP): A device used by some female-to-male transgender individuals that allows them to urinate while standing up. The use of STP devices is considered an aspect of social transition.

---

3. Transgender Map, www.transgendermap.com.

Surgical Transition: Surgical treatments designed to alter the appearance, voice, and/or functioning of an individual's body to align the individual with a gender identity that is different from their birth gender. Surgical treatments commonly associated with gender reassignment include "top surgery" (bilateral mastectomies or breast augmentation), "bottom surgery" (vaginoplasty, phalloplasty, or metoidoplasty), surgical contouring of the forehead, nose, jawline, and Adam's apple, cheek implants, lip reshaping, and lip lifts.

Therapy First: An organization formerly titled Gender Exploratory Therapy Association (GETA), whose position statement pertaining to therapy is: *"Individuals who are exploring gender identity or struggling with their biological sex should have access to therapists who will provide thoughtful care and tend to legitimate mental health concerns, without pushing an ideological or political agenda."* Therapy First is an excellent resource with an informational website for those who would like to explore their sense of gender identity but have encountered barriers to doing so in the traditional psychotherapy and medical climate. The organization has been falsely criticized for being an entity providing conversion therapy.

Top Surgery: Bilateral double mastectomies (for a female-to-male person) or breast augmentation or enhancement (for a male-to-female person). The term "top surgery" has become a commonly used euphemism to describe these invasive surgical procedures. Potential complications include infection, scarring, chronic pain, and lifelong regret.

Trans Activist / Trans Rights Activist: An individual who promotes the legal status of transgender people and seeks to eliminate violence and discrimination against transgender individuals. Not all trans activists recognize that many children who identify as transgender are not actually transgender. With that in mind, the definition changes to one that is far less altruistic, as the activist comes to be defined as someone who supports an ideology rather than the individual. Most people who suffer from gender dysphoria are not trans activists. Many of them reject the activists' claims and have been harmed by the trans activist agenda.

Trans Female: A woman who was designated as male at birth by a physician, likely by the observation of male external genitalia, but whose gender identity is female. These people are usually genetically male (with XY sex chromosomes). Although commonly used, "trans female" is a lay term.

Trans-Identified: An individual who identifies as transgender, although there is no objective evidence other than the individual's own declaration that they are transgender. There is usually no long-standing history or evidence of authentic gender dysphoria meeting DSM criteria.

Trans Male: A man who was designated as female at birth by a physician, likely by the observation of female external genitalia, but whose gender identity is male. These people are usually genetically female (with XX sex chromosomes). Although commonly used, "trans male" is a lay term.

Transvestic Disorder: Classified as a paraphilic disorder in the DSM-5, it is a disorder in which individuals experience sexual arousal from cross-dressing. The degree of cross-dressing varies between individuals. A man might wear women's undergarments beneath his three-piece suit at work, while another man might wear a full feminine outfit with associated makeup and hairstyle, attempting to present as female in public. Contrary to autogynephilia, arousal from the fantasy of being a woman or from the fantasy of having female physiologic functions is not an inherent component of transvestic disorder. Although individuals with transvestic disorder experience sexual arousal from cross-dressing, not all individuals who cross-dress have transvestic disorder. (*See* Cross-Dressing.)

Vaginoplasty: *See* Bottom Surgery.

World Professional Association for Transgender Health (WPATH): This is a nonprofit interdisciplinary professional and educational organization devoted to transgender health. Their mission is to promote evidence-based care, education, research, public policy, and respect in transgender health. WPATH recently came under scrutiny due to leaked internal messages and an audio recording (referred to as the "**WPATH files**") from one of its meetings. In these transcripts, doctors acknowledged that patients are often too young to understand the consequences of puberty blockers and hormone therapy, including loss of fertility and sexual function. Lack of proper informed consent for life-altering procedures was openly discussed, including a case in which a patient with schizophrenia requested and underwent surgical castration. Another case involved a patient with dissociative identity disorder (aka multiple personality disorder) who was seeking gender reassignment surgery, although not all of her identities shared the same gender. Revelations from the WPATH files highlight acknowledged shortcomings in informed consent for patients seeking medical and/or surgical transition. By their own admission in these leaked communications, some WPATH members do not follow their own published standards of care.

About the Author

Lisa Bellot, MD, is a board-certified psychiatrist who has practiced in California for the past twenty years. She has many faults, a few good traits, and is the mother of two extraordinary daughters.